RANDOM JUSTICE

RANDOM JUSTICE

On Lotteries and Legal Decision-Making

NEIL DUXBURY

CLARENDON PRESS · OXFORD

OXFORD
UNIVERSITY PRESS
Great Clarendon Street, Oxford OX2 6DP

Oxford University Press is a department of the University of Oxford.
It furthers the University's objective of excellence in research, scholarship,
and education by publishing worldwide in

Oxford New York

Athens Auckland Bangkok Bogotá Buenos Aires Calcutta
Cape Town Chennai Dar es Salaam Delhi Florence Hong Kong Istanbul
Karachi Kuala Lumpur Madrid Melbourne Mexico City Mumbai
Nairobi Paris São Paulo Singapore Taipei Tokyo Toronto Warsaw

with associated companies in Berlin Ibadan

Oxford is a registered trade mark of Oxford University Press
in the UK and in certain other countries

Published in the United States
by Oxford University Press Inc., New York

British Library Cataloguing in Publication Data

Data available

Library of Congress Cataloging in Publication Data
Duxbury, Neil.
Random justice: on lotteries and legal decision-making/Neil
Duxbury.
p. cm.
Includes index.
1. Law—Methodology 2. Judicial process. 3. Lotteries.
I. Title.
K212.D89 1999 99–24515
340′.11—dc21

ISBN 0–19–826825–4

1 3 5 7 9 10 8 6 4 2

Typeset in Times by
Cambrian Typesetters, Frimley, Surrey

Printed in Great Britain
on acid-free paper by
Bookcraft Ltd., Midsomer Norton, Somerset

For Tom and Joyce

Acknowledgements

Had I planned to write this book, it would have never materialized. A few summers ago, I read Jon Elster's trilogy of monographs on the value and limitations of rationality—*Ulysses and the Sirens, Sour Grapes,* and *Solomonic Judgements*—in an effort to develop a better critical perspective on neo-classical law and economics. Various of Elster's analyses—in particular, his discussions of strategies of precommitment and of states that are essentially by-products—influenced my research around that time. But I was not especially interested in his discussion, in *Solomonic Judgements*, of randomized social decision-making. In the course of teaching, however, I found myself increasingly asking students why a randomized solution to one or another legal issue would not have been appropriate. Little by little, the notion of decision-making by lot was reining me in: the examples discussed with students were written up as notes, the notes became a staff seminar, the staff seminar became the basis for a projected article, the projected article began to resemble a book, and . . . here I am.

The immediate and most obvious inspiration for this book is Elster's work on randomized social decision-making, upon which I have, perhaps rather foolishly, tried to build. I am also indebted to various institutions and people for helping me to complete this project. The Faculty of Law at the University of Manchester generously granted me leave to finish the book during the first semester of the 1998–9 academic session. During work on this project, I also benefited immensely from a number of small grants—so essential for covering inter-library loans and photocopying expenses—obtained from the Faculty's Research Support Fund. In all of my dealings with them, the staff of the John Rylands Library have demonstrated collective and exemplary courtesy and efficiency; I ought especially to mention the people in the Document Supply Unit, who have worked hard to obtain all sorts of articles and books on my behalf. I wish also to thank the library staff of the Institute of Advanced Legal Studies, London, and the Robert Crown Law Library at Stanford University. The few days which I spent at the latter institution were funded by a British Academy Overseas Conference Grant.

Three groups of people have ensured that this book is better than it would otherwise have been. First, there are those who endured and criticized my presentations at the University of Manchester, Faculty of Law; at Hull University Law School; at King's College London, School of Law; at Manchester Metropolitan University, School of Law; at the University of Aberdeen, Faculty of Law; at the University of Liverpool, Faculty of Law; at the University of California, Santa Barbara, Interdisciplinary Humanities Center; at Stanford Law School; and at UCLA Law School. These events often left me with the rather sobering realization that there are plenty of academics around who could tackle the theme of this book so much better than I have.

Secondly, there are those people who kindly provided feedback on, or other forms of help with, different parts of the project. Listed randomly, they are: Craig Rotherham, Albert Alschuler, Henrik Palmer Olsen, Anthony Ogus, Martin Wainwright, James Carrier, Mary Childs, Stephen Weatherill, Tom Gibbons, Christine Bell, Barbara Goodwin, Annette Lundby Kelsall, Christopher Hood, John Stanton-Ife, José Miola, David Milman, John Murphy, Ted White, Tim Murphy, Bernard Jackson, Joseph Jaconelli, John Harris, James Miller, David Miers, Jack Schlegel, Colin Scott, Andrew Griffiths, Ron Keegan, Maleiha Malik, Pauline Matthews, Jean McHale, Mohammed Rasekh, Caroline Bridge, William Lucy, Geoffrey MacCormack, Volodymyr Kuznetsov, Rodney Brazier, Sean Doran, Richard Posner, Alan Norrie, and Neil Walker. That some of the people in this second group belong also to the first surely proves that masochism is alive and kicking. Finally, I am especially grateful to Brian Bix, Matthew Kramer, Martin Loughlin, and Mike Redmayne for reading carefully and commenting in detail on every chapter of this book. I hate to think what it would have looked like without their help.

Manchester
14 November 1998

Contents

Introduction

Within the literature of legal philosophy, the idea of deciding by lot is almost wholly insignificant. It is a quirky idea that sometimes serves as a foil for those endeavouring to develop themes which are considered far more compelling and enlightening. At other times, the notion of deciding by lot is given the most cursory of treatments—examined and packed away within, say, the space of a footnote. Devoting a book to the idea may, to many legal philosophers, seem rather fanciful. That the idea in fact deserves serious and sustained examination will, it is hoped, become evident as this project unfolds.

Lotteries take many forms. They may be constructed or natural. They may be simple or complex. They may accord even chances or they may be (deliberately or naturally) biased. They may operate in isolation or in combination with other modes of decision-making. Certain lotteries we choose to enter, others are imposed upon us. With some lotteries we can select our lots, with others our lots are predetermined. Some lotteries allow each lot to be drawn only once (so that the choice of lots becomes more restricted as the lottery proceeds), others permit multiple selections of the same lot. No attempt is made in this study to present a taxonomy of the lottery. Suffice it to say that much of the ensuing discussion is informed by the distinctions which have just been listed.

Chapter 1 is founded on the distinction between the lotteries which we impose on life and the lotteries which life imposes on us. In law, as elsewhere, chance generates ambivalent feelings. The consequences of leaving chance uncontrolled can be good and bad. Yet it is simply not possible to regulate away all of the undesirable workings of chance. Efforts to use law to tame chance will sometimes—rather like British adaptations of Italian cuisine—prove over-inclusive and counter-productive. Not only might our efforts to regulate chance fail to eradicate much of that which we consider to be undesirable, but many of the salutary effects of leaving chance undisturbed may be destroyed. The unruliness of chance might go some way to explaining why it is usually to be found inherent within, rather than consciously imported into, legal systems.

We see in Chapter 2 that conscious appeal to, and reliance on, chance are practices not uncommon to certain cultures and historical periods. Such practices are largely attributable to the fact that lot-casting has often been invested with divinatory significance. Determining the contexts in which it is appropriate to cast lots to discover divine intent is a thorny theological issue. The fact that there has been so much theological disagreement over the correctness of lot-casting appears to be part of the explanation as to why the divinatory significance of the practice eventually disappeared. It is tempting to venture that this practice fell into decline primarily because we have become more rational. For various reasons, however, this speculation is resisted. Within the context of this study, the most significant of these reasons is that the modern aversion to the determination of important social and legal outcomes by lot might, according to one line of argument, be considered irrational. This particular line of argument is developed in section 4 of Chapter 4.

Chapter 2 also contains an inquiry into the use of lotteries to select political representatives. This practice was much more common in the past than it is today. As compared with the demise of divination by lot, the reasons for the declining use of sortition in politics appear to be more obvious. Given the size of most modern democracies, a political system which requires that members of the community be randomly selected to hold political office would leave the majority of citizens feeling disempowered. Furthermore, one might envisage that, among those selected, rather too many would be politically apathetic, resentful of having to serve in office, or unable to resist abusing their positions. It may also be the case that too many of those selected would be considered politically naive or even dangerous. In the city-states of antiquity and the Renaissance, political representation was not the professional activity that it is today. Within modern democracies, even if political representatives were to be picked from a pool of self-nominated candidates, there would probably still exist a fundamental worry that many of those selected would lack the qualities for the job.

This is not to suggest that sortition in politics is dead and buried. We see in Chapter 2 that the idea still has some practical significance—electoral tie-breaks, for example, are quite frequently resolved by lot—and that proposals for the greater use of lotteries for the purpose of selecting political representatives, for all that they are not unproblematic, are not uncommon either. Especial attention is accorded to the idea that proportional representation might be facilitated by introducing lotteries into voting systems. While the proposal for 'lottery voting' is not particularly persuasive, it illustrates how lotteries might be combined with other decision-making methods. The questions of whether such combinations might ever prove workable and valuable are taken up in Chapter 5.

Chapters 3 and 4 were originally to be one single chapter. The unwieldiness of this intended chapter became obvious as soon as it had been planned, and so a division was imposed: Chapter 3 would address the advantages of randomized social decision-making, Chapter 4 the disadvantages. But things have not quite worked out this way. Certainly these two chapters consider the pros and cons of social decision-making by lot, and Chapter 3, as compared with Chapter 4, focuses primarily on arguments in favour of randomization. As is intimated in the conclusion to Chapter 4, nevertheless, arguments concerning randomized social decision-making cannot satisfactorily be presented in an unequivocal fashion. What we encounter in Chapters 3 and 4, accordingly, is a considerable amount of toing and froing. The intention in these chapters has been to develop fairly detailed and nuanced arguments for and against social decision-making by lot. To virtually every argument presented there attaches a qualification or counter-argument. With some of the discussions this leads to digression, and there is no doubt that the material to be found in these chapters might have been more rigidly compartmentalized. Compartmentalization has been sacrificed, however, in the hope that specific arguments might be best appreciated when they are considered in the light of related, and sometimes opposing, arguments. Leniency is not expected from anybody who considers this strategy to be ill-judged.[1] The deliberateness of the strategy, however, perhaps ought to be noted.

It is suggested in Chapter 3 that numerous advantages attach to social decision-making by lot. The lottery offers a fair way of dealing with many uncomfortable, or even inherently unfair, dilemmas. A non-weighted lottery will be blind and so above corruption. That decisions reached by lot lack an element of human agency (excepting the initial decision to resort to lot) means that responsibility for especially troublesome decisions can be removed from the shoulders of particular people or groups. Lottery decisions may be economical, may generate positive incentives, and may promote a particular conception of equality. Randomization will sometimes be the best method by which to assign scarce indivisible resources, a good method by which to select a cross-section of a particular community, and a highly effective regulatory strategy. Each of these various advantages is qualified. Certain of them even end up recast as disadvantages. In Chapter 4, the disadvantages of randomization are categorized under four headings: lotteries, it is suggested, are blind, are constructed, generate uncertainty, and deny reason. It perhaps ought to be emphasized that these are but organizational categories: by no means is it claimed that there are only four drawbacks to social decision-making by lot (the blindness of the lottery, for example, is the source of numerous possible objections to this form of decision-making). Furthermore, the disadvantages of randomization can, like the advantages, be qualified and to a significant extent recast. Given that this is so, one might be forgiven for anticipating that Chapter 4 will be but a mirror-image of Chapter 3. This, however, is not the case. In Chapter 4, the arguments presented in favour of randomized social decision-making—which are developed in response to the arguments emphasizing the drawbacks of such decision-making—are not the same as the arguments for randomization which were considered in Chapter 3.

In Chapter 4, there are considered two particular advantages of randomized decision-making—these having first been presented as disadvantages—which were not discussed in Chapter 3. First of all, it is shown that randomization may prove beneficial when introduced into decision-making contexts precisely because of its capacity to generate uncertainty. The possible advantages of introducing randomizing mechanisms into decision-frameworks is explored more

---

[1] Compare Roberto Mangabeira Unger, *Social Theory: Its Situation and its Task (A Critical Introduction to* Politics, *a Work in Constructive Social Theory)* (Cambridge: Cambridge University Press, 1987), 9: 'When the larger argument falls into confusion and obscurity, when I stagger and stumble, help me. Refer to the purpose described in this book and revise what I say in the light of what I want.'

concretely in section 3 of Chapter 5. Secondly, it is argued at length that contemplation of the use of lotteries for legal decision-making purposes is especially valuable because it provides some insight into what we expect such decision-making to entail. The use of lotteries to resolve legal disputes, it is suggested, may sometimes be defended on rationalistic grounds. Generally, however, we appear to want adjudication to be reasoned rather than rational. The provision of reasons tends to render decision-makers accountable and to satisfy the expectation that disputants be subjected to an adjudicative system which exhibits procedural fairness. It is observed, however, that the provision of reasons comes at a price, and that in certain legal decision-making contexts—we focus especially on child-custody adjudication—that price might not always be worth paying. Where, owing to legal indeterminacy, adjudication is inordinately drawn out, the costs incurred may, for those affected by the case, be emotional as well as temporal and financial in nature. In short, where the elaboration of reasons comes at a very high price, the determination of legal outcomes by lot, even if considered impracticable, might at least be shown to be rational.

The question of whether lotteries might be put to greater practical use within social and (primarily) legal decision-making contexts is addressed in Chapter 5. The basic thesis of this chapter is that if lotteries are to be used more extensively in such contexts, they will most likely have to be combined with other decision-mechanisms. Lotteries in fact combine naturally with various other such mechanisms. This chapter, however, focuses on certain contrived combinations. It is argued that it may, on occasions, prove advantageous to combine lotteries with markets. Imposition of a price for entry into a lottery may sometimes be economically defensible where a number of similarly situated commercial concerns are competing for scarce resources (such as broadcasting licences). Although such schemes will not be so defensible if they impede competition, there exist certain instances—the allocation of onshore oil-drilling leases in the United States is illustrative—where the market-and-lottery combination actually stimulates economic activity. Imposition of a price for exemption from a lottery can also, on occasions, be defended on grounds of allocative efficiency. Military commutation might be defended thus, for all that history does not flatter the practice.

Chapter 5 also advances a distinctly tentative argument for what is termed adjudication in the shadow of a lottery. There may sometimes be a reasonable case for stipulating that legal decision-makers have a definite amount of time to settle on an outcome and that, should this period of time expire without a decision having been reached, the outcome will thereupon be determined by lot. Only rarely might such a procedure be defensible—indeed, much of the discussion focuses on arguments against adjudication in the shadow of a lottery. Where such a procedure is defensible, however, it might focus the minds of decision-makers and also encourage them to use their decision-making time efficiently. There may be scope for adjudicating in the shadow of a lottery where decision-makers are entrusted to allocate resources which are not only scarce but also require speedy distribution. This method of adjudication may be appropriate, furthermore, where decision-making bodies are burdened with large numbers of small claims disputes. The chapter concludes with the decidedly speculative proposition that it may even be appropriate to impose the shadow of the lottery on higher courts if there exists genuine and widespread concern that those courts are taking too expansive an approach to reasoning and, in consequence, dealing with too few cases.

A Gary Larson cartoon from 1981 depicts a lifeboat stranded at sea and containing four survivors. At the stern of the boat there sits a forlorn figure holding a short straw. At the bow there sits a man who is obviously speaking. The caption reads: 'Fair is fair, Larry . . . We're out of food, we drew straws—you lost.' The humour of the cartoon derives from the fact that one of the other two survivors is a very smug-looking dog. The blindness of the lottery outcome means that it will sometimes seem unfair. Yet it is precisely because the lottery is blind that we often believe it to be the fairest means by which to resolve an essentially unfair situation—such as when a disadvantage or burden exists which must be distributed but which cannot be shared equally. Although this study is an attempt to depict randomized legal decision-making positively, it is also an effort to show that randomization is an idea about which surprisingly little can be said without qualification. Depending largely upon context, lotteries may, among other things, be considered fair or unfair, just or unjust, efficient or inefficient. The equivocality of the lottery should not be underestimated. Nor, however, ought we to ignore the adaptability of the device. Even if this study fails satisfactorily to meet with either of these injunctions, both deserve emphasis.

1

The Spectre of Chance

We have an uneasy relationship with chance.[1] We need and yet fear it. Life without chance would be dull, possibly unbearable, indeed hardly conceivable. Natural endowments, evolution, existence itself—all might be seen as matters of chance.[2] The instinct to put one's faith in chance runs throughout societies and history;[3] indeed, a good deal of human activity can be explained as an expression of this faith.[4] Surrendering to chance is often liberating[5] and it seems beyond doubt that, through chance discoveries and occurrences, our lives often change for the better.[6]

Yet chance is disturbing. It offers no guarantee that one will get the outcome that one desires.[7] Just as we can be its beneficiaries, so too we may be its victims;

[1] I prefer to use the term 'chance' to denote occurrence without the presence of design or recognizable cause and the term 'luck' to denote the state of being a beneficiary or victim of chance. Nevertheless, at certain points throughout this work I consider it to be stylistically appropriate to use the terms as if they were all of a piece.

[2] Evolutionary theory has tended to highlight most vividly the role of chance in these matters: see Charles R. Darwin, *The Origin of Species* (London: John Murray, 1859); Jacques Monod, *Chance and Necessity: An Essay on the Natural Philosophy of Modern Biology* (London: Collins, 1972), 121–2; Richard Dawkins, *The Selfish Gene* (Oxford: Oxford University Press, orig. publ. 1976, new edn. 1989), 55–7. See also Daniel C. Dennett, *Darwin's Dangerous Idea: Evolution and the Meanings of Life* (Harmondsworth: Penguin, 1995), 458–60; and Gerd Gigerenzer et al., *The Empire of Chance: How Probability Changed Science and Everyday Life* (Cambridge: Cambridge University Press, 1989), 123–62.

[3] See F. N. David, 'Dicing and Gaming (A Note on the History of Probability)' (1955) 42 *Biometrika* 1–15; and Ian Hacking, *The Emergence of Probability: A Philosophical Study of Early Ideas about Probability, Induction and Statistical Inference* (Cambridge: Cambridge University Press, 1975), 1–10. According to Hacking (ibid. 2), 'it is hard to find a place where people use no randomizers', even though 'theories of frequency, betting, randomness and probability appear only recently [sc., since around the mid-17th cent.]'. Yet, 'no one knows why' there should have been no attempt to theorize about randomness until the Renaissance. Such theorization, Sambursky has argued, was unable to develop in ancient Greece 'because Greek mentality saw precision restricted to the heavens and failed to see laws in the fluctuations and irregularities on earth.' S. Sambursky, 'On the Possible and the Probable in Ancient Greece' (1956) 12 *Osiris* 35–48 at 48. More generally, cf. O. B. Sheynin, 'On the Prehistory of the Theory of Probability' (1974) 12 *Archive for History of Exact Sciences* 97–141; Ernest Coumet, 'La Théorie du hasard: Est-elle née par hasard?' (1970) 25 *Annales. Economies, Sociétés, Civilisations* 574–98.

[4] See Vilhelm Aubert, 'Chance in Social Affairs' (1959) 2 *Inquiry* 1–24.

[5] In popular fiction, the classic portrait is Luke Rhinehart, *The Dice Man* (London: HarperCollins, 1994 (1972)), though my own feeling about that book is that it also serves as a demonstration of how chance can be oppressive.

[6] For an illustrative discussion, see Ernst Mach, 'On the Part Played by Accident in Invention and Discovery' (Eng. trans. T. J. MacCormack) (1896) 6 *The Monist* 161–75.

[7] In 'games of mere chance', Raz observes, 'there is no question of choosing moves in order to win'. Joseph Raz, *Practical Reason and Norms* (2nd edn., Princeton: Princeton University Press, 1990), 120. While this is surely right, participants in games of chance often see the matter differently

and while it can liberate, equally it can oppress.[8] To attribute events to chance is to own up to the limits of our knowledge: it is to say that something occurred but that we do not really know why.[9] The phenomenon becomes especially sobering when we reflect upon its capacity to strike indiscriminately. Indeed, the randomness of misfortune and suffering is sometimes a prospect difficult to tolerate. Chance can also impress upon us the contingency of moral valuation. It would be comforting if the disposition to correct moral judgement (whatever we take that to mean) could be rendered immune to chance. This, however, is not the case, since those factors which determine the moral status of a person's actions are themselves subject to luck.[10] How one judges the actions of others may depend on whether those others are responsible for the actions in question. Yet consistent application of this responsibility criterion undermines many of the moral evaluations that we find it natural to make, for the matters on which people are morally assessed will often be beyond their control. That is, we tend to judge people on their actions and

---

(i.e. they regard the games in which they engage primarily as 'games of skill'). See David Oldman, 'Chance and Skill: A Study of Roulette' (1974) 8 *Sociology* 407–26; John Cohen, *Chance, Skill, and Luck: The Psychology of Guessing and Gambling* (Harmondsworth: Penguin, 1960), 84–112; Ellen J. Langer, 'The Illusion of Control' (1975) 32 *Journal of Personality and Social Psychology* 311–28; and, for the common law idea that a lottery is a venture the outcome of which is dependent on chance rather than skill, cf. *Taylor* v. *Smetten* (1883) 11 QBD 207; *Hall* v. *Cox* [1899] 1 QB 198; *Scott* v. *Director of Public Prosecutions* [1914] 2 KB 868; *Moore* v. *Elphick* [1945] 2 All ER 155; and *Boucher* v. *Rowsell* [1947] 1 All E.R. 870.

[8] For a vivid fictional portrait of the oppressiveness of chance, see Jorge Luis Borges, 'The Lottery in Babylon' (1959), in Borges, *Labyrinths: Selected Stories and Other Writings* (Eng. trans. J. M. Fein, Harmondsworth: Penguin, 1970), 55–61. On Borges's essay, see further Barbara Goodwin, 'Justice and the Lottery' (1984) 32 *Political Studies* 190–202. For another such portrait (which centres upon the lottery as a gambling device), cf. the classic *film noir*, *Force of Evil* (dir. Abraham Polonsky, 1948).

[9] See, generally, Hubert Saget, *Le Hasard et l'anti-hasard* (Paris: Vrin, 1991), 174–86. That chance serves as a constant reminder that much of what happens to us eludes explanation is, of course, frustrating to anyone who makes their living from seeking explanations. Perhaps it is for this reason that those who do make their living in this way are, now and again, rather dismissive of the phenomenon. See, e.g., Geoffrey Hawthorn, *Plausible Worlds: Possibility and Understanding in History and the Social Sciences* (Cambridge: Cambridge University Press, 1991), 61.

[10] We might understandably condemn a Nazi prison guard for his actions during the War, for example, and yet that person might have lived a morally unremarkable life had his parents, say, emigrated to the USA during his childhood. For a complex exploration of the general theme, see B. A. O. Williams, 'Moral Luck' (1976) 50 *Proceedings of the Aristotelian Society* 115–35; T. Nagel, 'Moral Luck' (1976) 50 *Proceedings of the Aristotelian Society* 137–51. The Nazi prison guard example is a variant on one provided by Nagel (ibid. 147–8). One can, of course, be legally lucky in much the same way as one can be morally lucky: whether or not one is guilty of an offence will very often depend on whether or not one does harm—and this in itself may be a matter of chance. Consider, in this regard, the example of culpability for gross negligence as discussed by J. C. Smith, 'The Element of Chance in Criminal Liability' [1971] *Criminal L. Rev.* 63–75 at 65–8; and see also Lloyd L. Weinreb, 'Desert, Punishment, and Criminal Responsibility' (1986) 49 *Law and Contemporary Problems* 47–80 at 66–7, 74–9; and Jeremy Horder, 'A Critique of the Correspondence Principle in Criminal Law' [1995] *Criminal L. Rev.* 759–70 at 763–7. For other examples (drawn from tort law), see H. L. A. Hart and Tony Honoré, *Causation in the Law* (2nd edn., Oxford: Clarendon Press, 1985), 170; and Peter Cane, 'Retribution, Proportionality, and Moral Luck in Tort Law', in Peter Cane and Jane Stapleton (eds.), *The Law of Obligations: Essays in Celebration of John Fleming* (Oxford: Clarendon Press, 1998), 141–73.

omissions, not on how they might have acted had circumstances been different; and yet the fact that circumstances were not different is a matter of chance. Luck, in other words, rests at the foundation of our moral judgements: the actions on which we are judged emerge from a world which we do not control.[11]

The notion of 'moral luck' is especially unnerving because there seems to be something in our conception of morality 'that arouses opposition to the idea that moral responsibility, or moral merit, or moral blame, should be subject to luck.'[12] Perhaps we are bothered by the claim that morality cannot be rendered resistant to luck because we like to think that there is something about morality itself— about the disposition to correct moral judgement—that somehow guards us against the ill consequences of luck.[13] Certainly some find reassurance and hope in the idea that bad luck—be it bad moral luck or other forms of misfortune (such as inequalities of birth)—can be controlled and redressed.[14] Yet it is evident that chance sometimes refuses to be tamed and that some matters of luck are simply beyond our control.[15] What, then, are we to do? Are we to surrender ourselves to chance? Or ought we to endeavour to master it?

---

[11]   See Nagel (above, n. 10), 140: 'Our beliefs are always, ultimately, due to factors outside our control, and the impossibility of encompassing those factors without being at the mercy of others leads us to doubt whether we know anything.' It perhaps ought to be noted that Nagel's position on the subject of moral luck is somewhat different from—I would say rather more ambitious than—that presented by Williams. For explorations and critiques of both positions, see Judith Andre, 'Nagel, Williams, and Moral Luck' (1983) 43 *Analysis* 202–7; Margaret Urban Coyne, 'Moral Luck?' (1985) 19 *Journal of Value Inquiry* 319–25; and, generally, Daniel Statman (ed.), *Moral Luck* (Albany, NY: State University of New York Press, 1993).

[12]   Bernard Williams, 'Moral Luck: A Postscript' (1993), in Williams, *Making Sense of Humanity and Other Philosophical Papers* (Cambridge: Cambridge University Press, 1995), 241–7 at 241.

[13]   See Martha C. Nussbaum, *The Fragility of Goodness: Luck and Ethics in Greek Tragedy and Philosophy* (Cambridge: Cambridge University Press, 1986), 3–8; and Sigmund Freud, 'The Future of an Illusion' (1927), in Freud, *Civilization, Society and Religion: Group Psychology, Civilization and its Discontents and Other Works* (Eng. trans. J. Strachey, Harmondsworth: Penguin, 1985), 181–241 at 194–200. Consider also Melvin J. Lerner, 'All the World Loathes a Loser' (June 1971) *Psychology Today*, 51–5, 66 at 51: 'All of us need to believe that we live in a world in which we and others like us can get what we deserve—and deserve what we get. Most of us care about justice for ourselves and for others, not justice in the legal sense, but in a more basic sense. Good things should happen to good people and intolerable suffering comes only to bad people.' When we refer to someone as 'lucky', I would suggest, what we actually mean is that this person can be identified, *ex post*, as having done well in some situation, or situations, in which chance can be seen to have played a role; our tendency, however, is to conceive 'lucky' to mean being in possession of 'luck', as if this were a property which is mysteriously granted to some people and largely, or even totally, withheld from others.

[14]   On the control and redress of bad moral luck, see Claudia Card, *The Unnatural Lottery: Character and Moral Luck* (Philadelphia: Temple University Press, 1996). On the idea of redress for unequal natural endowments, see John Rawls, *A Theory of Justice* (Oxford: Oxford University Press, 1972), 74–5, 100–8; and compare Robert Nozick, *Anarchy, State, and Utopia* (Oxford: Blackwell, 1974), 213–31; John E. Roemer, *Theories of Distributive Justice* (Cambridge, Mass.: Harvard University Press, 1996), 232–4.

[15]   On the difficulties of redressing inequalities of natural endowments, for example, see Anthony T. Kronman, 'Talent Pooling', in J. Roland Pennock and John W. Chapman (eds.), *Nomos XXIII: Human Rights* (New York: New York University Press, 1981), 58–79. See also Barbara Goodwin, *Justice by Lottery* (Hemel Hempstead: Harvester Wheatsheaf, 1992), 27–8: '[T]he biggest chance

The answer seems to be that we do both. We want, as it were, to get the best from chance, and so we both resist and embrace it.[16] We try to exert control when we both fear what the consequences of leaving matters to chance might be and also sense that control is there to be exerted; but we leave chance alone when we recognize that it is simply not for taming or that any effort to do so is likely, more than anything else, to make us unhappy. Fate, in short, is something which human beings both oppose and desire.[17]

The trick, of course, is in the balance. 'What we want, Heaven help us, is simultaneously to be perfectly ruled and perfectly free.'[18] Similarly with chance: we would like to be able to control chance to the best extent possible and yet also derive optimum benefit from it—which is unlikely to be possible if we are concerned with controlling it.[19] Perhaps the best that we can do is aspire to the ideal of a perfect balance by trying, so far as is possible, to make chance work to our advantage (by, for example, making the best of unexpected opportunities) while also attempting to tame chance (through paternalistic or precommitment strategies, for example,[20] or through less 'rational' actions such as indulging superstitions) when we fear its potentially disadvantageous consequences. The

distribution of all takes place when we are born . . . [T]hough we have the illusion that we choose our roles, they are really chosen for us. The nature of society is in principle already determined; our lots are cast once, at birth, and these determine to a large extent our actions and successes and failures for a whole lifetime.'

[16] For an illustrative discussion of this point which focuses on insurance (as an example of how we try to combat the ill consequences of chance) and gambling (as the classic example of how we embrace chance), cf. Milton Friedman and L. J. Savage, 'The Utility Analysis of Choices Involving Risk' (1948) 56 *Journal of Political Economy* 279–304.

[17] Perhaps, in modern times, we are more inclined to oppose than to desire it: see Anthony T. Kronman, '*Amor Fati* (The Love of Fate)' (1995) 45 *Univ. Toronto LJ* 163–78 at 174–5. Assuming the correctness of Kronman's observation, part of the explanation for why we have become more resistant to fate may be that we are now more prone to equating fate with chance or luck—with the idea that *anything* might happen—whereas, in the past, the tendency was to see fate primarily in terms of fatalism (the belief, that is, that *only this* could happen). One might expect that there will exist a stronger tendency to oppose fate where it is associated with the accidental as well as with the deterministic. On earlier understandings of fate *vis-à-vis* chance, see Jerold C. Frakes, *The Fate of Fortune in the Early Middle Ages: The Boethian Tradition* (Leiden: E. J. Brill, 1988), 25–8, 55–63, 148–56.

[18] Arthur Allen Leff, 'Unspeakable Ethics, Unnatural Law' [1979] *Duke LJ* 1229–49 at 1229. For a development of the theme, see Lloyd L. Weinreb, *Natural Law and Justice* (Cambridge, Mass.: Harvard University Press, 1987), 4–7.

[19] For a very impressive exploration of one particular dimension of this point, see Jon Elster, *Sour Grapes: Studies in the Subversion of Rationality* (Cambridge: Cambridge University Press, 1983), 43–108.

[20] Certain paternalistic strategies—such as requiring motorcyclists to wear safety helmets or forbidding people from swimming at public beaches when lifeguards are not on duty—can be viewed as interferences with a person's liberty so as to reduce the likelihood of that person falling victim to chance occurrences. Certain precommitment strategies—such as placing one's alarm clock away from one's bed, thus making it impossible to switch it off without getting up—might be viewed as efforts to ensure that there is less chance that one will end up taking an undesirable course of action. On paternalism, see generally Gerald Dworkin, 'Paternalism' (1972) 56 *The Monist* 64–84. On precommitment, see generally Jon Elster, *Ulysses and the Sirens: Studies in Rationality and Irrationality* (rev. edn., Cambridge: Cambridge University Press, 1984), 36–111.

likelihood, of course, is that people will not very often conceive of chance in such an explicitly strategic fashion. Nevertheless, it does seem to be the case that, in general, human beings implicitly aspire to the perfect balance by trying both to exploit potentially beneficial situations and to protect themselves against bad luck.[21]

Something akin to this aspiration is evident within law.[22] Chance is an integral, ineradicable feature of the legal process. Just as in other areas of life, being a beneficiary or a victim of the legal system will often be a matter of luck.[23] Sometimes, the chance element of the legal process is lamented—the observation that a particular part of the process 'is a lottery', for example, is invariably offered as a condemnation[24]—and there are those who argue that minimizing the undesirable consequences of the operation of chance in law is both a feasible and important project.[25] Holmes famously observed that a task of the legal profession is to advise clients on their prospects of avoiding bad legal consequences when engaging in particular activities—so that those clients, rather than simply hoping to get lucky, might try to assess their options in a calculated fashion.[26]

---

[21] See also Nicholas Rescher, *Luck: The Brilliant Randomness of Everyday Life* (New York: Farrar, Straus, Giroux, 1995), 180–8.

[22] See, generally, Alain Bénabent, *La Chance et le droit* (Paris: Librairie Générale de Droit et de Jurisprudence, 1973).

[23] For an example of how, in principle, one could (literally) be a chance beneficiary of the legal system, see Justinian, *Institutes* 2, 20, s. 23, as applied in *Re Knapton* (1941) Ch. 428. More generally, on the use of lotteries to determine property inheritance, see Harry L. Levy, 'Property Distribution by Lot in Present-Day Greece' (1956) 87 *Transactions and Proceedings of the American Philological Association* 42–6 (Levy notes at p. 44 n. 10 that inheritance by lot is a feature of Turkish as well as of Greek law); Michael Herzfeld, 'Social Tension and Inheritance by Lot in Three Greek Villages' (1980) 53 *Anthropological Quarterly* 91–100; Oluf H. Krabbe, 'Om Lodtrækning i Fortid og Nutid [On Lotteries in the Past and in the Present]' (1944) 26 *Juristen* 157–75 at 172–3 (providing details of a 17th-cent. Danish law which stipulated that, when more than one heir to an estate wished to inherit the same object, allocation would be made by lottery); and John Winsor Pratt and Richard Jay Zeckhauser, 'The Fair and Efficient Division of the Winsor Family Silver' (1990) 36 *Management Science* 1293–1301 (cf. also R. Burns (correspondence), *Guardian*, 24 Nov. 1997, G2, p. 17). For an example of how one might become a chance victim of the legal system, see David Lewis, 'The Punishment that Leaves Something to Chance' (1989) 18 *Philosophy and Public Affairs* 53–67 (on the criminal justice system as a penal lottery). More generally, see Note, 'The Luck of the Law: Allusions to Fortuity in Legal Discourse' (1989) 102 *Harvard L. Rev.* 1862–82.

[24] Academic lawyers have sometimes developed this observation when considering personal injury awards. See Terence G. Ison, *The Forensic Lottery: A Critique on Tort Liability as a System of Personal Injury Compensation* (London: Staples Press, 1967); Marc A. Franklin, 'Replacing the Negligence Lottery: Compensation and Selective Reimbursement' (1967) 53 *Virginia L. Rev.* 774–814; and P. S. Atiyah, *The Damages Lottery* (Oxford: Hart Publishing, 1997), 143–50. See also William T. Harris, 'A Public Choice Analysis of the Evolution of Tort Law: Liabilities, Lotteries, and Redistribution' (1992) 51 *American Journal of Economics and Sociology* 1018–8; and, more generally, Christopher P. Bowers, 'Courts, Contracts, and the Appropriate Discount Rate: A Quick Fix for the Legal Lottery' (1996) 63 *Univ. Chicago L. Rev.* 1099–137; and Evan Osborne, 'Courts as Casinos? An Empirical Investigation of Randomness and Efficiency in Civil Litigation' (1999) 28 *Journal of Legal Studies* 187–203.   [25] See, e.g., Smith (above, n. 10), *passim*.

[26] See Oliver Wendell Holmes, 'The Path of the Law' (1897) 10 *Harvard L. Rev.* 457–78 at 457 ('People want to know under what circumstances and how far they will run the risk of coming against what is so much stronger than themselves, and hence it becomes a business [of the legal profession] to find out when this danger is to be feared'); and compare Sir James Fitzjames Stephen, *A General*

Yet it was Holmes too who recognized that, in law, chance raises its head in a variety of ways and that, in certain of its manifestations, chance resists eradication. The idea that the legal system should somehow try to give redress to those who are disadvantaged by natural inequalities of birth, for example, cut no ice with Holmes.[27] At the heart of that legal-economic perspective which is often labelled 'Chicagoan' there rests a similar sentiment: namely, that efforts to use state regulation to counter the adverse effects of luck tend to be impotent (rather like regulating so as to ensure that we have sunshine at weekends, as Stigler once remarked[28]), not to mention arbitrary.[29] Furthermore, according to some Chicagoans, regulation may sometimes force us to confront something similar to—though not quite the same as—the moral luck problem.[30] In short, just as there are those who worry about and wish to exercise control over chance as it operates within law, so too there are those who are inclined to regard such efforts as hubristic,[31] who regard luck, both good and bad, as an inevitable feature of law and life and who prefer—and believe that it is generally to our advantage—to accept the rough with the smooth.[32]

View of the Criminal Law of England (2nd edn., London: Macmillan & Co., 1890), 83: 'There is more harm than good in telling people precisely how far they may go without risking punishment in the pursuit of an unlawful object.'

[27] See, e.g., O. W. Holmes, Jr., *The Common Law* (Boston: Little, Brown & Co., 1881), 108.

[28] George J. Stigler, *The Citizen and the State: Essays on Regulation* (Chicago: University of Chicago Press, 1975), 168.

[29] In the sense, that is, that there can be no right way to determine which instances of bad luck ought to be compensable (and, indeed, to what degree those instances ought to be compensable). See, generally, Richard A. Epstein, 'Luck' (1988) 6 *Social Philosophy and Policy* 17–38.

[30] Obviously, one can envisage instances where regulators take risks and get lucky. How, in moral terms, ought such risk-taking to be viewed? Consider a situation in which absence, or insufficient enforcement, of regulations results in a drug being approved and marketed before thorough testing has been carried out. The consequences may be tragic, but if the drug has no harmful side-effects and improves or even saves lives, its early approval may ensure that people who would have suffered (or suffered for longer) under a more strict regulatory regime in fact benefit. Chicago regulatory theorists, among others, have claimed that penalties tend to be imposed when drugs are approved too early but not when they are approved too late: i.e. haste is considered to be morally blameworthy while risk-aversion is not, even though the latter may sometimes turn out to be just as costly as the former. See George J. Stigler, 'The Formation of Economic Policy', in *Current Problems in Political Economy* (Dr Paul L. Morrison Lectures in Political Economy, 1962–5, Greencastle, Ind.: DePauw University, 1965), 57–76 at 74–5; R. H. Coase, *Essays on Economics and Economists* (Chicago: University of Chicago Press, 1994), 59; also Kirstin Schrader-Frechette, *Risk and Rationality: Philosophical Foundations for Populist Reforms* (Berkeley: University of California Press, 1991), 131–45; and compare Stephen Breyer, *Regulation and its Reform* (Cambridge, Mass.: Harvard University Press, 1982), 148–53.

[31] For illustrations of both attitudes, see George Sher, *Beyond Neutrality: Perfectionism and Politics* (Cambridge: Cambridge University Press, 1997); and compare Richard A. Epstein, *Simple Rules for a Complex World* (Cambridge, Mass.: Harvard University Press, 1995). Sher develops a 'pro-perfectionist' argument to the effect that there exists a defensible conception of the good life which ought to be embraced and promoted by the state, whereas the essence of Epstein's argument is that, since there exists no satisfactory criterion to facilitate objective comparisons of values and since regulations often fail to remedy the problems which they address, state-regulatory regimes are inevitably imperfect.

[32] Though, of course, Chicagoans would not object to the use of private personal insurance to try to counter the ill effects of chance; nor would many of them (Epstein, I think, would be an exception here) deny the utility of tort negligence principles where the inflicter could deal with the risk more cheaply than could the victim.

The fact that it is often not possible—and may even be unwise to try—to exert control over chance is part of the explanation as to why, traditionally, there has been a reluctance consciously to import elements of randomness into the legal system. By and large, chance is inherent within the system: that is, in so far as it is there, it is there without design. Rarely do we set out specifically to introduce elements of chance into law. Of course, there are exceptions to this claim—the most glaring being that of jury selection[33]—and we shall consider some of these exceptions in due course. Particularly in relation to legal decision-making, however, there appears—certainly in modern legal systems—to exist a distinct aversion to making (as opposed to accepting that we may have to let) chance play a part. Legal decision-making by lot, in short, is something on which we are not especially keen.

There seems to be little doubt that legal decision-making by lot is in many ways highly problematic, and one of the purposes of this study is to try to articulate the main problems. Another purpose of this project, however, is to try to demonstrate that these problems may be overstated. Although the prospects for the use of the lottery as a means of social and legal decision-making may be limited, they perhaps need not be as limited as they currently are. Indeed, not only do examples of such decision-making abound throughout history, but models, explorations, and proposals for the use of the lottery as a decision-making tool are common within political philosophy. This study considers what sort of case might be made for the use of lotteries in social and legal decision-making contexts. As already intimated, I shall argue that decision-making by lot has more social and legal potential than we have been prone to assume, that it is an idea which deserves to be taken seriously.[34]

But just how seriously? If people are by and large wary about resort to lot as a method of social and legal decision-making, it might be considered otiose to

---

[33] Although even randomness in jury selection can be compromised—as, traditionally, it has been in the United States—owing to the existence of 'filters' such as the prosecutorial right of peremptory challenge at voir dire. For the classic study of how random jury selection can be compromised, cf. Hans Zeisel, 'Dr Spock and the Case of the Vanishing Women Jurors' (1969) 37 *Univ. Chicago L. Rev.* 1–18. In English law, peremptory challenge in criminal trials was abolished for defendants by the Criminal Justice Act 1988, s. 118 (the number of possible occasions for such challenge having been already reduced by successive statutes).

[34] The emphasis in this book is on the actual and potential use of the lottery as a social decision-making device. I am not concerned with the use of lotteries as means of generating state income (though the two uses are, in fact, historically connected: see Jon Elster, *Solomonic Judgements: Studies in the Limitations of Rationality* (Cambridge: Cambridge University Press, 1989), 36 n. 3). Nor am I especially concerned with other instances of randomization, such as random inspections or sampling (although I shall have some observations to offer on random decisions to inspect and on randomized clinical trials in Chapters 3 and 4 respectively). On the notion of randomization generally, cf. Deborah J. Bennett, *Randomness* (Cambridge, Mass.: Harvard University Press, 1998); Nicholas Rescher, 'The Concept of Randomness' (1961) 27 *Theoria* 1–11; Peter Kirschenmann, 'Concepts of Randomness' (1972) *Journal of Philosophical Logic* 395–414; Gregory J. Chaitin, 'Randomness and Mathematical Proof' (1975) 232 *Scientific American* 47–52; Alonzo Church, 'On the Concept of a Random Sequence' (1940) 46 *Bulletin of the American Mathematical Society* 130–5; and Mervin E. Muller, 'Random Numbers' (1968) 13 *International Encyclopedia of Social Science* 307–14.

suggest that the method ought to be adopted more widely.[35] Why try to make a serious case for a practice to which people are significantly averse? The answer to this question is that what interests me most of all about decision-making by lot is not the prospects for its adoption but aversion to its adoption. If one grants that the social and legal potential and advantages of decision-making by lot are frequently underestimated, it might be interesting then to explore why this should be the case. A fundamental feature of decisions reached by lot is that they are stripped of human agency; indeed, where lotteries are used, human choice is present within the decision-making process only to the extent that a determination has been made to resort to the lottery in the first place (and also, where a lottery is weighted, to the extent that there must be a decision concerning how it should be weighted). Absence of human agency is sometimes highlighted as a primary virtue of the lottery decision. Where difficult choices have to be made, resort to lot reduces the possibility of some person or group being blamed for—or, for that matter, feeling guilty about—the consequences. Furthermore, that decisions by lot are attributable to chance rather than to human intent may sometimes make them more tolerable to those who are unlucky: to be rejected by chance, after all, might be considered less of an affront—less of an occasion for loss of self-esteem—than would rejection by others.[36] Yet it is precisely because lottery decisions are lacking in human agency that we are very often troubled by them. Such decisions are, after all, mindless. They cannot be ascribed to any particular person or persons. They are decisions for which no one can be held responsible or accountable.[37]

What especially troubles us about lottery decisions, I think, is the fact that they are not reasoned: the outcome of a lottery rests on a process that bears no relevance to the issue in relation to which a decision is being reached.[38] Reason does not, of course, exhaust human agency: decisions made on the basis of stated reasons are only one category of decisions which human beings can reach and for which they can be held accountable. When considering aversion to lottery use, nevertheless, I think that they are the most significant type of decision. The reason

---

[35] Though it might be observed more generally that the fact that there exists a widespread disinclination to engage in certain activities has traditionally not stopped legal and political theorists from advocating the pursuit of those activities where it is believed that such pursuit will generate benefits. See, e.g., Elisabeth M. Landes and Richard A. Posner, 'The Economics of the Baby Shortage' (1978) 7 *Journal of Legal Studies* 323–48.

[36] See Hank Greely, 'The Equality of Allocation by Lot' (1977) 12 *Harvard Civil Rights-Civil Liberties L. Rev.* 113–41 at 123. Even if to be rejected by chance is somehow less dishonourable than to be rejected by others, however, we might still consider selection by chance to be less honourable than selection by those others and so actually prefer to accept the risk of being rejected by others as the necessary price to be paid for the chance of being selected by them. (The notion that lottery outcomes may actually generate or exacerbate loss of self-esteem is taken up in Chapter 4.)

[37] Though of course, as already noted, somebody will be responsible for the initial decision to decide by lot. See also John Broome, 'Selecting People Randomly' (1984) 95 *Ethics* 38–55 at 52.

[38] See Serge-Christophe Kolm, *Modern Theories of Justice* (Cambridge, Mass.: MIT Press, 1996), 36.

for this is that decisions reached by resort to chance—or even decisions made on the basis of instinct or emotion—will usually be less articulated or elaborated than are decisions which rely explicitly upon reasoning. And while we can ask of a person why it is that he or she resolved particular issues by relying on chance, instinct, or emotion (or, for that matter, why it is that this person exhibits the instincts or emotions that he or she does), these resolutions do not offer much scope for dialogue or engagement and will normally, I suspect, provide rather little to focus on and contend with as compared with resolutions which deal with the same issues but which are furnished with reasons.

This brings me to the primary thesis of this book.[39] Aversion to decision-making by lot is, I believe, indicative of a distinct attraction, possibly even an addiction, to reason. It is possible to envisage instances in which resort to lot will produce decisions that are impartial and extremely cost-efficient and in which, moreover, reasoning one's way to a decision will most likely take considerable time and expose one to the accusation of partiality. Yet, even in these cases, there rarely exists any inclination to decide by resort to sortition. The process of legal decision-making is generally, if often only implicitly, considered to be more important than the quality of decisions reached; and so a highly contentious legal decision furnished with reasons is likely to meet with greater approval than would a genuinely impartial (and, in consequentialist terms, welcome) decision arrived at by lot. Why should this be so?

The answer to this question, I think, is that what we seek, particularly in legal decision-making, is not right answers but attributable answers—answers for which somebody can be held responsible or accountable. More than this, we commonly want legal answers which are serious as well as attributable—answers, that is, which are furnished with reasons as opposed to being based on instinct or caprice or some other emotional response. By taking seriously the notion of deciding by resort to lot, and through an examination of why there exists considerable reluctance to embrace this form of decision-making, I hope to be able to offer some insight into the place which reason occupies in law.

---

[39] This thesis is developed in Chapter 4, section 4. The thesis is to be distinguished from the book's main proposal concerning the more extensive use of lotteries in social and legal decision-making contexts (see Chapter 5).

2

Contextualizing the Lottery

The practices of past or distant societies sometimes appear, when we compare them with our own, to be marked by a deficiency of reason. Yet closer, more contextualized inspection of those practices often reveals them to be not nearly as unreasonable as we originally believed.[1] Once arrangements which previously seemed unreasonable begin to make sense, furthermore, the likelihood is that our own current ways of doing things will no longer seem quite so inevitable.

One can imagine a community of the future in which social decisions are generally reached through resort to sortition.[2] While the lottery has never been adopted as a general social decision-making tool, we shall see in due course that it has, in the past, been used to resolve a fairly wide variety of matters.[3] Yet, today, seriously to entertain the prospect of extensive social decision-making by resort to lot would probably strike most people as absurd. 'To a modern educated man,' Tylor remarked over a century ago, 'drawing lots or tossing up a coin is an appeal to chance, that is, to ignorance.'[4] To argue that, in general, social goods and burdens ought to be distributed randomly is to take no account of criteria such as merit, desert, competence, and need. Why, when important decisions have to be made, should we place our trust in the luck of the draw?

This question cannot be cursorily dismissed. The most appropriate answer to it very well may be that, in general, social decision-makers ought not to rely upon

---

[1] For a compelling demonstration of this point in relation to systems of proof, see Mirjan Damaška, 'Rational and Irrational Proof Revisited', in J. F. Nijboer and J. M. Reijntjes (eds.), *Proceedings of the First World Conference on New Trends in Criminal Investigation and Evidence* (Lelystad: Koninkijke Vermande, 1997), 75–83.

[2] For a detailed depiction, see Barbara Goodwin, *Justice by Lottery* (Hemel Hempstead: Harvester Wheatsheaf, 1992), 3–23.

[3] Social decisions are decisions about social policy (e.g. decisions concerning resource allocation or dispute settlement) and are broadly distinguishable from decisions concerning individual choice (such as, say, whether or not to take up a hobby). In this book, I am concerned principally with the lottery as a social decision-making tool, although now and again my concern is with the lottery as a method of private decision-making between or among individuals (which private decisions may or may not have wider social implications). Similarly, my concern here is mainly, though not exclusively, with the lottery as something which is resorted to wilfully (as a means of procuring what Dworkin calls 'option luck') as opposed to something which occurs without human intent (i.e. as a reflection of 'brute luck'). See Ronald Dworkin, 'What is Equality? Part 2: Equality of Resources' (1981) 10 *Philosophy and Public Affairs* 283–345 at 293. On the latter form of lottery, cf., e.g., Hobbes, *Leviathan*, I. 15; and Paine, *Rights of Man*, II. 3 (on 'the lottery of human faculties').

[4] Edward B. Tylor, *Primitive Culture: Researches into the Development of Mythology, Philosophy, Religion, Language, Art, and Custom* (2 vols., 2nd edn., London: John Murray, 1873), i. 78. On the archaism of lot-casting, cf. also J. Huizinga, *Homo Ludens: A Study of the Play-Element in Culture* (Eng. trans. R. F. C. Hull, London: Routledge & Kegan Paul, 1949), 78–9.

the luck of the draw. Indeed, we will see that there are plenty of reasons to be wary of social decision-making by lot. Yet wariness of the practice is not the same thing as wholesale aversion to it, and it is possible to identify instances in which the lottery tends to be valued positively as a social decision-making mechanism. Making sense of these instances—that is, understanding why there should exist a willingness randomly to allocate some resources and tasks but not others—is difficult, not least because views concerning the utility of the lottery as a social decision-making device vary throughout history and cultures.

That these views may vary considerably is obvious from the fact that once acceptable aleatory practices are now basically extinct. In the second part of this chapter we shall observe that, although, considered historically, the lottery can be seen to be a significant political decision-making device, in modern political systems its function, where it has one, is usually marginal. This observation can be viewed as a specific illustration of a more general point, one which we shall explore immediately: namely that there seems to have existed, in the past, a greater willingness to use lotteries in order to reach decisions of considerable social magnitude.

1. DIVINATION BY LOT

The principal explanation for this greater willingness is, I think, that the outcome of casting lots was once regarded not as random but as the revelation of divine intent.[5] In essence, the idea is expressed in Proverbs 16: 33.[6] Indeed, in the Old Testament scriptures,[7] lot-casting is quite frequently engaged in for the purpose of ascertaining God's will.[8] While divination by lot can be traced back at least as

---

[5] For a discussion of, and an attempt to defend, the idea that there can be no such thing as a chance occurrence which is completely independent from the will of God, see Donald M. MacKay, *Science, Chance and Providence* (Oxford: Oxford University Press, 1978), 21–40.

[6] 'The lots may be cast into the lap, but the issue depends wholly on the Lord.'

[7] The practice of divination by lot seems to occur in the New Testament only once, in the choice of Matthias as successor to Judas (Acts 1: 26). Certainly there are other instances of lot-casting in the New Testament (see, e.g., Matt. 27: 35; Mark 15: 24; Luke 1: 9–11; John 19: 23–4), but none of these other instances is an example of divination by lot. On lot-casting in the New Testament, see generally P. A. Gordon Clark, 'Lots', in James Hastings (ed.), *Dictionary of the Apostolic Church* (2 vols., Edinburgh: T. & T. Clark, 1915–18), i. 710–13 at 712–13.

[8] See, e.g., Joshua 7: 14–18; Jonah 1: 7; and 1 Samuel 14: 40–2. The ancient Jews resorted to lot-casting to determine God's will concerning, among other matters, allocation of land (see, e.g., Numbers 26: 52–6), conscription of soldiers (Judges 20: 9–10) and dispute-settlement (Proverbs 18: 18). More generally, see A. M. Hasofer, 'Random Mechanisms in Talmudic Literature' (1967) 54 *Biometrika* 316–21; J. Lindblom, 'Lot-Casting in the Old Testament' (1962) 12 *Vetus Testamentum* 164–78; David Werner Amram, 'Chapters from the Biblical Law. IX: The Trial of Achan by Lot' (1900) 12 *The Green Bag* 659–61; Bernard S. Jackson, *Theft in Early Jewish Law* (Oxford: Clarendon Press, 1972), 233–6; and the entries by Murray Lichtenstein and Louis Isaac Rabinowitz under 'Lots' at (1971) 11 *Encyclopaedia Judaica* 510–14. It would none the less appear that the ancient Jews were not always entirely convinced of the reliability of determining divine will by lot: cf. Nachum L. Rabinovitch, *Probability and Statistical Inference in Ancient and Medieval Jewish Literature* (Toronto: University of Toronto Press, 1973), 23.

far as the ninth century BC,[9] however, it would be wrong to regard the practice as wholly archaic. In some cultures, modern anthropologists have shown, it remains extant.[10] Yet lot-casting becomes especially interesting when it is considered not in anthropological but in historical terms. Anthropological investigation into the casting of lots appears generally to reveal that the practice is still resorted to in many societies, and that it serves a variety of objectives,[11] but that it is only rarely relied upon for the purpose of reaching important social or communal decisions. By contrast, when lot-casting is examined historically, it becomes clear that it once had much greater social significance than it does today.

In modern times, one of the primary anxieties about the lottery as a social decision-making device concerns its capacity to trivialize important issues. 'To use a lottery to allocate risks or benefits is not only a denial of rationality,' according to a *Science* editorial of the 1970s, 'it is also a denial of man's humanity; each man is reduced to a cipher, distinguished from other ciphers only by the uniqueness of the combination of digits that identify his records in a growing number of office files.'[12] Yet, in the past, resort to lot was considered very differently: the primary concern about the lottery as a decision-making method has traditionally been not that it might trivialize important matters but that such an important device might be used inappropriately—that is, to settle trivial affairs. Although divination by the casting of lots is not forbidden (*illicita*) by natural law, Aquinas believed, such practice must only be undertaken where there appears to be no other way of discovering the correct course of action: since lotteries can be 'misapplied to earthly business', only in cases

---

[9] See A. Leo Oppenheim, *Ancient Mesopotamia: Portrait of a Dead Civilization* (Chicago: University of Chicago Press, 1964), 99–100, 208–9.

[10] See, e.g., Robert Jaulin, 'Formal Analysis of Geomancy' (Eng. trans. A. Holden) (1970) 2 *Semiotica* 195–246 (explaining 'geomantic revelation' as a lottery-based form of divination). A similar point might be made with regard to ordeals and duels. On ordeals, see e.g. E. Adamson Hoebel, *The Law of Primitive Man: A Study in Comparative Legal Dynamics* (New York: Atheneum, 1979 (1954)), 251–2. On duels, see e.g. R. F. Barton, *Ifugao Law* (Berkeley: University of California Press, 1969 (1919)), 90–2.

[11] For example, certain anthropologists have attempted to demonstrate that, in some instances, divinatory lot-casting serves a strategic purpose. Moore has argued that scapulimancy among Naskapi caribou hunters works in this way. In deciding where to hunt by interpreting the cracks and spots which appear in the shoulder-blade of the caribou when it has been held over hot coals for a short time, the Naskapi do not determine where to hunt on the basis of personal preference or judgement but rather base their decision 'on the outcome of an impersonal and relatively uncontrolled process'. Omar Khayyam Moore, 'Divination: A New Perspective' (1957) 59 *American Anthropologist* 69–74 at 71. By rendering their hunting strategies pretty much random in this way, Moore suggests, the hunters possibly maximize their chances of out-foxing the game, since it becomes more or less impossible for the caribou to anticipate the emergence of a pattern in hunting activity. 'If it may be assumed that there is some interplay between the animals they [i.e. the Naskapi] seek and the hunts they undertake, such that the hunted and the hunters act and react to the other's actions and potential actions, then there may be a marked advantage in avoiding a fixed pattern in hunting' (ibid.). See also William Davenport, 'Jamaican Fishing: A Game Theory Analysis' (1960) 59 *Yale University Publications in Anthropology* 3–11.

[12] Dael Wolfle, 'Chance, or Human Judgment?' (1970) 167 *Science* 168.

of 'urgent necessity is it lawful, provided due reverence be observed, to call upon God for a judgement by casting lots'.[13]

The lottery, as Aquinas's position suggests, was regarded in medieval times as a means of getting God to speak.[14] If God directs everything in the universe, so the argument went, the way lots fall represents not randomness but divine choice.[15] None the less, behind this lottery earthly hands were at work. For determining what constitutes business appropriate for settlement by lot is a matter for human beings. It is well known that many forms of ordeal were not so much methods of crime-detection as means by which to justify a verdict which had already been reached.[16] Since the lottery would provide an outcome not dictated by human judgement, it was sometimes considered to be fairer than certain other medieval systems of trial.[17] Yet lotteries are not divorced from human judgement: people decide where lotteries should be used, what forms those lotteries should take and who falls into the pool of eligible candidates.

---

[13] Aquinas, *Summa Theologiae*, II. ii. 95. 8.

[14] See F. N. David, *Games, Gods and Gambling: The Origins and History of Probability and Statistical Ideas from the Earliest Times to the Newtonian Era* (London: Charles Griffin & Co., 1962), 13–20. A much earlier illustration of the belief that lot-casting may reveal supernatural intent is to be found in the *I Ching*, or *Book of Changes*, a Chinese oracular book of wisdom supposedly written or compiled by Confucius for use as a source of guidance in personal, social, political, and military decision-making. This consists of a series of epigrams (with accompanying commentaries) which are related to a sequence of 64 hexagrams composed of lines which may be broken or unbroken and which may also be static or moving. To consult the *I Ching* for guidance, an inquirer must have a specific question in mind and must engage in divination to locate the appropriate hexagram. Divination originally involved the heating and cracking of tortoise shells, but the *I Ching* has subsequently been consulted through elaborate rituals involving the casting of either divining sticks (usually yarrow stalks) or coins. The purpose of divination is not to ascertain the will of God but to determine how the Path (*Tao*) is configured and where one stands upon it. See C. G. Jung, *Synchronicity: An Acausal Connecting Principle* (Eng. trans. R. F. C. Hull, London: Routledge & Kegan Paul, 1972 (1952)), 50–3 (*I Ching*), also 96–101 (on *Tao*); and Deborah J. Bennett, *Randomness* (Cambridge, Mass.: Harvard University Press, 1998), 36–42.

[15] See Elaine Pagels, *The Gnostic Gospels* (Harmondsworth: Penguin, 1982 (1979)), 66.

[16] See Keith Thomas, *Religion and the Decline of Magic: Studies in Popular Beliefs in Sixteenth- and Seventeenth-Century England* (Harmondsworth: Penguin, 1973 (1971)), 252–64. More generally, on the ordeal as a form of adjudication, cf. Robert Jacob, 'Le Jugement de Dieu et la formation de la fonction de juger dans l'histoire européene' (1995) 39 *Archives de Philosophie du Droit* 87–104.

[17] See Charlotte Leitmaier, *Die Kirche und die Gottesurteile: Eine rechtshistorische Studie* (Vienna: Herold, 1953), 28–30. Elster suggests that if the outcome of a lottery represents God's decision, it should hardly matter that the lottery is conducted in a fair manner, 'since God's hand could always steer the die or the coin so as to make the right side come up . . . Nor would there be any need to take great care in selecting the pool of eligibles for a lottery.' The fact that 'people did in fact care about these procedural matters testifies to their ambiguous attitude towards the methods'. Jon Elster, *Solomonic Judgements: Studies in the Limitations of Rationality* (Cambridge: Cambridge University Press, 1989), 51. This line of argument seems questionable: (1) for the believer, the relevant issue is surely not whether God could, but whether he would, correct the imperfect procedure of the lottery; (2) that people cared about procedural matters probably reveals not ambiguity but a disinclination to be seen to be challenging God (something against which the Bible repeatedly counsels: see, e.g., Deut. 6: 16). To conduct the lottery in an imperfect manner would have been to test God, and so to exhibit a lack of faith.

From early medieval times, the issue of where lotteries should and should not be used—as with the more general question of what were legitimate and what were improper forms of divination[18]—was of especial concern to theologians. The basic line of argument which emerged with regard to lot-casting was, in essence, that which was espoused by Aquinas: since to resort to lot is to ask for God's word, we must use lotteries sparingly and reverentially. To resort to them for trivial or self-serving purposes would be sacrilegious. Hence, 'games of chance were from a very early period prohibited, not simply on account of the many evils that result from them, but as a species of blasphemy, being an appeal on trivial matters to the adjudication of the Deity'.[19] This line of reasoning is particularly prominent in Puritan casuistic literature.[20] The use of lots for the purpose of sport—so-called 'lusory' lots—was wrong, according to James Balmford, because such practice represents a vain and disrespectful summoning of God's special providence.[21] Much the same argument was advanced by Puritan writers with regard to divination by lot for the purposes of, among other things, fortune-telling, detecting criminals, and raising money.[22] While a tone of utter certainty concerning the proper use of lots runs throughout a good deal of this literature, however, the matter was in reality far from settled. It is all very well to claim that, when troublesome decisions have to be made, lots can be cast and God will thereby show his hand. But what are genuinely troublesome decisions? How

---

[18] On which cf. Hermann Nottarp, *Gottesurteilstudien* (Munich: Kösel Verlag, 1956), 34–9.

[19] W. E. H. Lecky, *History of the Rise and Influence of the Spirit of Rationalism in Europe* (2 vols., London: Longmans, Green & Co., 1910 (1865)), i. 280.

[20] See Thomas (above, n. 16), 142–3; and, more generally, D. R. Bellhouse, 'Probability in the Sixteenth and Seventeenth Centuries: An Analysis of Puritan Casuistry' (1988) 56 *International Statistical Review* 63–74.

[21] James Balmford, *A Short and Plaine Dialogue Concerning the unlawfulness of Playing at Cards or Tables, or any other Game consisting in Chance* (London: Richard Boile, 1593; repr. London: Ellen Boyle, 1623), 5–6.

[22] See, e.g., Thomas Cooper, *The Mystery of Witchcraft. Discovering the Truth, Nature, Occasions, Growth and Power Thereof* (London: Nicholas Okes, 1617; repr. London: Bernard Alsop, 1622), 149–50. Of course, that Puritan divines tended to oppose such practices does not mean that people generally abstained from them. The first English state lottery was established by Elizabeth I in 1566 to raise revenue for the repair of harbours. Such lotteries were used intermittently until they were outlawed in the 1820s. See, generally, John Ashton, *A History of English Lotteries* (London: The Leadenhall Press, 1893); and also Jacob Cohen, 'The Element of Lottery in British Government Bonds, 1694–1919' (1953) n.s. 20 *Economica* 237–46 at 241–5. Nor were the Puritans alone in opposing revenue-raising lotteries. In the 18th cent. Adam Smith objected to such lotteries not on religious grounds, but because they exploit the propensity of individuals to overestimate their chances of good fortune. 'That the chance of gain is naturally over-valued,' he observed, 'we may learn from the universal success of lotteries . . . There is not . . . a more certain proposition in mathematics, than that the more tickets you adventure upon, the more likely you are to be a loser. Adventure upon all the tickets in the lottery, and you lose for certain; and the greater the number of your tickets the nearer you approach this certainty.' Smith, *Wealth of Nations*, I. x. b. 27. For a rather more sanguine view of revenue-raising lotteries, see John Venn, *The Logic of Chance: An Essay on the Foundations and Province of the Theory of Probability, with Especial Reference to its Logical Bearings and its Application to Moral and Social Science* (2nd edn., London: Macmillan & Co., 1876), 110–11; and cf. also D. H. Mellor, *The Matter of Chance* (Cambridge: Cambridge University Press, 1971), 162–70.

can one be sure that one resorts to lot-casting for reasons which are not disrespectful to God?

Indication that there existed, in medieval times, uncertainty over this matter is apparent from the not entirely consistent attitude of the courts with regard to lot-casting by criminal trial juries. The criminal jury was introduced into English law during the early thirteenth century when the ordeal by edict of the Roman Church was abolished.[23] Although the criminal jury replaced a divinatory practice, however, members of juries have, over the centuries, been known from time to time to engage in forms of divination or supernatural ritual when seeking to reach a verdict. Only a few years ago, a Crown Court conviction was quashed by the Court of Appeal because four jurors had used a ouija board, purportedly in an effort to receive answers from one of the defendant's alleged victims.[24] Over the centuries, Winfield remarked in the early 1920s, '[c]asting lots seems to have been a pretty frequent piece of impropriety committed by jurors who were puzzled by the facts'.[25] Yet resort to lot by juries has not always been a straightforward matter of misconduct. While, for example, most seventeenth- and early eighteenth-century case-law indicates that verdicts would be set aside,[26] and that jurors would on occasions be fined,[27] when decisions were reached by resort to sortition, there exists at least one instance from this period in which the casting of lots by jurors was judicially approved. In *Prior* v. *Powers*, decided in 1665, it was held that where members of a jury are equally divided, reaching a verdict by recourse to lot would be an acceptable alternative to a retrial, since it 'is as good a way of decision as by the strongest body . . . and is suitable in such cases to the law of God'.[28]

Even the Puritan divines of this period expressed some disagreement over the appropriate use of lots. In *Of the Nature and Use of Lots*, originally published in 1619, Thomas Gataker departed radically from orthodox Puritan opinion by claiming that it is not divine law but the laws of nature which determine the outcomes of

---

[23] See Roger D. Groot, 'The Early-Thirteenth-Century Criminal Jury', in J. S. Cockburn and Thomas A. Green (eds.), *Twelve Good Men and True: The Criminal Trial Jury in England, 1200–1800* (Princeton: Princeton University Press, 1988), 3–35. Frank attributes to F. W. Maitland the observation that 'the jury was not by any means immediately popular', and that 'at first the ordeals were generally considered more desirable, more safe'. Jerome Frank, *Courts on Trial: Myth and Reality in American Justice* (Princeton: Princeton University Press, 1973 (1949)), 109.

[24] *R.* v. *Young* [1995] QB 324.

[25] Percy Henry Winfield, *The History of Conspiracy and Abuse of Legal Procedure* (Cambridge: Cambridge University Press, 1921), 190. In a similar vein, see also Jerome Frank, *Law and the Modern Mind* (Gloucester, Mass.: Peter Smith, 1970 (1930)), 184–5 n. 3.

[26] See, e.g., *R.* v. *Fitz-Water* (27 Car. II) 2 Lev. 139; and *Hale* v. *Cove* (1725) 1 Stra. 643.

[27] See, e.g., *Foster* v. *Hawden* (29 Car. II) 2 Lev. 205; and *Foy* v. *Harder* (29 Car. II) 3 Keb. 805. Cf. also the later case of *Vaise* v. *Delaval* (1785) 1 TR 11 (court refusing to hear evidence of jury coin-tossing).

[28] *Prior* v. *Powers* (16 Car. II) 1 Keb. 811 (*per* Windham J). It should be noted, nevertheless, that, according to the reporter in this case, Twisden J considered that it would be 'of ill example' if a new trial were not granted.

lotteries.[29] 'For example: In the blending of scrolls or tickets together, the motion of the vessel wherein they are blended . . . causes some to lie this way and some to lie that way . . . [No] man [can] say certainly that there is ordinarily any special hand of God, in the shuffling and sorting of them, crossing the course of nature'.[30] God plays no greater role in events which are accidental than he does in those which are contingent or inevitable, and so '[t]he casualty of an event does not simply of itself make it a work of God's special or immediate providence'.[31] If the results of lotteries are a representation of God's will, Gataker argued, God would have to be capricious, for these results are inevitably inconsistent. '[T]han an ordinary Lot there is nothing more uncertain, ready upon every new shaking of the Lot pot to give out a new sentence . . . [Is] it not frivolous, if not impious, therefore to say, that upon every second shaking or drawing God alters his sentence . . . and so to charge him with contradiction or contrariety?'[32] Since God is not capricious, Gataker concluded, he cannot play any special role in determining the outcomes of lotteries.

By separating chance from divine providence, Gataker was suggesting that there is, in principle, nothing blasphemous about using lots for secular purposes. Indeed, he believed that resort to lot is appropriate for settling civil matters (such as determining the composition of committees or appointing magistrates) and for sporting and recreational purposes.[33] Such thinking ran very much against the grain of seventeenth century theological orthodoxy and attracted considerable opposition.[34] The American Puritan, Increase Mather, for example, condemned as impious Gataker's sanctioning of the use of lotteries for recreational ends.[35] Yet, even in the early seventeenth century, Gataker was not a lone voice. 'Many too nicely take exceptions at cards, tables, and dice, and such mixed lusorious lots', wrote Robert Burton in the 1620s; although such pastimes 'may justly be otherwise excepted at, as they are often abused', they are 'honest recreations in themselves'.[36] By the early decades of the following century, Gataker's views on the use of lotteries for secular purposes were not only being replicated and defended but also developed.[37] Although at first considered radical and strongly contested,

---

[29] Thomas Gataker, *Of the Nature and Use of Lots: A Treatise Historicall and Theologicall* (London: Edward Griffin for William Bladen, 1619; 2nd edn., London: John Havilland for William Bladen, 1627). On Gataker, cf. *Encyclopaedia Britannica* (11th edn., Cambridge: Cambridge University Press, 1910), xi. 527. [30] Gataker, *Nature and Use of Lots* (1st edn.), 146–7. [31] Ibid. 22. [32] Ibid. 159. [33] Ibid. 130. [34] See, generally, Thomas (above, n. 16), 144; Bellhouse (above, n. 20), 70–2; and cf. also Thomas Gataker, *A Just Defence of Certain Passages in a Former Treatise Concerning the Nature and Use of Lots* (London: John Havilland for William Bladen, 1623). Critical reaction to Gataker's views on lotteries apparently jeopardized his clerical career: see Nicholas Rescher, *Luck: The Brilliant Randomness of Everyday Life* (New York: Farrar, Straus, Giroux, 1995), 119. [35] Increase Mather, *Testimony against Prophane Customs* (repr. of 1687 edn., Charlottesville, Va.: University of Virginia Press, 1953), 13–15. [36] Robert Burton, *The Anatomy of Melancholy* (ed. H. Jackson, London: Dent & Sons, 1932 (1621)), 82. [37] See, in particular, Jean Barbeyrac, 'Discours sur la nature du sort', in Gerardus Noodt, *Du pouvoir des souverains, et de la liberté du conscience* (Fr. trans. J. Barbeyrac, 2nd edn., Amsterdam: no publisher, 1714), 82–207.

his position 'gradually influenced educated men'[38] and 'eventually was commonly accepted'.[39] The challenge to orthodoxy became orthodoxy.[40]

That the idea of divination by lot began to seem less theologically compelling does not mean that the practice similarly fell into disuse. 'Among the people the lot retained its appeal for divination and decision-taking.'[41] Even the idea did not become wholly disreputable.[42] By the late seventeenth-century, nevertheless, the secularism which had initially been prompted by the Reformation was sufficiently well established in English society to ensure that both the practice and the idea of divination by lot were beginning to fade from view.[43] With increasing secularization, the practice of attributing events to chance came to be seen not as a form of explanation but as a failure to comprehend, an inability to understand what caused those events to occur.[44]

It would be easy to determine from this that the movement away from divinatory lot-casting is part of the evolution of human rationality. If we believe that the practice of casting lots in order to get God to show his hand is an irrational one, and if we no longer engage in that practice whereas once we did, then we might indeed very easily conclude that we have become more rational. For at least four reasons, however, such a conclusion ought to arouse suspicion. The conclusion would demand, first of all, both that we define rationality to suit our own modern, secular purposes and that we deny that there could ever be a genuinely rational

---

[38] Clark (above, n. 7), 713.

[40] See Tylor (above, n. 4), i. 79.

[39] Bellhouse (above, n. 20), 72.

[41] Thomas (above, n. 16), 146.

[42] Consider, here, an American example: where a ship is at sea and its passengers and crew are *in extremis*, Judge Baldwin observed in the famous case of *United States* v. *Holmes* in 1842, the selection of a sacrificial victim by lot 'is resorted to as the fairest mode, and, in some sort, as an appeal to God'. *United States* v. *Holmes* (CC Pa. 1842) 26 Fed. Cas. 360, 367. When circumstances along these lines came before the Queen's Bench Division in the even more famous English case of *R*. v. *Dudley and Stephens* (1884) 14 QBD 273, however, lots had not been cast by the survivors and were not contemplated by the court. According to one legal historian, *United States* v. *Holmes* 'is notable . . . as the only case [in Anglo-American law] that explicitly accepts the propriety, in appropriate circumstances, of selecting victims by lot'. A. W. Brian Simpson, *Cannibalism and the Common Law: A Victorian Yachting Tragedy* (London: The Hambledon Press, 1994 (1984)), 176.

[43] See C. John Sommerville, *The Secularization of Early Modern England: From Religious Culture to Religious Faith* (New York: Oxford University Press, 1992), 147–9 (discussing providence generally). According to Sommerville (p. 186), '[b]y 1700 we have seen many of the marks of completed secularization: the appearance of religious movements as a reaction to the failure of religious establishment, reductionistic explanations of the religious sense, the state's power to define religion. A further sign of the times was that the enemy of religion was now seen, not as a spiritual opponent, Satan, but as simple indifference.' Of course, with industrialization the process of secularization would evolve still further. On this matter, cf. Alasdair MacIntyre, *Secularization and Modern Change* (London: Oxford University Press, 1967).

[44] See also Peter C. Fishburn, 'Acceptable Social Choice Lotteries', in Hans W. Gottinger and Werner Leinfellner (eds.), *Decision Theory and Social Ethics: Issues in Social Choice* (Dordrecht: Reidel, 1978), 133–52 at 137: 'Modern attitudes towards social choice lotteries have been shaped in large measure by Enlightenment thought that led to the doctrine of the freedom and moral responsibility of men to shape and control their destiny . . . According to the freedom-responsibility doctrine, the use of a lottery to make a social decision subverts man's control over his own affairs, denies his proper role as a moral agent responsible for the health and improvement of the social organism, and otherwise constitutes a step backwards into the dark ages by relegating the decision to blind chance.'

motive behind divination by lot. Secondly, it would be questionable to conclude that the turn away from divinatory lot-casting marked, somehow, an increase in human rationality given that we have hardly witnessed the death of superstition and that we appear today to be as inclined to believe in the mystical and the super-natural as we have ever been. Certainly it can be argued that modern and past practices differ, and that we may well have become more rational, to the extent that we are no longer inclined to allow such beliefs to dictate political and legal—much as we may now and again allow them to influence our private—decision-making.[45] Yet it may sometimes be the case that refusal to entertain the possibility of political and legal decision-making by resort to randomization betrays not human rationality but quite the opposite. Indeed, thirdly, contemporary applications of the lottery for the purpose of decision-making can hardly be less tainted by irrationality than earlier applications if it is sometimes the case—and I intend, in due course, to show that it is sometimes the case—that decision-making by lot is resisted (or, for that matter, accepted) even though it is not possible rationally to justify our practice. Finally, if looking for God's wisdom in the fall of the dice (or whatever) seems irrational, the impulse to exert control over the uncontrollable may itself be irrationally motivated and, even where this is not the case, may still reveal the limits of human rationality. Indeed, the very belief that we have become more rational could in itself be a symptom of irrationality—that is, of an unwillingness to acknowledge, or at least an inability to appreciate, the degree to which rationality is bounded.[46]

2. ELECTION BY LOT

Perhaps the principal indication of how our estimation of the lottery as a decision-making device has changed over the centuries is that it no longer has much divinatory significance. A further indication of how our estimation has changed rests in the fact that, as a decision-making tool, the lottery no longer has much political significance.[47] Nowadays, choice of political representatives by random selection

---

[45] Why should we no longer be inclined to resort to chance, superstition, or whatever for the purpose of reaching decisions of public (as opposed to personal) significance? Possibly the answer to this question rests in Hacking's observation that, in earlier times, people lacked an understanding of evidence (or at least of anything analogous to our modern understanding of evidence). See Ian Hacking, *The Taming of Chance* (Cambridge: Cambridge University Press, 1990), 1–11. We might speculate that the emergence of the ability to understand evidence explains why political and legal decision-makers gradually stopped looking to the divine and the mystical for answers.

[46] Elster (above, n. 17), 17, calls the irrational belief in the omnipotence of rationality 'hyperra-tionality'. A symptom of hyperrationality is the inability to see that it is sometimes more rational to be irrational than it is to be rational—an example would be the failure to appreciate that where the best possible decision is by no means obvious, the most rational course of action may be to abandon the outcome to chance.

[47] Although I am discussing divination by lot and election by lot as separate practices, it is of course possible that the two may merge. The obvious example is the appointment of religious lead-ers by lot—as was possibly once the Tibetan practice, for instance, with regard to the election of the

virtually never occurs. San Marino has traditionally chosen its governors by lot,[48] and some political systems permit the use of lotteries as electoral tie-breakers.[49] There may even sometimes be a lottery-like quality to policy-selection within contemporary political systems.[50] In the House of Commons, for example, whether or not Private Members' Bills stand any chance of being presented—whether or not, that is, they are accorded the free time which has not been reserved for government business—is normally dependent on what is, in effect, a lottery.[51] For the most part, however, lotteries do not feature within modern political processes.

Reluctance to use lotteries for political purposes is understandable. The notion of general random policy-selection seems to be a non-starter, not only because such a practice would require that capriciousness be regarded as the central principle of sound government and that insecurity and uncertainty among citizens be treated as a desideratum, but also because it would, ironically, require an excessive amount of political planning: a policy of random policy-selection would have to be settled upon and, on every political issue, there would have to be formulated a repertoire of policies from which a random choice could be made.

With a lottery-based electoral system at least eight drawbacks emerge.[52] First,

---

Dalai Lama: see J. G. Frazer, *The Golden Bough: A Study in Magic and Religion. Part I: The Magic Art and the Evolution of Kings* (2 vols., 3rd edn., London: Macmillan and Co., 1911), i. 411–12. On lot-casting in Tibet, cf. further Rebecca Redwood French, *The Golden Yoke: The Legal Cosmology of Buddhist Tibet* (Ithaca, NY: Cornell University Press, 1995), 129–36.

[48] For details of the system, see Vilhelm Aubert, 'Chance in Social Affairs' (1959) 2 *Inquiry* 1–24 at 16; and Aldo Garosci, *San Marino: Mito e storiografia tra i libertini e il Carducci* (Milan: Edizioni di Comunità, 1967), 143–6.

[49] In the UK, if two or more candidates for parliamentary election have an equal number of votes (even after recounts), the returning officer must decide the ballot by lot and proceed as if the winner of the lottery had obtained one more vote than the other candidate (or candidates): see Representation of the People Act 1983, Sched. 1, Rule 49. Elster (above, n. 17), 62–3 n. 89, cites a number of similar examples relating to certain North American states. Resort to lotteries to settle tie-breakers in municipal elections and mayoral contests appears to be a fairly regular occurrence in the USA: see, e.g., Reuters, 'A Coin, Then Cards and Finally a Mayor', *New York Times*, 8 Mar. 1998, § 1, p. 29, col. 5; Associated Press, 'N. Dakota Town Has Coin Flip Vote', *New York Times*, 22 June 1998, § 1, p. 28, col. 3; and Pam Belluck, 'Coin Takes a Jersey Bounce in a Little House on the Prairie', *New York Times*, 25 July 1998, § A, p. 6, col. 1. More generally, on the potential of the lottery as a tie-breaking device, cf. Peter C. Fishburn, 'Even-Chance Lotteries in Social Choice Theory' (1972) 3 *Theory and Decision* 18–40; also Peter C. Fishburn, 'Lotteries and Social Choices' (1972) 5 *Journal of Economic Theory* 189–207; and, on difficulties with the use of lotteries on alternatives in tie-breaking situations, cf. Richard Zeckhauser, 'Majority Rule with Lotteries on Alternatives' (1969) 83 *Quarterly Journal of Economics* 696–703.

[50] On the idea that policy-choice will often inevitably involve an element of randomness, see e.g. Richard Zeckhauser and Donald Shepard, 'Where Now for Saving Lives?' (1976) 40 *Law and Contemporary Problems* 5–45 at 11: '[W]e have no commonly accepted measures for the outputs of alternative policies. The benefits of policy A may be measured in lives saved; those of B in years of life preserved . . . In effect, we are considering an individual standing at a node in a decision tree, choosing among alternative lotteries on quality and quantity of life.'

[51] See Rodney Brazier, *Constitutional Practice* (2nd edn., Oxford: Clarendon Press, 1994), 220–2.

[52] Since, at this point, my discussion is pitched in very general terms, I am considering the lottery as what might be called a 'pure' form of political selection. As will become clear once we turn to specific applications of randomization for political purposes, however, lotteries have often been used not instead of, but alongside, elections.

there is the problem of determining just who should be eligible to be chosen as a political representative. If certain people are to be excluded from the pool of eligibles, those exclusions have to be justified. Secondly, and relatedly, a decision would have to be reached as to whether or not individuals could exclude themselves from the pool (and, if so, on what grounds). Thirdly, assuming that the pool of eligibles is very large, a lottery system would engender political discontinuity since the strong likelihood would be that, with every new election,[53] a wholly new set of representatives would be chosen. This would mean, fourthly, not only that politicians would tend to be inexperienced in governmental affairs but also that there would be little incentive for them to endeavour to learn from what little experience they were to acquire. Few, after all, would wish to invest considerable time and energy in performing a task to which one has been assigned, and from which one will eventually be discharged, by virtue of random selection. Fifthly, a lottery system would be unlikely to encourage long-term planning by politicians while in office.[54] In fact, sixthly, under a system where government is constituted by a collection of disparate individuals, the likelihood of any sort of political consensus emerging would be remote. Factionalism would probably be endemic, and even if a majority of representatives were to find themselves in agreement on certain issues, the incentive to capitalize on this fact would not only be negligible, given the near impossibility of reappointment to political office, but also undesirable to the extent that random selection of political representatives creates the risk of placing power in the hands of people who turn out to share extremist views.[55] Another problem with choice of representatives by lottery—and we shall encounter this seventh drawback more than once in this study—is that no account is taken of the fact that there are those with a genuine talent for, and indeed desire to do, the job. '[N]o appointment by lot', Burke observed, 'can be generally good in a government conversant in extensive objects. Because they have no tendency, direct or indirect, to select the man with a view to the duty, or to accommodate the one to the other.'[56] Finally, if political representatives are randomly chosen to

---

[53] Which might themselves be randomly timed. The idea is noted as 'a theoretical possibility' by Assar Lindbeck, 'Stabilization Policy in Open Economies with Endogenous Politicians' (1976) 66 *American Economic Review: Papers and Proceedings* 1–19 at 18 n. 8, and is developed and criticized by Elster (above, n. 17), 91, who argues that under such a system governments would be unlikely, if not unable, to engage in effective planning for the future.

[54] Although one way in which some degree of stability and future-orientedness could be facilitated under such a system would be through the establishment of a constitution containing clauses which cannot be easily changed and which commit future generations to the pursuit of certain fundamental political goals. The essence of the idea is captured by Spinoza when he claims (rather idealistically) that, 'if a state is to be capable of lasting, its administration must be so organized that . . . its rulers . . . cannot be induced to break faith or act badly'. Spinoza, *Tractatus Politicus* 1. 6. In defence of constitutional precommitment, see Stephen Holmes, *Passions and Constraint: On the Theory of Liberal Democracy* (Chicago: University of Chicago Press, 1995), 100–235.

[55] See Elster (above, n. 17), 90.

[56] Edmund Burke, *Reflections on the Revolution in France, And on the Proceedings in Certain Societies in London Relative to that Event* (ed. Conor Cruise O'Brien, Harmondsworth: Penguin, 1968 (1790)), 139.

serve for a finite term with next to no prospect of reappointment, they are unlikely to consider themselves particularly accountable to (or be responsive to the concerns of) citizens, nor will citizens generally be able to exert much influence over formulation of policy. Decision-making by lot, in short, can have a disempowering effect.[57] Such a system, if it causes citizens to feel that they cannot generally affect the political process, will breed among the populace a sense of political indifference, alienation, and even resentment.[58]

These drawbacks no doubt explain why the use of lotteries to select political representatives is a virtually extinct practice today. There have, nevertheless, been some notable applications of lotteries for this purpose in the past. Furthermore, the idea that lotteries may have a place in modern political arrangements has received considerable support among certain contemporary political theorists.[59]

Past Applications

Consider, first of all, historical examples of political selection by lot. It is perhaps hardly surprising to discover that there have been times in the past

[57] For an illustration of this point, see William J. Boyes and Stephen K. Happel, 'Auctions as an Allocation Mechanism in Academia: The Case of Faculty Offices' (1989) 3 *Journal of Economic Perspectives* 37–40. The illustration is discussed in Chapter 4.

[58] See Hank Greely, 'The Equality of Allocation by Lot' (1977) 12 *Harvard Civil Rights-Civil Liberties L. Rev.* 113–41 at 122–3.

[59] We ought, at this point, to note a distinction between selection by lot and selection through rotation. The two practices are not mutually exclusive—goods and burdens could, for example, initially be allocated randomly and subsequently rotated periodically (see, e.g., Thomas More, *Utopia* (Eng. trans. P. Turner, Harmondsworth: Penguin, 1965 (1516)), 73)—though they are analytically distinct. Distribution by rotation is usually operated where a limited number of people have to carry out among themselves an undesirable task: hence, doctors in a general practice will usually have an on-call rota, onerous administrative tasks may be rotated among colleagues within university departments, and so on. On the rotation of the burden of collecting taxes in 18th-cent. China, cf. Jonathan D. Spence, *The Search for Modern China* (London: Hutchinson, 1990), 125. In political and legal theory, rotation has sometimes been defended as a democratic and egalitarian method of allocating goods and burdens. See, e.g., James Harrington, 'The Commonwealth of Oceana' (1656) in Harrington, *The Commonwealth of Oceana and a System of Politics* (ed. J. G. A. Pocock, Cambridge: Cambridge University Press, 1992), 1–266 esp. at 33–7, 123–4; Roberto Mangabeira Unger, *False Necessity: Anti-Necessitarian Social Theory in the Service of Radical Democracy (Part I of Politics, a Work in Constructive Social Theory)* (Cambridge: Cambridge University Press, 1987), 491–502; and Duncan Kennedy, *Legal Education and the Reproduction of Hierarchy: A Polemic Against the System* (Cambridge, Mass.: Afar, 1983), 79, 117, 123. A system whereby political offices are filled on a rotative basis might, as with randomization, ensure government by a representative cross-section of the community (though of course, as with the lottery system, there would be no guarantee of this). The representational quality of rotation can be seen at work within the European Community: the presidency of the Council is rotated among member states every six months. See Stephen Weatherill and Paul Beaumont, *EC Law* (2nd edn., London: Penguin, 1995), 69–70. Rotation also governs the appointment of advocates-general to the smaller member states (cf. ibid. 156). More generally, rotation has an advantage over randomization since individuals are likely to know in advance that they have been selected for office and therefore will have time to prepare themselves for the task. This advantage could, none the less, turn out to be a drawback if advance notice of who one's political representatives are to be leads some citizens to engage in bribery and other forms of manipulation. On rotation, cf. generally Goodwin (above, n. 2), 125–41.

when appointment of political representatives by lot has been undertaken on an *ad hoc* basis.[60] In England from the sixteenth through to the nineteenth century, for example, a lottery system was sometimes used for the purpose of selecting borough officers.[61] What is, I think, rather more interesting than such occasional applications is the fact that certain past societies were committed to the more extensive and systematic use of lotteries for political purposes. The most obvious case in point is ancient Greece. In Athens from the mid-fifth until the late fourth century BC, when the city fell to the Macedonians, virtually all officials were chosen by lot.[62] Although certain officers, particularly military leaders, were appointed by direct election,[63] it was assumed that the majority of the (male) populace was fit to govern.[64] Participation in the lottery was by and large voluntary and the normal term of office was one year with, in almost every instance, a ban on reappointment.[65] In order to determine whether or not they were formally eligible (but not, apparently, whether they were competent) to hold office, candidates were required to submit to a *dokimasia* or preliminary scrutiny.[66] Furthermore, probably in order to try to

[60] Various examples are to be found in Bernhard Heisterbergk, *Die Bestellung der Beamtem durch das Los: Historische Untersuchungen* (published as 16/5 of *Berliner Studien für klassische Philologie und Archäologie*. Berlin: Calvary & Co., 1896), esp. at 99–119, although this study deals in the main with election by lot at Athens.

[61] For this particular example, see Charles Gross, 'The Early History of the Ballot in England' (1897–98) 3 *American Historical Review* 456–63 at 456; and also Mark A. Kishlansky, *Parliamentary Selection: Social and Political Choice in Early Modern England* (Cambridge: Cambridge University Press, 1986), 36.

[62] See, generally, J. W. Headlam, *Election by Lot at Athens* (2nd edn., Cambridge: Cambridge University Press, 1933); and also Gustave Glotz, 'Sortitio' (1907) 4 *Dictionnaire des antiquités grecques et romaines* 1401–17.

[63] 'All the officials concerned with civilian administration are appointed by lot, apart from the treasurer of the army fund, the men in charge of the festival fund and the curator of the water supply: these are elected . . . All the military officers are elected also.' Aristotle (attr.), *The Athenian Constitution* 43: 1. On military posts in Athens, see also ibid. 30: 5 and 61: 1–7.

[64] Thus, one of 'the characteristics of democracy', Aristotle believed, is 'that the appointment to all offices, or to all but those which require experience and skill, should be made by lot'. *Politics* 1317ᵃ 20–1 (and cf. also 1298ᵃ 27). It is important to stress, nevertheless, that the Athenians did not randomly select those who were to occupy positions of major political responsibility. See A. H. M. Jones, *Athenian Democracy* (Oxford: Blackwell, 1957), 48; and also Michael Walzer, *Spheres of Justice: A Defence of Pluralism and Equality* (Oxford: Blackwell, 1983), 305–6.

[65] See M. I. Finley, *The Ancient Greeks* (Harmondsworth: Penguin, 1966 (1963)), 75–6.

[66] See Headlam (above, n. 62), 96–8. According to Headlam (p. 97), '[t]he object of the δοκι-μασία was simply to keep out of office men who were legally incapacitated'. Staveley, by contrast, speculates that '[b]y all but the most misguided idealist some protection must have been seen to be needed against appointment by lot of the truly incompetent. The procedure of the *dokimasia* . . . was no doubt as effective a method of providing that protection as any which could be devised.' E. S. Staveley, *Greek and Roman Voting and Elections* (London: Thames and Hudson, 1972), 60. More generally, cf. Gabriel Adelaye, 'The Purpose of the *Dokimasia*' (1983) 24 *Greek, Roman and Byzantine Studies* 295–306. In Adelaye's view, 'if a candidate of questionable character and political inclination appeared at the *dokimasia*, there can be no doubt that he would be made to answer some embarrassing questions and disqualified if unable to satisfy the board of examiners' (ibid. 306).

prevent manipulation of the selection process, the lottery would often be carried out in two stages.[67]

Athenians were committed to the use of the lottery, it seems, not because they invested it with divinatory significance but because they associated it with political virtue.[68] '[E]lection by lot', Finley comments, 'translated equality of opportunity from an ideal to a reality'.[69] Resort to lot for political purposes was regarded, indeed, as an affirmation of faith in democracy.[70] '[S]electing administrative officials by lot, particularly officials who occupied positions of prestige, such as the *archons* or the president of the Council and assembly, was a public expression of democracy's commitment to the equality of all citizens.'[71] The political virtue of the lottery did not end there. A lottery system would make competition for political office pointless and thereby reduce the likelihood of conflicts and factionalism.[72] Where representatives are replaced annually and selected randomly, opportunities, and indeed the incentive, to suborn those who hold office will most likely be diminished. The outcome of a properly conducted lottery cannot be attributed to—or, more pertinently, blamed on—any specific person or group and is therefore unlikely to generate political resentment (thus it is that Plato wrote of 'avoid[ing] the anger of the man in the street by giving him

---

[67] That is, randomly choosing an eligible pool and then randomly choosing from this pool. Goodwin's claim (above, n. 2), 154 (and cf. also p. 97) that 'double sortition was used [at Athens] to prevent corruption or partiality' is probably an overstatement. Staveley observes that '[n]o entirely satisfactory explanation as to why the Athenians employed this elaborate procedure has yet been offered', though he notes (above, n. 65), 39, that, without the double-sortition requirement, it might have proved fairly simple for candidates to be bought off by powerful tribesmen. '[T]his double process of sortition', he ventures, 'perhaps . . . rendered manipulation of the lot more difficult than when lots were drawn by or on behalf of candidates in a predetermined order' (ibid. 67).

[68] For the argument that the lot was, for Athenians, a secular device (certainly when used for political purposes), see Headlam (above, n. 62), 4–11.

[69] Finley (above, n. 65), 77. The Athenian conception of equality of opportunity was, of course, rather different from modern conceptions given that the ancient Greeks considered certain categories of people (slaves, in particular) to be inherently unequal to others. See Jennifer Tolbert Roberts, *Athens on Trial: The Antidemocratic Tradition in Western Thought* (Princeton: Princeton University Press, 1994), 77–8.

[70] See Mogens Herman Hansen, *The Athenian Democracy in the Age of Demosthenes: Structure, Principles and Ideology* (Eng. trans. J. A. Crook, Oxford: Blackwell, 1991), 235–7.

[71] Richard G. Mulgan, 'Lot as a Democratic Device of Selection' (1984) 46 *Review of Politics* 539–60 at 546. Specifically on selection of *archons* by lot, cf. Mabel Lang, 'Allotment by Tokens' (1959) 8 *Historia* 80–9; and Fustel de Coulanges, 'Sur le tirage au sort appliqué à la nomination des archontes athéniens' (1878) 2 *Nouvelle Revue Historique de Droit Français et Étranger* 613–43. Coulanges's work has to be read with circumspection, since he proceeds on the incorrect assumption that the ancient Greeks regarded sortition as a specifically divinatory method for selecting officials.

[72] Aristotle noted that, 'at Heraea . . . instead of electing their magistrates, they took them by lot, because the electors were in the habit of choosing their own partisans'. *Politics*, 1303ᵃ 15–16. In a modern context, cf. Fredrik Engelstad, 'The Assignment of Political Office by Lot' (1989) 28 *Social Science Information* 23–50 at 30: 'Drawing lots [for the purpose of selecting political representatives] may . . . prevent important social conflicts. Electoral campaigns easily lead to unnecessary polarization between candidates, unfounded election promises and hostility between groups. Such social costs disappear when the choice is made by a neutral mechanism that is not susceptible to influence'. Note, however, that the ancient Greeks' use of political lotteries did not eliminate factionalism entirely: see Mulgan (above, n. 71), 548.

an equal chance in the lot'[73]). Political humility might be encouraged where officials are selected both randomly and for a period rarely extending beyond one year.[74] Possibly the most significant of the lottery's virtues, for Athenians, was its capacity to combat oligarchical tendencies. The idea, it seems, was that sortition would keep political power permanently weak, that it would provide a safeguard to the extent that no one would be able to exert anything more than temporary control over the majority of political offices.[75]

Such virtues have been appreciated in places other than ancient Greece. Even at Rome during the Republican era (which, in practice, was governed by an oligarchy), lots were used for two political purposes.[76] Roman citizens voted as members of tribes rather than as individuals. But not everyone with the right to vote was a citizen. Before their enfranchisement in 90 BC, the Latins were non-citizens who nevertheless, while present in Rome, enjoyed among their special privileges the right to cast their vote at tribal legislative assemblies. Although the Latins themselves were unlikely to place much store in exercising this right, any particular tribe would probably have been reluctant to have been assigned their vote, 'for it was at least conceivable that the voice of the citizen tribesmen, if attendance [at assembly] was poor, would be nullified by that of the Latins temporarily added to their ranks'.[77] Since permanently to assign the Latins' votes to any one tribe would most likely have been considered disadvantageous by the tribe in question, the Romans determined which tribe should receive those votes by resorting to lot on each occasion that a voting assembly was called.

The second purpose of the lottery was to determine which tribe should vote first. The Roman voting system was flawed in so far as, in certain elections, tribes voted successively and the one which voted first, the *centuria praerogativa*, would have its returns announced before the others had been called to vote. This meant that the *centuria praerogativa* was able 'to set a pattern for voting and to exercise not a little influence on the uncommitted members of later centuries'.[78] The Romans therefore resorted to sortition from one election to the next so as to vary the order in which tribes were called to vote and ensure that one tribe did not always enjoy the advantage of being the prerogative century.[79]

---

[73] *Laws*, 6. 757ᶜ.

[74] Election by lot is preferable to suffrage, Servius Tullius is supposed to have remarked, because whereas 'suffrage might occasion mortification to those who were excluded, and undue pride to the favoured ones . . . chance preclude[s] this danger, for it does not deal in humiliation or inflation'. Cited after Montesquieu, *The Spirit of the Laws* (Eng. trans. T. Nugent, New York: Hafner, 1949 (1748)), 11 n. *l*. As for the ancient Greeks, Hignett contends that, '[a]s sortition carried with it no religious sanction in political appointments, an official selected by the chance of the lot could not enjoy the same prestige as one chosen by the will of the people'. C. Hignett, *A History of the Athenian Constitution to the End of the Fifth Century BC* (Oxford: Clarendon Press, 1952), 230–1.

[75] See Headlam (above, n. 62), 180; Hansen (above, n. 70), 84.

[76] In general, see Staveley (above, n. 66), 154–6, 230–2; and, for other applications of the lottery at Rome, cf. C. Lécrivain, 'Sortitio—Rome' (1907) 4 *Dictionnaire des antiquités grecques et romaines* 1417–18.   [77] Staveley (above, n. 66), 154.   [78] Ibid. 155.

[79] A similar system was used in the Spanish city of Málaga in the 1st cent. BC: cf. *lex Malacitana*, s. 57, as reproduced in Staveley (above, n. 66), 235.

Throughout, and indeed prior to, the Renaissance period, a number of European city-states devised electoral systems which involved sortition. During the thirteenth century, numerous Italian communes introduced electoral conventions which required, in different ways and to varying degrees, the drawing of lots.[80] In the 1430s, the city of Barcelona introduced a fairly complex lottery procedure for choosing its twelve principal councillors.[81] Rousseau noted the perverse intricacy of the system which fifteenth-century Venetians developed for the purpose of appointing their chief magistrate or doge.[82] Lasting for five days, election for the dogeship entailed a procedure which might well have come straight from the pages of Kafka. Whereas the ancient Athenians resorted to double sortition, the Venetians practised quintuple sortition.[83] Thirty members of the city's main council, the *maggior consiglio*, would be selected by lot. This group of thirty would then conduct a further lottery so as to reduce their number to nine. These nine men would then be required to elect forty nominees by a majority of no fewer than seven votes each. This group of forty would reduce their number by sortition to twelve, who would then elect a further twenty-five nominees by at least seven votes apiece. The twenty-five nominees were reduced by lot to nine, and this group of nine would elect a further forty-five nominees who would reduce themselves by lot to eleven. These eleven elected forty-one nominees and it was this group of forty-one, the *Quarantuno*, that was charged with responsibility for electing the doge by a majority of at least twenty-five votes.

The point of this complex system was not—as was probably the case with the Athenian practice of double-sortition—to try to eliminate the possibility of rigged lotteries; rather, it was both to prevent any particular political faction from controlling the electoral process and to ensure that the ultimate choice of doge was not wholly down to chance. Apparently, the third stage in the procedure—the election of the forty by the nine—was the most crucial one, for it was presumed that this group of nine, having been selected by two successive lotteries, would be 'safely out of the hands of the Republic's sovereign assembly' and, rather than be subject to any particular political influence, would elect the forty politicians which 'it considered most suitable for office.[84] 'In short, nine arbitrarily selected

---

[80] For sketches of lottery-based electoral conventions at Genoa, Bologna, Parma, Brescia and Sienna during the 13th cent., see Arthur M. Wolfson, 'The Ballot and Other Forms of Voting in the Italian Communes' (1899) 5 *American Historical Review* 1–21 at 10–13.

[81] See Claude Carrère, *Barcelone: Centre économique à l'époque des difficultés, 1380–1462* (2 vols., Paris: Mouton & Co., 1967), i. 37–40. A randomized system for selecting political officers is also described in the constitution of medieval Raetia: cf. generally Otto P. Clavadetscher, 'Die Herrschaftsbildung in Rätien', in Ursus Brunold and Lothar Deplazes (eds.), *Rätien im Mittelalter. Verfassung, Verkehr, Recht, Notariat: Ausgewählte Aufsätze (Festgabe zum 75. Geburtstag Otto P. Clavadetscher)* (Disentis: Desertina, 1994), 326–43.

[82] See Rousseau, *Du contrat social*, IV. 3.

[83] For a more detailed account of what follows, see Robert Finlay, *Politics in Renaissance Venice* (London: Ernest Benn, 1980), 141–2.   [84] See ibid. 142–3.

and relatively undistinguished patricians were charged with electing forty men of political significance, who would then maintain others of like position in subsequent stages of the election.'[85] While, throughout these subsequent stages, a good deal of hard bargaining for votes would take place, 'the crucial element of chance meant that no one was assured of victory'[86] and that it would be difficult, if not impossible, for 'any group to impose its will without an overwhelming majority or substantial good luck'.[87] Being not entirely at ease with either a system of voting or with a straightforward lottery, the Venetians were attempting to devise a middle route which would ensure that election to doge was not a possibility for just about anyone, and therefore was not open to the popular orders, but at the same time was sufficiently random to ensure that the office was unlikely to be ceded to an unscrupulous politician backed by a powerful clique.

Whereas the fifteenth-century Venetians combined election and sortition so as to sustain something along the lines of moderate oligarchy, the citizens of fourteenth-century Florence developed a remarkably open electoral system the proper functioning of which, they believed, was best guaranteed if there was incorporated into it an element of random selection. The purpose of Florentine electoral politics was to appoint members to the city government, the *Signoria*, and its various committees.[88] So reluctant were the Florentines to see anyone hold political power for any significant length of time that, near the end of the thirteenth century, they instituted the practice of appointing new officials to the entire *Signoria* and its committees every two months.[89] Hardly surprisingly, the creation of such a short term of office generated political instability. Rather than abandon their scheme, however, the Florentines endeavoured to make it work by introducing a lottery-based system whereby the officials for numerous successive bi-monthly governments would be simultaneously selected, nominated, and approved.[90] Every three years, various institutions and organizations within the city would nominate candidates for the *Signoria* and its committees. This process would result in a large number of nominees, usually several thousand, who would then be considered by a scrutiny committee (most of whose members would have been appointed by the existing government). The committee would vote in secret on each nominee—a two-thirds majority being required for approval—and the names of approved candidates would then be placed in bags from which were randomly drawn, every two months, the names of those who were to serve on the *Signoria* for the next two-month term.[91] These bags would not be exhausted, nor would they be discarded, at the end of the three-year period, and so there was

[85] Ibid. 143.   [86] Ibid.   [87] Ibid. 143–4.

[88] See John M. Najemy, *Corporatism and Consensus in Florentine Electoral Politics, 1280–1400* (Chapel Hill, NC: University of North Carolina Press, 1982), 14–15.

[89] See ibid. 30.

[90] What follows is drawn from ibid. 99–125; and Elster (above, n. 17), 83–4.

[91] A similar system apparently operated in 13th-cent. Perugia: see Philip Jones, *The Italian City-State: From Commune to Signoria* (Oxford: Clarendon Press, 1997), 41.

almost always more than one bag in existence. At the outset of each three-year period, once the process of scrutiny had been completed, the rule was to draw names at random from the oldest bags and, as those emptied, to proceed to the most recent.

'These mechanisms', Najemy observes, 'had the effect of transforming the electoral process into a giant political lottery.'[92] With various modifications, this system survived at Florence into the fifteenth century. Yet one might reasonably wonder how it ever survived beyond the first two-month term.[93] Besides impairing political stability and long-term planning, and leaving aside the fact that the process of scrutinizing the many nominees must have been a massive administrative burden in itself, the system offered those who were to take office no incentive to act prudently: it is, after all, difficult to envisage many people being especially dedicated to a post from which they will be removed within a matter of weeks.[94] It seems that the Florentine electoral system was accepted because it opened up the political process to the populace. More or less all male citizens were, in principle, eligible for nomination to office, and the suspicion that one's name could well be in one of the bags—that one's turn may soon come[95]—might well have prevented many people from making life difficult for those who did currently hold political power. Opportunities and incentives to bribe officials were diminished owing to the randomness and the fluidity of the political process; and, since the scrutiny committee voted on nominees in secret and individuals were unlikely to discover that they had not been approved, there was little prospect for complaints about disenfranchisement and discrimination among the electorate.

Selection of political representatives by lot obviously has numerous drawbacks. Yet it is obvious also that, in certain past societies, there existed a belief that the benefits to be gained from resorting to sortition in political affairs would, in one way or another, outweigh the costs which might be incurred. Why is it, then, that modern societies are generally unwilling to tolerate the disadvantages which come with political selection by lot? Why do we differ from certain of our ancestors in this regard? To these questions there are, perhaps inevitably, no satisfactory simple answers. Nevertheless, at least three observations seem apposite.

First, there is the simple matter of size: not only do contemporary democracies tend to have larger populations than did the city-states of antiquity and the

---

[92] Najemy (above, n. 88), 299.

[93] Indeed, there inevitably existed among the Florentine citizenry reservations regarding the use of lots for political and legal purposes. Consider, for example, the reservations of Francesco Guicciardini, a jurist of the late Florentine republic, as discussed by J. G. A. Pocock, *The Machiavellian Moment: Florentine Political Thought and the Atlantic Republican Tradition* (Princeton: Princeton University Press, 1975), 134–5, 234, 254. Guicciardini, it seems, was more enamoured of the Venetian model of political sortition (see ibid., 261–2).

[94] See Najemy (above, n. 88), 313–14.

[95] While the Florentine system did not outlaw re-election, the scrutiny committee treated as ineligible nominees who had either held office recently or whose close relatives had held office recently. See ibid. 108–9.

Renaissance, but a greater proportion of these modern populations is eligible to participate in political affairs. Any appeal that the idea of using sortition to select representatives may have will probably be diminished if the individual's chances of being selected for political participation are extremely remote.[96] Citizens in general will be less likely to take seriously the possibility that their turn may come, while those who concern themselves with political affairs will be more likely to express their dissatisfaction with the individuals who have been selected to hold political office (and, indeed, with the general process of government). Where the electorate is anything other than small in number, political selection along lines similar to any of those which have been discussed here would very likely be considered not only administratively unworkable but also more or less guaranteed to generate political discontent, or at least apathy.[97]

Secondly, there is this matter of apathy. One of the reasons for promoting aleatory politics in certain of the city-states, particularly Athens and Florence, appears to have been to try to ensure fairly widespread political participation and to sustain a culture in which a significant proportion of the population stood a very good chance of being actively involved in the political process at some point in their lives. In general, it seems, this is what the ancient Athenians and the Florentines would have wanted.[98] That the majority of citizens in modern democracies would want the same is, at best, debatable. In the 1830s, Tocqueville confessed to being bewildered to find that in the United States, 'where the inhabitants have only recently migrated to the land' and 'the instinctive love of country can scarcely exist . . . everyone, in his sphere, takes an active part in the government of society'.[99] However, modern commentators—for all that many of them long for a citizenry more involved in political affairs—detect widespread political indifference rather than engagement.[100] No doubt such a state of affairs is lamentable. My point, however, is not so much to pass judgement as to observe that a system which incorporates randomness into the process of political selection would hardly be suited to a culture in which many people would neither relish nor accept, but actually resent, being chosen for office.

---

[96]   See further Walzer (above, n. 64), 133–4.

[97]   Garosci (above, n. 48), 54–6 notes that one of the reasons for the survival of political sortition at San Marino is that, in terms of size, the principality bears more resemblance to the various ancient city-states than it does to modern European democracies.

[98]   On Athens (and ancient Greece more generally), cf. Alasdair MacIntyre, *After Virtue: A Study in Moral Theory* (2nd edn., London: Duckworth, 1985), 133. On Florence, see Najemy (above, n. 88), 9–10. None the less, it ought also to be noted that, within certain Italian city-states of the Renaissance era, although '[a] belief existed that wide participation in office was desirable . . . office-holding and council service were deemed as much a duty as a privilege, a liability imposed by oaths of citizenship and ordained by statute'. Jones (above, n. 91), 410.

[99]   Alexis de Tocqueville, *Democracy in America* (2 vols., New York: Vintage, 1990; vol. i orig. publ. 1835, vol. ii 1840), i. 243.

[100]   See, e.g., Mary Ann Glendon, *Rights Talk: The Impoverishment of Political Discourse* (New York: Free Press, 1991), 128–30; and Nina Eliasaph, *Avoiding Politics: How Americans Produce Apathy in Everyday Life* (Cambridge: Cambridge University Press, 1998).

Finally, there is the matter of how political representation is perceived. Lewis Namier once suggested that our political system would not suffer were we to choose representatives randomly, for, were this done, our politicians would speak for the same range of interests as would an elected body. 'Were it decided that the 615 heaviest men in the country should constitute the House of Commons, the various interests and parties could be trusted to obtain their proportionate weight in it.'[101] The issue here is not whether such a claim is supportable,[102] but whether such a proposal would be considered acceptable. That the proposal would be unlikely to receive much support seems obvious. The interesting question is why this should be so. One of the reasons, I think, is that, in modern societies, there is a tendency to favour politicians who are not only willing to speak up for particular interests but who are also able to represent those interests skilfully. Indeed, one of the virtues of election as a democratic device is that it enables citizens to choose their political representatives on merit, and perhaps the most important criterion of merit is the demonstration of a distinct talent for the job. As both Montesquieu and Rousseau recognized, sortition, unlike voting, cannot satisfy an electorate which regards politics as a profession and which expects its representatives to possess political expertise.[103] The ancient Greeks in particular differed from citizens of contemporary democracies in that they did not conceive of politics in this way. It was more important to the Greeks that there existed what they considered to be equality of opportunity to hold office rather than that political posts go to those who seemed most suited to particular jobs.[104] Sortition accorded with their conception of politics. When, however, the holding of political office is generally viewed not as an honour which ought to be shared around but as a vocation to be pursued by those with the necessary talents, selection of representatives by lot seems decidedly less appropriate.[105]

---

[101] Lewis Namier, *England in the Age of the American Revolution* (2nd edn., London: Macmillan, 1961), 3. A similar outlook—albeit one which exhibits cynicism towards intellectuals as opposed to political elections—can be detected in the American political journalist William F. Buckley's apparent remark that 'he would rather be governed by a random drawing of names from the Cambridge, Massachusetts, phone book than by the faculty of Harvard University'. Cited after Diego Gambetta, ' "Claro!": An Essay on Discursive Machismo', in Jon Elster (ed.), *Deliberative Democracy* (Cambridge: Cambridge University Press, 1998), 19–43 at 34.

[102] For an argument that Namier's is not, cf. M. J. C. Vile, *Constitutionalism and the Separation of Powers* (Oxford: Clarendon Press, 1967), 298–300.

[103] See Montesquieu (above, n. 74), 11–12; Rousseau, *Du contrat social*, IV. 3.

[104] See Mulgan (above, n. 71), 556–7.

[105] There is also, of course, the point that random selection for political office would, for many citizens of contemporary democracies, be a massive inconvenience. That people often regard selection for jury service in this way is widely acknowledged: see, e.g., *Royal Commission on Criminal Justice* (London: HMSO, 1993), 131–2. Since holding political office would very likely require more of an individual's time and commitment than would jury service, one can imagine that a proposal in favour of political selection by lot would meet with considerable resistance from those worried about, say, possible loss of earnings or career interruptions. Were it ever to be put forward as a serious proposal, I suspect that Goodwin's suggestion (above, n. 2), 164–5, that magistrates ought to be randomly selected—to serve 'for five or ten years (say) rather than a lifetime'—would meet with much the same resistance, notwithstanding the fact that magistrates were sometimes chosen by lot at

Modern Proposals

There is, then, a very obvious conclusion to be reached: it is hardly surprising that selection by lot should rarely feature within contemporary political systems, for the practice is demonstrably unsuited to the needs and concerns of modern democracies. Yet the obviousness of this conclusion does not necessarily make it wholly convincing. Although various arguments can be developed against using lotteries for the purpose of political selection, numerous claims might be offered in support of the practice. Some of these claims have already emerged from our discussion: that lotteries can prevent the formation of elites and promote equality of political opportunity; that, where there exists widespread belief, be it correct or mistaken, that the lottery can be manipulated, scheming for political power will most likely be considered futile; that, since they separate outcome from human contrivance, decisions by lot cannot be blamed on any particular person or group;[106] and that, since representatives selected by lot will most likely attribute their political status to fortuitousness rather than to popularity or talent, they might be expected, as compared with representatives selected by vote, to demonstrate a greater degree of political humility.

There are still other arguments which might be advanced in support of randomness in political selection, although many of these arguments are highly contentious. On the assumption that a system of selection by lot would have the effect of encouraging people to become politically knowledgeable in case they should be chosen for office, for example, it might be argued that such a system has the potential to improve general political awareness. However, the plausibility of the assumption at the heart of this argument depends on just how many people within the population are eligible for selection. If the pool of eligibles is extremely large, the assumption will be extremely questionable—as questionable as, say, the assumption that most citizens of the United Kingdom tend to acquire some general legal knowledge in case they should be selected for jury service.

Certain other arguments in favour of random political selection are implausible because they stem from the belief that the political arrangements and ideals of ancient Athens can be replicated in modern democracies. According to Burnheim, for example, modern democracies are not genuinely democratic since politicians are not a representative sample of the population that they are supposed to serve. 'In order to have democracy we must abandon elections . . . and revert to the ancient principle of choosing by lot those who are to hold various public

---

both Athens and Rome (see Douglas M. MacDowell, *The Law in Classical Athens* (Ithaca, NY: Cornell University Press, 1978), 40; and V. Ehrenberg, 'Losung' (1927) 13 *Realencyclopädie der klassischen Alternumwissenschaft* 1451–90 at 1468).

[106] Unless, of course, resentment is directed at those responsible for instituting a system of political selection by lot.

offices.'[107] Callenbach and Phillips similarly argue that real democracy demands a system of political selection by lot resembling that which existed at Athens and that, if genuine democracy is to prevail in the United States, the House of Representatives ought to be comprised of 435 people randomly selected to hold office for a two-year term. Just as the Greeks kept some posts open to election, the Senate would, under the Callenbach and Phillips scheme, continue to be an elected body representing state and party interests, and the balance of power between the two Houses would remain the same. If membership of the House of Representatives were determined according to random selection, Callenbach and Phillips believe, the House would be cross-sectionally typical of the population and each member would promote the interests of those in society with whom he or she identifies. The purpose of the proposed reform, in short, would be to make Congress (or certainly one of its chambers) more representative of the American people.[108] Recently, in the United Kingdom, a similar proposal has been advanced by the think-tank, Demos. Random selection of 'peers', according to Demos, would establish a more cross-sectionally representative House of Lords.[109]

---

[107] John Burnheim, *Is Democracy Possible? The Alternative to Electoral Politics* (Cambridge: Polity Press, 1985), 9.

[108] See Ernest Callenbach and Michael Phillips, *A Citizen Legislature* (Berkeley, Calif.: Banyan Tree Books (co-published Bodega, Calif.: Clear Glass), 1985), 9–13.

[109] For details of the Demos proposal, cf. Anthony Barnett and Peter Carty, *The Athenian Option: Radical Reform for the House of Lords* (London: Demos, 1998); Nicholas Wood, 'Ancient Greece Inspires House of Lords Reform', *The Times*, 30 May 1998, p. 19; Anthony Barnett, 'Is Labour too Old-Fashioned for Athens?', *The Times*, 3 June 1998, p. 18; and compare Daniel Lightman, 'Ancients Go Modern' (1998) 10/2 *Oxford Today* 48. Barnett and Carty (p. 16) suggest that certain mechanisms ought to be built into the random selection process so as to ensure that all regions and both sexes are adequately represented in the House of Lords. Although they clearly recognize that randomness and representation do not necessarily go hand in hand, however, it is not clear why the qualified random selection procedure which they propose would be any more representative of 'the people' than would an unqualified one. Indeed, endeavouring to tame randomness so as to guard against disproportionate representation in the House of Lords may turn out to be a cure worse than the disease, not least because the endeavour requires justification. If random selection of peers is to be compromised for the sake of representativeness, one might ask, why should we only be worried about adequate representation of regions (however they might be defined) and the sexes?

The notion that random selection might play a part in revitalizing representative democracy also informs work by the Institute of Public Policy Research (IPPR) on the use of so-called 'citizens' juries' to enhance public participation in political decision-making. See John Stewart, Elizabeth Kendall, and Anna Coote, *Citizens' Juries* (London: IPPR, 1994); and Anna Coote and Jo Lenaghan, *Citizens' Juries: Theory into Practice* (London: IPPR, 1997). Citizens' juries—rather like the German 'planning cells'—'are small groups of citizens, selected to represent the general public rather than any interest or sector, who meet to deliberate upon a policy question' (Stewart *et al.*, *Citizens' Juries*, p. iii). 'Between 12 and 16 jurors are recruited, using a combination of random and stratified sampling, to be broadly representative of their community. Their task is to address an important question about policy or planning. They are brought together for four days, with a team of two moderators ... The jury's verdict need not be unanimous, nor is it binding. However, the commissioning authority is required to publicise the jury and its findings' (Coote and Lenaghan, *Citizens' Juries*, p. ii). Note that the IPPR has been wary of selecting all jurors randomly. 'We decided that a jury recruited to achieve some degree of representativeness was less likely to incur criticism than a randomly selected jury that by chance excluded one or more significant groups' (Coote and Lenaghan, p. 73). On the German use of planning cells (members of which are selected at random),

The basic difficulty with Callenbach's and Phillips's proposal is that it depends on too straightforward an equation of randomness with representativeness. The authors fail to acknowledge that, while random selection may ensure cross-sectional representation in the long run, it is unlikely to do so at any particular point in time. Indeed, under such a scheme, minority groups may have a long wait before they find a voice within the House of Representatives (and even then, of course, this representation will only be temporary). Furthermore, leaving aside the question of whether democracy necessarily would be more genuine were it to be reformed along lines such as those proposed by Burnheim, Callenbach and Phillips, and Demos (never mind the matter of how such reforms might be instituted), a fundamental problem with these proposals is that they could only ever be plausible so long as no account were taken of what has already been noted: namely, that ancient Athens was in various ways very different from any modern democracy and that these differences explain in large measure why we no longer use sortition to select political representatives.

Another contentious, although rather different argument concerning political selection by lot is advanced by Thaler, who advocates the random assignment of members of US Congress to congressional committees—a proposal which, he concedes, is 'probably politically infeasible'.[110] He begins by asking us to picture the large restaurant party which decides that everyone at the table will contribute equally to the bill irrespective of what each individual has ordered. Imagine also, he continues, that this party decides that all food and drink will be ordered by committee: that is, that within this party of diners there should be separate committees responsible for ordering drinks, starters, main courses, and so on; and that each person should be allowed to serve on the committee of his or her choice. The likely outcome is obvious: '[t]he lushes will have a bottle of wine with each course, the sweet-tooths two rounds of dessert, and if by chance a lush finds himself on the dessert committee we can be sure that rum cake will be served'.[111] Where people are able to choose the committees on which they serve, there will be a tendency towards overspending. The restaurant party scenario, according to Thaler, captures the fundamental problem with modern US congressional arrangements: members of Congress determine for themselves on which committees they shall serve and then, in the absence of strict limits on government expenditure, overspend in endeavouring to protect and promote their own interests. While the system possesses the advantage of ensuring that members end up on the committees which reflect their concerns and experience, it is disadvantageous

see Peter C. Dienel, *Die Planungszelle: Der Bürger plant seine Umwelt. Eine Alternative zur Establishment-Demokratie* (Opladen: Westdeutscher Verlag, 1997); and, for the argument that random selection might be used in the UK for the purpose of staffing quangos, cf. Martin Wainwright, *It* Should *Be You. Using Random Choice to Open Up Quangos: A Proposal for a Pilot Scheme Using the National Lottery Distribution Bodies* (Leeds: Tomolly, 1998).

[110] Richard H. Thaler, 'Illusions and Mirages in Public Policy' (1983) 73 *The Public Interest* 60–74 at 72. [111] Ibid.

in so far as it encourages excessive public spending and creates the possibility of particular committees being dominated, if not controlled, by long-serving members. Hence the argument for random assignment to committees.

Whether one is convinced by Thaler's metaphor of Congress as dining party will depend, I suspect, upon whether or not one shares his view that, in the committee scenario, diners and politicians alike are likely to be motivated not so much by self-interest as by selfishness or even greed. As Thaler has noted elsewhere, political actors, like human actors generally, often recognize that pursuit of self-interest requires that one behaves cooperatively rather than selfishly.[112] Since Congress is responsive to public opinion, it seems implausible to suggest that its members will never feel compelled to exercise economic restraint. Perhaps a more interesting facet of Thaler's argument is his implicit claim that selection by lot ought to be viewed positively if one is distrustful of any system which allows for the establishment of a body of political experts. According to Amar, although politicians selected by lot may, on average, possess less expertise as compared with their elected counterparts, 'they would'—I prefer might—'be in closer touch with the needs and concerns of fellow citizens in the real world of the polity. Furthermore, the fact that incumbents could not guarantee themselves re-election might well encourage them to adopt a longer decisional time-horizon than the next election.'[113] Indeed, representatives chosen by lot, having little chance of reselection, would have less reason than do elected politicians to respond to the lobbying of special-interest groups.

It has already been observed that sortition is far more suited to the political arrangements of small communities than it is to those of large modern democracies. Perhaps, then, lotteries might be put to good use in regional rather than national politics. Random selection of local representatives—an idea by no means alien to English government[114]—may operate so as to promote equal access to, and cross-sectional representation on, regional councils where direct and widespread involvement with local issues is considered to be desirable but the number of citizens wishing to participate is too great to permit everyone to assemble. Sortition might prove to be particularly appropriate, furthermore, for the purpose of filling local offices which require neither specialist knowledge nor an inordinate amount of individual commitment. In relation to North American municipalities, Barber has argued that random selection might be suitable for determining membership of, among other bodies, school committees, zoning

---

[112] See Robyn M. Dawes and Richard H. Thaler, 'Anomalies: Cooperation' (1988) 2 *Journal of Economic Perspectives* 187–97.

[113] Akhil Reed Amar, 'Choosing Representatives by Lottery Voting' (1984) 93 *Yale LJ* 1283–1308 at 1298–9. Of course, another possibility—to reiterate a point which has already been noted—would be that incumbents, or at least some of the incumbents, selected in this manner would demonstrate little in the way of commitment either to political affairs or to the people that they are supposed to represent. If quality of performance in office cannot affect chances of re-election, political representatives will have little, if any, incentive to govern well.

[114] See Kishlansky (above, n. 61), 36.

boards, conservation commissions, housing authorities, and licensing boards; if their members were chosen by lot, 'such boards and committees would simultaneously function as genuinely representative civic institutions of the town and as schools of citizenship and statesmanship'.[115] As at Athens, sortition could be accompanied by a system of scrutiny to try to ensure suitability for office, and members of boards might be paid a per diem to compensate for private time devoted to the public weal. It would be wrong, however, to treat such a proposal as unproblematic. Since not all citizens will want to participate in local politics, the creation of a lottery system may require that only those who volunteer themselves as eligible should be included within the pool of candidates. Such a requirement would most likely favour those individuals who have political ambition while generating a sense of political disconnectedness among those who do not choose to be involved.

A basic problem with political selection by lot is what we might term the possibility of random dictatorship. A pure lottery separates outcome from human judgement. Accordingly, if the selection of political office-holders were entirely down to chance, we could find ourselves being governed by the most repugnant of people—people, indeed, who might be unwilling to forfeit power once they have had a taste of it.[116] Thus it is that modern proponents of political sortition sometimes advocate not pure lotteries but systems which combine lotteries with voting—in shorthand, systems of 'lottery voting'. Under such a system, citizens would be given the chance to vote for those representatives whose policies they favour. Instead of demanding that votes be counted to determine the majority winner, however, the system requires that each vote be placed into a vessel from which, at random, a ballot will be drawn. The lottery is weighted—or, as Ackerman says, responsive[117]—in the sense that any representative's chances of being selected will be greater or smaller depending on the number of votes that he or she has received. Although the person with the majority of votes stands the best chance of winning, however, they will not necessarily be the winner.

What advantages might such a system have over one which elects simply on the basis of majority vote? There are at least three possible advantages to a system of lottery voting. First, such a system creates an obvious disincentive for voter dishonesty—that is, for citizens to try to advance their own interests by voting in such a way as not to register their true preferences. When representatives are elected by virtue of majority of votes, some voters will be inclined to misrepresent their preferences in the hope of ensuring an outcome which they consider

---

[115] Benjamin R. Barber, *Strong Democracy: Participatory Politics for a New Age* (Berkeley: University of California Press, 1984), 292.

[116] We ought at least to mention here Chesterton's delightful counter-argument: namely, that there is a stronger possibility of dictatorship where those who are chosen to govern have demonstrated a desire to govern, and so we do better to select our governors randomly. See Gilbert K. Chesterton, *The Napoleon of Notting Hill* (London: John Lane, 1904), 43–7.

[117] See Bruce A. Ackerman, *Social Justice in the Liberal State* (New Haven: Yale University Press, 1980), 286.

preferable to that which would obtain were they to report their preferences sincerely.[118] The problem with such misrepresentation is not so much that it is cynical or manipulative as that, in certain (admittedly rare) instances, it may lead to political decisions being reached which are not at all representative of popular will. Since, under a system of lottery voting, every vote that a candidate receives enhances his or her chance of being randomly selected, citizens are in effect deterred from registering votes inconsistent with their true preferences.[119]

Secondly, as compared with traditional cumulative voting, lottery voting is less likely to generate among certain of the electorate the feeling that to vote for one's preferred candidate is basically a waste of time. Under a cumulative system, some citizens are likely not to vote because they believe that there is little point in supporting either a candidate who stands more or less no chance of being elected or even one whose victory is confidently expected.[120] By contrast, under a system of lottery voting each vote counts equally in the sense that every citizen's vote increases by the same amount the likelihood of their preferred candidate being randomly chosen in the ballot.[121]

Thirdly, a system of lottery voting throughout constituencies diminishes the possibility of any minority being permanently unrepresented. The random element of the system would increase the likelihood that, in some electoral districts, minority candidates would be chosen for office (the possibility of those candidates being chosen will obviously be greater in those constituencies where they attract the greatest support).[122] Indeed, the law of averages dictates that, in the long run, a parliament selected by a system of lottery voting would more or less mirror the underlying distribution of votes among the electorate. Since, under

---

[118] See Allan Gibbard, 'Manipulation of Voting Schemes: A General Result' (1973) 41 *Econometrica* 587–601; Peter Gärdenfors, 'Manipulation of Social Choice Functions' (1976) 13 *Journal of Economic Theory* 217–28; and also William H. Riker, *Liberalism Against Populism: A Confrontation Between the Theory of Democracy and the Theory of Social Choice* (San Francisco: W. H. Freeman & Co., 1982), 143.

[119] See, generally, Allan Gibbard, 'Manipulation of Schemes that Mix Voting with Chance' (1977) 45 *Econometrica* 665–81.

[120] What we tend to find within majoritarian voting systems, according to Jaconelli, 'is a formal equality of voting power, matched by a strategic inequality. As actually cast, certain votes may turn out to have less weight than others.' Joseph Jaconelli, 'Majority Rule and Special Majorities' [1989] *Public Law* 587–616 at 596.

[121] See Elster (above, n. 17), 87–8. American courts have, on occasions, upheld the use of lotteries to reduce wasted votes by permitting the random reallocation of 'surplus' votes to voters' second-choice candidates in particular electoral districts: cf. *Moore* v. *Election Commissioners* (1941) 35 NE 2d 222, 240; *Campbell* v. *Board of Education* (EDNY 1970) 310 F. Supp. 94, 103–4. Random re-allocation of votes is, however, a practice distinct from lottery voting.

[122] See Ackerman (above, n. 117), 298: 'The advantage of the [responsive] lottery, of course, is that it gives the egalitarian minority at least *some* chance of determining the political outcome in a way consistent with its conscientious beliefs.' Cf. also Robert Paul Wolff, *In Defense of Anarchism* (New York: Harper & Row, 1970), 45: '[L]egislation by lot would offer some chance to the minority, unlike rule by the majority, but it would not offer to each citizen an equal chance that his preference be enacted. Nevertheless, it does seem to come closer to the ideal of equal chances than majority rule.'

such a system, all parties could expect political representation proportionate to number of votes won, not only might the problem of voter apathy among minorities be reduced but parties who establish as their main agenda the representation of those minorities might be treated more seriously.[123]

CONCLUSION

In modern times, lotteries have been—and still are—used for reaching numerous important social decisions. Yet the practice of lot-casting no longer has much religious or political significance. The two basic objectives of this chapter have been to explain how and why the practice had such significance in the past and to try to shed some light on why it no longer does. I have suggested that rationality is not the key to understanding modern reluctance to settle important social matters by resort to sortition. To eschew chance is not necessarily to be more rational; indeed, I shall argue in due course that there are instances where abandoning an outcome to chance is as rational a strategy as any other, no matter that we may sometimes be disinclined to believe as much.

Although I shall presently endeavour to show how chance, and by extension chance devices, can sometimes be undervalued or unduly resisted, the argument in this chapter has not been that we have somehow committed a fundamental error by abandoning faith in either divination or election by lot. Indeed, I have tried to show why loss of faith in both practices is, from a modern perspective, quite understandable. I think it is also understandable, however, why that faith should have been present in the past. More than this, I would argue that there is a very simple and important lesson to be learnt from past developments of, and modern proposals favouring, systems which combine lotteries with voting: namely that the lottery need not operate in isolation and that, in certain contexts, proper appreciation of its potential as a social decision-making tool will require that one conceives of its being used in combination with some other decision-mechanism. While it is not my claim that the possible advantages of lottery voting somehow outweigh the disadvantages that would attach to any such scheme, I would contend that such a system is distinctly more attractive than is a 'pure' lottery system which entrusts selection of political representatives entirely to chance.

Indeed, in so far as this book advances any sort of case for more extensive use of randomization in social decision-making, the argument is usually that lotteries

---

[123] See Amar (above, n. 113), 1295–8. Amar suggests that there are two further advantages to a system of lottery voting: first, that in the context of the USA such a system eliminates incentives to gerrymander, since, no matter how the boundaries of electoral districts are drawn, 'so long as districts contain equal numbers of voters' any particular political party will not be able to alter the number of districts that it might expect to win (ibid. 1294–5); secondly, that 'lottery voting would tend to erode the two-party system by allowing minor parties to spring up and flourish' (ibid. 1296). Whether this second advantage really would be an advantage seems debatable. I pursue this point in Chapter 5.

ought to be utilized in combination with other decision-making mechanisms and processes (such as the market and adjudication). That we should, in modern times, very often be averse to the use of pure lotteries for the purpose of reaching important social decisions seems understandable. The thesis of Chapter 5, nevertheless, is that there may sometimes be instances where it makes good sense to allow an element of randomness to operate within a broader process of decision-making. Before we develop that thesis, however, we need to consider what sorts of advantages and drawbacks randomization might bring to social decision-making.

3

Relying on Luck

The previous chapter suggests that we are no longer as inclined as we once were to resolve matters of considerable social importance by resort to lot. This suggestion should not be read as a claim that the lottery is no longer used as a device of social decision-making. Lotteries are still put to social uses. Most obviously, randomization rests at the heart of the Anglo-American jury system. '[N]o one has identified a convincing alternative means of selecting jurors', the Royal Commission on Criminal Justice commented in 1993.[1] But apart from jury selection, and leaving aside the fact that lotteries are often used for the purpose of raising state revenue, there appear to be no other areas of social life in which sortition is, as a matter of course, the preferred method of reaching decisions or allocating tasks and resources.

There are, nevertheless, plenty of what we might term local instances of social decision-making by lot. These instances, while numerous, are exceptional. Certain of them have been mentioned already. Others include the use of random devices to select military conscripts,[2] to settle sporting matters,[3] to determine

---

[1] *Royal Commission on Criminal Justice* (London: HMSO, 1993), 131.

[2] A practice which was periodically subscribed to in France from the 17th to late 19th cent. and which has been resorted to intermittently in the USA from the time of the Civil War through to Vietnam. On France, see Francis Choisel, 'Du tirage au sort au service universel' (1981) 37 *Revue Historique des Armées* 43–60; Claude Sturgill, 'Le tirage au sort de la Milice en 1726 ou le début de la décadence de la Royauté en France' (1975) 31 *Revue Historique des Armées* 27–38; and Bernard Schnapper, *Le Remplacement militaire en France: Quelques aspects politiques, économiques et sociaux du recrutement au XIXᵉ siècle* (Paris: SEVPEN, 1968), 36–9, 271–2. With regard to the USA, see Jack Franklin Leach, *Conscription in the United States: Historical Background* (Rutland, Vt.: Tuttle, 1952), 255–7 (Civil War); John Whiteclay Chambers II, *To Raise an Army: The Draft Comes to Modern America* (New York: Free Press, 1987), 184–5, 189, 198 (First World War); Edward A. Fitzpatrick, *Conscription and America: A Study of Conscription in a Democracy* (Milwaukee, Wis.: Richard, 1940), 55 (Second World War); and James M. Gerhardt, *The Draft and Public Policy: Issues in Military Manpower Recruitment, 1945–1970* (Columbus: Ohio State University Press, 1971), 248, 319–23, 343–6.

[3] Such as determining, in sporting events, which teams or individuals will compete with one another. In certain sports, particularly in the USA, lottery systems are sometimes used to determine which individuals should play for which teams. In some sports, the matching—as opposed to the selection—of competitors by lot appears to be avoided: one purpose of the seeding system in tennis, for example, seems to be to prevent the best players from competing in the early rounds of tournaments (thus maintaining audience interest in the later stages). The practice of settling some football—what Americans call soccer—matches by penalty shoot-out is now and again described as a resort to lottery. This description is, however, inaccurate. Penalty-taking and lot-casting are not analytically indistinct since scoring—and, of course, saving—penalties involves skill as well as luck. (Although we may overestimate the role of skill and underestimate that of luck: see Amos Tversky and Thomas Gilovich, 'The Cold Facts about the "Hot Hand" in Basketball' (1989) 2 *Chance* 16–21.) Penalty

which citizens should be subject to tax inspection,[4] to recruit employees,[5] to determine which immigration applications should be successful,[6] to assign judges to cases,[7] even (in certain small-scale communities) to determine sexual partnerships.[8] Lotteries have been either used or approved, furthermore, to allocate plots of land,[9] public housing,[10] church pews,[11] proceeds of charity,[12] oil-drilling

shoot-outs first appeared in Britain at the beginning of the 1970s as a means of settling European cup matches which were drawn on aggregate. Prior to this, such matches had been settled by the flip of a coin. Determining the winner by coin-tossing has always been either rejected or accepted reluctantly, I think, because it takes no account of skill. Thus there has been a tendency, in football, to seek out other more 'responsive' methods of tie-breaking, such as penalty shoot-outs, away goals counting double, and sudden-death. More generally, on luck as compared with merit, cf. Joel Feinberg, *Doing and Deserving: Essays in the Theory of Responsibility* (Princeton: Princeton University Press, 1970), 62–5.

   [4] See Jon Elster, *Solomonic Judgements: Studies in the Limitations of Rationality* (Cambridge: Cambridge University Press, 1989), 63.

   [5] *Isonor* v. *Department of Social Security* (18. iv. 94, EAT 965/93), summarized at (Nov. 1994) 508 *Industrial Relations Law Bulletin* 14–15 (recruitment of suitable job applicants by random selection held to be non-discriminatory).

   [6] See Jon Elster, *Local Justice: How Institutions Allocate Scarce Goods and Necessary Burdens* (Cambridge: Cambridge University Press, 1992), 57–9, 72.

   [7] To cite but one example of this practice, when deciding cases the European Court of Human Rights is comprised of a chamber of nine judges, eight of whom are chosen randomly from a panel of forty (i.e. panel comprised of one judge from each member state). The ninth judge will be a legal expert from the member state in which the case has arisen. See Clare Ovey, 'The European Convention of Human Rights and the Criminal Lawyer: An Introduction' [1998] *Criminal L. Rev.* 4–15 at 5.

   [8] For example, the San Francisco commune, Kerista village, employed randomization and rotation for the purpose of maintaining non-monogamous, 'polyfidelitous' relationships among group members. See Ayala Pines and Elliot Aronson, 'Polyfidelity: An Alternative Lifestyle Without Jealousy?' (1981) 4 *Alternative Lifestyles* 373–92. For a historical account of, and reflections on, Kerista (which disbanded in 1991), cf. Eve Furchgott, 'What Happened to Kerista?' at <http://www.leftbank.com/CosWeb/text/T/kerista> (visited 13 Nov. 1998). In his autobiography (written in 1771), Benjamin Franklin reports the story that Moravian marriages would be determined by lot in instances where 'two or three young women were to be found equally proper for the young man'. *The Autobiography of Benjamin Franklin and Selections from His Writings* (New York: Random House, 1944), 169–70.

   [9] As has been the case in the past, for example, in New Zealand and in certain North American states. On New Zealand, see W. J. Gardner, 'A Colonial Economy' in W. H. Oliver with B. R. Williams (eds.), *The Oxford History of New Zealand* (Oxford: Clarendon Press, 1981), 57–86 at 60; and Peter Adams, *Fatal Necessity: British Intervention in New Zealand, 1830–1847* (Auckland: Auckland University Press, 1977), 141–4. With regard to the US, cf. Douglas C. Wilms, 'Georgia's Land Lottery of 1832' (1974) 52 *Chronicles of Oklahoma* 52–60; and Edward Everett Dale, 'Oklahoma's Great Land Lottery' (1983) 22 *Great Plains Journal* 3–41. In medieval England, plots of land were sometimes allocated randomly under the so-called 'open-field' system. See W. O. Ault, *Open-Field Farming in Medieval England: A Study of Village By-Laws* (London: Allen & Unwin, 1972), 26; Oliver Rackham, *The Illustrated History of the Countryside* (London: Weidenfeld & Nicolson, 1994), 74; and also Carl J. Dahlman, *The Open Field System and Beyond: A Property Rights Analysis of an Economic Institution* (Cambridge: Cambridge University Press, 1980), 31–6.

   [10] As has been done in Israel and the USA. On Israel, see Elster (above, n. 3), 63. With regard to the US, see *Holmes* v. *New York City Housing Authority* (2d Cir. 1968) 398 F.2d 262, 265 (holding that, where applicants for public housing are indistinguishable on grounds of entitlement but not all applications can be satisfied, selection by lot meets with due process requirements); and Hank Greely, 'The Equality of Allocation by Lot' (1977) 12 *Harvard Civil Rights-Civil Liberties L. Rev.*

leases,[13] broadcasting licences,[14] prospecting rights,[15] tickets for public events,[16] vaccines and other drugs,[17] haemodialysis machines,[18] and places at medical and other schools.[19] It would be wrong, in short, to assume that jury selection is the only modern example of randomized social decision-making.

113–41 at 126–30. More generally, on the constitutionality (in the North American context) of social decision-making by lot, cf. *Hornsby* v. *Allen* (5th Cir. 1964) 330 F.2d 55 (random selection of equally qualified applicants for scarce liquor licences constitutionally permissible); and also John Hart Ely, *Democracy and Distrust: A Theory of Judicial Review* (Cambridge, Mass.: Harvard University Press, 1980), 137; though compare *Delaware* v. *Prouse* (1979) 440 US 648, 655–7, 663 (police randomly stopping motor vehicles to check driver's licence and vehicle registration held to violate privacy interests protected by the Fourth Amendment prohibition against unreasonable search and seizure).

[11] See Keith Thomas, *Religion and the Decline of Magic: Studies in Popular Beliefs in Sixteenth- and Seventeenth-Century England* (Harmondsworth: Penguin, 1973 (1971)), 140.

[12] Ibid. and note also Augustine, *De Doctrina Christiana* 1. 28. 61. Krabbe, in his study of ancient and modern uses of lotteries, notes that old Norwegian and Icelandic laws required lot-casting to take place in order to determine the order in which farmers in particular localities would assume temporary responsibility for taking care of the poor. See Oluf H. Krabbe, 'Om Lodtrækning i Fortid og Nutid' (1944) 26 *Juristen* 157–75 at 170.

[13] See Abraham E. Haspel, 'Drilling for Dollars: The Federal Oil-Lease Lottery Program' (1985) 9 *Regulation: American Enterprise Institute Journal on Government and Society* 25–31.

[14] For early arguments advocating random allocation of broadcasting licences, see *Star Television Inc.* v. *FCC* (DC Cir. 1969) 416 F.2d 1086, 1095 (Leventhal J, dissenting); and Robert A. Anthony, 'Towards Simplicity and Rationality in Comparative Broadcast Licensing Proceedings' (1971) 24 *Stanford L. Rev.* 1–115 at 102; and, for more recent legal provisions permitting lottery use in this context, cf. Jeremy Tunstall, *Communications Deregulation: The Unleashing of America's Communications Industry* (Oxford: Blackwell, 1986), 157; Harvey L. Zuckman and Martin J. Gaynes, *Mass Communications Law in a Nutshell* (2nd edn., St Paul, Minn.: West Publishing Co., 1983), 384–7.

[15] See Christopher Zinn, 'Hapless Gold-Digger sees £100m Slip Away', *Guardian*, 17 Dec. 1997, p. 1.

[16] See Willem K. B. Hofstee, 'Allocation by Lot: A Conceptual and Empirical Analysis' (1990) 29 *Social Science Information* 745–63 at 745; and Greely (above, n. 10), 118 n. 28.

[17] See John F. Kilner, 'A Moral Allocation of Scarce Lifesaving Medical Resources' (1981) 9 *Journal of Religious Ethics* 245–85 at 252 (random allocation of polio vaccine in England); James F. Childress, *Practical Reasoning in Bioethics* (Bloomington: Indiana University Press, 1997), 190–1 (random allocation of protease inhibitors to HIV and AIDS patients); and Tamar Lewin, 'Prize in an Unusual Lottery: A Scarce Experimental Drug', *New York Times*, 7 Jan. 1994, at § A, pp. 1, 17 (random allocation of Betaseron to patients with multiple sclerosis).

[18] See Gerald R. Winslow, *Triage and Justice* (Berkeley: University of California Press, 1982), 101–5; Paul Ramsey, *The Patient as Person: Explorations in Medical Ethics* (New Haven: Yale University Press, 1970), 252; and Note, 'Scarce Medical Resources' (1969) 69 *Columbia L. Rev.* 621–92 at 660.

[19] On medical schools, consider the Dutch experiment with weighted admissions lotteries as presented by Willem K. B. Hofstee, 'The Case for Compromise in Educational Selection and Grading', in Scarvia B. Anderson and John S. Helmick (eds.), *On Educational Testing* (San Francisco: Jossey-Bass, 1983), 109–27. (The Dutch system, which gives higher graded students a 75% chance of admission as compared with a 50% chance for average students, has met with considerable resistance and has recently been subjected to judicial criticism: see Mark Fuller, 'News of the World', *The Times Magazine*, 26 Sept. 1998, p. 12.) Use of lotteries to determine entry into medical school has also been considered in the USA: cf. Andre E. Hellegers, 'A Lottery for Lives?' (1977) 12 *Obstetrics and Gynaecology News* 20–1 at 21. Certain popular secondary schools in the North of England have customarily allocated some of their places on a random basis (this practice is probably also undertaken in other parts of the UK, though I am only aware of its adoption by particular schools in Lancashire: on the Lancashire experience, see Fran Abrams, 'Parents Challenge School-Places

Yet the fact of the matter is that the examples listed above do represent exceptions rather than the norm. Resort to lot in social decision-making is not an especially common occurrence. I suggested in the previous chapter that the primary reasons for the demise of the lottery as a device of social decision-making are religious, cultural, and logistical. In this chapter and the next, my approach is more analytical than historical. In this chapter, I shall consider and try to illustrate the main advantages that lotteries hold for decision-makers. These advantages, we shall see, are more often than not subject to qualification. Indeed, while there are numerous attractions to randomized social decision-making, it is also very clearly the case, as I will show in Chapter 4, that deciding by lot is frequently beset by disadvantages. Yet there will emerge from that chapter a fairly positive depiction of social decision-making by lot; indeed, the chapter contains a detailed argument to the effect that claims in favour of randomized legal decision-making in particular may sometimes possess a peculiarly rationalistic appeal. It is suggested, furthermore, that such claims deserve serious consideration because they may prove to be heuristically valuable. I shall argue in Chapter 5 that, although the lottery is a controversial social decision-making device, the potential for its application in allocative and adjudicative contexts may generally have been somewhat underestimated. That chapter contains suggestions as to where, and how, lotteries might profitably be used for social, and particularly legal, decision-making purposes. Thus it is that the thrust of this book moves from historical to analytical and, ultimately, to normative.

1. WHY TRUST IN LUCK?

In fiction, the lottery frequently represents tyranny: to decide randomly is very often to engage in capricious, unnerving, malevolent behaviour.[20] Decision-making by lot can occasionally conjure up unsettling images in real life, too, not only because random selection is sometimes equated with arbitrariness,[21] but also because one of

---

Lottery', *The Independent*, 31 May 1994, p. 4). More generally, on the prospects for the use of randomization (and other social choice mechanisms) for allocating individuals to scarce positions, see Aanund Hylland and Richard Zeckhauser, 'The Efficient Allocation of Individuals to Positions' (1979) 87 *Journal of Political Economy* 293–314.

[20] See, e.g., Shirley Jackson, 'The Lottery' (1948), in Richard Ford (ed.), *The Granta Book of the American Short Story* (London: Granta, 1992), 62–70 (and compare Joshua 7); Graham Greene, *Doctor Fischer of Geneva or The Bomb Party* (London: The Bodley Head, 1980); and Jorge Luis Borges, 'The Lottery in Babylon' (1959), in Borges, *Labyrinths: Selected Stories and Other Writings* (Eng. trans. J. M. Fein, Harmondsworth: Penguin, 1970), 55–61.

[21] Breyer makes this equation, for example, when he suggests that regulatory initiatives are sometimes influenced by what he terms 'random agenda selection'. See Stephen Breyer, *Breaking the Vicious Circle: Toward Effective Risk Regulation* (Cambridge, Mass.: Harvard University Press, 1993), 19–21. Cf. also Cass R. Sunstein, *Legal Reasoning and Political Conflict* (New York: Oxford University Press, 1996), 165, where he claims that 'lotteries have an arbitrariness of their own, by virtue of their random character'. This, I would argue, is analytically incorrect: the arbitrary outcome

the few instances in which humans seem almost instinctively drawn to lot-casting is that of the situation of crisis which requires that, in some way or another, somebody must take a risk, suffer, or be sacrificed.[22] When preparing to enter into battle, for example, Nordic soldiers of the sixth century would apparently draw lots to determine which of them would stand at the head of the battalion as it advanced towards the enemy.[23] From the seventeenth through to the nineteenth century, the *de facto* law of the sea when survival demanded resort to cannibalism was to cast lots in order to select both victims and executioners.[24] Indeed, we noted in the previous chapter the case of *United States* v. *Holmes*, in which it was suggested that, where a ship is at sea and 'all sustenance is exhausted, and a sacrifice of one person is necessary to appease the hunger of others', the fairest mode of selecting a victim is by lot. 'In no other than this or some like way are those having equal rights put upon an equal footing, and in no other way is it possible to guard against partiality and oppression, violence and conflict.'[25] This idea—that drawing lots offers the most appropriate means by which to settle on a victim—arises also in Kohlberg's example of 'The Captain's Dilemma' and in Fuller's famous fable of the stranded speleologists.[26] Desperate situations sometimes demand that the lives of certain people be taken or threatened: that some individuals be held hostage or be conscripted, that someone be sent on a perilous mission or be sacrificed to provide food for others, or whatever. In such instances, casting lots seems to possess a rather grim appeal: where we lack criteria enabling us to say with conviction that one person or group of persons ought to be chosen to suffer or be put at risk, a common instinct, I think, is to trust in luck *faute de mieux*.[27]

differs from the random outcome in that it is a product of human preference. The random outcome depends on human preference only to the extent that a decision is made to resort to randomization in order to generate an outcome. The actual outcome which is produced by a (non-weighted) randomized procedure is independent of human agency.

[22] Even in real life, furthermore, tyranny is sometimes imposed randomly. Consider, for example, the apparently random acts of destruction engaged in by the French terrorist, Émile Henry, as described by George Woodcock, *Anarchism: A History of Libertarian Ideas and Movements* (Harmondsworth: Penguin, 1962), 292–3.

[23] See Krabbe (above, n. 12), 158–9. Another example is the mine-workers' convention of 'cavilling'. Throughout the 19th cent.—indeed, up until the early 1940s—miners at some collieries in North East England would, each quarter, cavil or draw lots to determine who should work in which coal pit (some pits being more hazardous than others). Cavilling was also, on occasions, used by colliery owners to determine redundancies: see, generally, Huw Beynon and Terry Austrin, *Masters and Servants. Class and Patronage in the Making of a Labour Organisation: The Durham Miners and the English Political Tradition* (London: Rivers Oram Press, 1994), 149–53.

[24] See A. W. Brian Simpson, *Cannibalism and the Common Law: A Victorian Yachting Tragedy* (London: The Hambledon Press, 1994 (1984)), 122–45.

[25] *United States* v. *Holmes* (CC Pa. 1842) 26 Fed. Cas. 360–7. For discussion of the case, see Sid Z. Leiman, 'The Ethics of Lottery' (1978) 4 *Kennedy Institute Quarterly Report* 8–11.

[26] See Lawrence Kohlberg, *The Philosophy of Moral Development* (New York: Harper & Row, 1981), 205–11; and Lon L. Fuller, 'The Case of the Speluncean Explorers' (1949) 62 *Harvard L. Rev.* 616–45 at 618. Kohlberg's example is strewn with errors, as is ruthlessly demonstrated by Brian Barry, *Justice as Impartiality* (Oxford: Clarendon Press, 1995), 237–41, 258–66.

[27] See further Torstein Eckhoff, *Justice: Its Determinants in Social Interaction* (Rotterdam: Rotterdam University Press, 1974), 215, 305–7.

Indeed, it is perhaps interesting to note that much of the philosophical and social-scientific literature discussing the potential for decision-making by lot assumes a primary utility of the device to be its capacity to resolve uncomfortable dilemmas which can arise under various conditions of scarcity and abundance. Thus it is that randomized redundancies have been considered for the purpose of reducing an over-expanded workforce;[28] that, on at least one occasion, random allocation of procreation rights has been suggested as a means by which to control population growth;[29] that random imposition of appropriate sentences on criminal offenders has been mooted as (among other things) a method by which to alleviate prison overcrowding;[30] that the use of a weighted lottery has been

[28]   See Norman J. Ireland and Peter J. Law, *The Economics of Labour-Managed Enterprises* (London: Croom Helm, 1982), 19–21.

[29]   See Greely (above, n. 10), 135–8. In summary, Greely's argument is that if, say, it was considered desirable to limit the birth-rate average to 1.7 children per woman, procreation rights should be randomly allocated so that only seven out of ten women would be permitted to bear a second child (ibid. 136–7). Ensuring compliance with such a policy would obviously pose immense, if not insurmountable, difficulties. Greely suggests (137 n. 109) that contraceptives might be added to the water supply, with antidotes being randomly distributed by government to every seven in ten women. Aside from the fact that such a proposal can be criticized on grounds of human autonomy and welfare, the random distribution of antidotes which Greely proposes would only make sense if the desired birth-rate average were 0.7 rather than 1.7 children per woman; in fact, it would hardly make sense even in this instance since, if such a policy were successfully implemented, it would have the effect of keeping the birth-rate average significantly below the level of 0.7, for there would be some women randomly allocated procreation rights who would either not want or not be able to have children.

[30]   See Elster (above, n. 4), 101–3; also David Lewis, 'The Punishment that Leaves Something to Chance' (1989) 18 *Philosophy and Public Affairs* 53–67 at 59–61. The idea here is that once the verdict has been pronounced and sentence chosen, the court might use a randomizing device to determine whether or not it should actually be carried out.

With capital punishment, the practice would resemble that of decimation for mutiny, desertion, or treason whereby one in every ten offenders would be executed, the remaining nine having their sentences commuted to life imprisonment. Resort to this practice is discussed by Wedberg, who notes also that in both Sweden and Finland during the 17th and 18th cent., death sentences would be determined by lot not only when the large number of people found guilty in relation to a particular episode meant that the courts were disinclined to execute all offenders, but also in instances where two or more persons were found to be involved in the murder of another but the courts could not identify the actual murderer. One might anticipate that divination explains resort to lot in such cases. According to Wedberg, however, where courts were unable to identify murderers, random decision-making was resorted to out of respect for *lex talionis*, which prescribes that one life—but not more than one—should be taken for another. See Birger Wedberg, *Tärningkast om liv och död: Rättshistoriska skisser* [*Dicing with Life and Death: A Legal-Historical Sketch*] (Stockholm: Norstedt & Söners, 1935), 10–37. Wedberg points out (p. 26) that a Swedish royal decree of 1724 stipulated that everyone included in a lottery for the imposition of the death penalty 'should be guilty of and punishable for homicide, although, out of regard for human life, only one, following the draw, should be submitted to punishment by death'. In the USA, the Supreme Court has held imposition of the death penalty by random means to be cruel and unusual punishment—see *Furman* v. *Georgia* (1972) 408 US 238—although the Court in that case equates randomness with capriciousness (cf., in particular, the concurring opinion of Stewart J, at 309–10).

With prison sentences, a system whereby convicted offenders stood, say, a one in three chance of not having to serve time would still pose a deterrent—albeit weaker than that posed by a system which does not incorporate this element of chance—to would-be offenders, but would have the advantage of reducing the size of the prison population and thereby reducing public expenditure. The primary, and surely much more compelling, disadvantages of such a system are that the guilty would

proposed for the purpose of allocating police attention to different categories of crime (the more serious crimes being accorded greater weight in the proposed lottery);[31] that randomization has been advocated by some moral philosophers as the fairest method of allocating scarce life-saving medical resources[32] (and indeed, by at least one academic lawyer, as a means by which to distribute scarce legal resources[33]), and that serious thought has even been given to the idea that

often go unpunished and in many instances would no doubt proceed to commit further crimes (for which they might still not be punished). Bruce J. Winick, 'Legal Limitations on Correctional Therapy and Research' (1981) 65 *Minnesota L. Rev.* 331–442 at 417–20 argues (in relation to the USA) that although the use of randomizing techniques in relation to sentencing is likely, in most instances, to be considered 'constitutionally offensive', it may, in the context of correctional research experiments, 'be constitutionally permissible when fundamental rights are not infringed, and perhaps even when they are infringed if other research designs would not be feasible'. For a similar argument, cf. Alexander Morgan Capron, 'Social Experimentation and the Law', in Alice M. Rivlin and P. Michael Timbane (eds.), *Ethics and Legal Issues of Social Experimentation* (Washington, DC: The Brookings Institution, 1975), 127–63 at 160–3.

[31] See Elster (above, n. 4), 49; Elster (above, n. 6), 112. Within the Chicago tradition of the economics of punishment there runs an argument to the effect that a random element is introduced into the criminal justice system when prison sentences are set at very high levels in order to compensate for low probabilities of apprehension and conviction. For Chicagoans such as Becker and Ehrlich, the advantage of the high penalty–low probability combination is that it is likely to maximize deterrence at minimum cost and so combat crime in an optimal fashion. The obvious objection to this combination is that it creates *ex post* inequalities among offenders: while many offenders will escape punishment, those who do not will serve lengthy sentences. Would it not be better to try to increase probabilities of apprehension and conviction while also reducing prison sentences, so that more offenders are imprisoned but punished less severely? The Chicagoan response to this question is that to object to the high penalty–low probability combination is rather like questioning the fairness of lotteries because their outcomes create inequalities among participants. The combination is fair, just as lotteries are fair, Chicago neo-classicists would argue, because *ex ante* costs and benefits are equalized among offenders. For the classic argument in favour of the high penalty–low probability combination, see Gary S. Becker, 'Crime and Punishment: An Economic Approach' (1968) 76 *Journal of Political Economy* 169–217; and, for the analogy with lotteries, cf. Isaac Ehrlich, 'The Optimum Enforcement of Laws and the Concept of Justice: A Positive Analysis' (1982) 2 *International Review of Law and Economics* 3–27 at 4–5.

[32] See, e.g., John F. Kilner, 'A Moral Allocation of Scarce Lifesaving Medical Resources' (1981) 9 *Journal of Religious Ethics* 245–85 at 252–4, 266; Al Katz, 'Process Design for Selection of Hemodialysis and Organ Transplant Recipients' (1973) 22 *Buffalo L. Rev.* 373–418 at 393, 395, 415–17; James F. Childress, 'Who Shall Live When Not All Can Live?' (1970), in Stanley Joel Reiser *et al.* (eds.), *Ethics in Medicine: Historical Perspectives and Contemporary Concerns* (Cambridge, Mass.: MIT Press, 1977), 620–6 at 623–5; Childress (above, n. 17), 180–92; and cf. also Nicholas Rescher, 'The Allocation of Exotic Medical Lifesaving Therapy' (1969) 79 *Ethics* 173–86 at 183–4. Rescher advocates what is, in essence, a weighted lottery which requires that applicants either be excluded from the lottery or given preference within it according to specific criteria (such as life-expectancy). The problem with this proposal is that it encounters incommensurability problems: that is, it requires that different patients' lives be accorded different values. A primary reason for resorting to lot in this context is to try to avoid making such judgements. As critics of Rescher's proposal have observed, the problem with weighted lotteries is that they do not sidestep incommensurability problems: different lives have to be accorded different weights for purposes of conducting the lottery, even though there exists no single acceptable formula by which to determine these weights. See further Hans Oberdiek, 'Who is to Judge?' (1976) 87 *Ethics* 75–86 at 84–5; and Marc D. Basson, 'Choosing Among Candidates for Scarce Medical Resources' (1979) 4 *Journal of Medicine and Philosophy* 313–33 at 328.

[33] See Marshall J. Breger, 'Legal Aid for the Poor: A Conceptual Analysis' (1982) 60 *North Carolina L. Rev.* 281–363 at 353–5. For a critique of Breger's arguments in favour of randomly allo-

people might be randomly selected to be killed so that their organs can be harvested in order to save a greater number of others.[34] While it is by no means the case that all proposals for resort to decision-making by lot concern situations which demand sacrifices, it seems very clear that a considerable proportion of the academic literature suggesting more extensive or novel use of lotteries focuses on instances where some person or group must draw the short straw for the sake of the greater good.[35]

It should, of course, be clear from some of the examples just listed that drawing the short straw is not always to be equated with bad luck. Sometimes, people may count themselves very fortunate to have been randomly selected. Even where this is the case, however, decision-making by lot can unsettle us for the simple reason that chance still has its victims. If random selection is used to determine who should receive scarce medical resources, public housing, places at medical school, or whatever, those who are not chosen become the unlucky ones. Decision by lot will very often constitute an unpleasant choice even when it does not impose an undesirable burden on the person or people selected.

Randomized decision-making often generates a sense of unease because the purpose of the exercise is frequently perceived to be that of assigning social burdens or denying social goods. One person's good may, of course, be another's burden: that some people actually enjoy gardening, for example, is almost beyond my comprehension. Perhaps the same point can be advanced with regard to social tasks such as military and jury service.[36] My intuition, however, is that where there exist unavoidable social tasks which are generally perceived to be burdensome and which people are by and large equally competent to undertake, selection by lot will quite often—particularly if the offering of a financial incentive to undertake the task is out of character with the task itself[37]—be considered a sensible strategy to adopt. The basic point here is that decision-making by lot is often associated with the assignment of tasks which are generally considered to be burdensome. The same point is advanced by, among others, Elster, who continues with the slightly

---

cating specific legal services, cf. Marie A. Failinger and Larry May, 'Litigating Against Poverty: Legal Services and Group Representation' (1984) 45 *Ohio State LJ* 1–56 at 22–4, 44–5.

[34] See John Harris, 'The Survival Lottery' (1975) 50 *Philosophy* 81–7; also John Harris, *Violence and Responsibility* (London: Routledge & Kegan Paul, 1980), 66–84.

[35] See, e.g., Torstein Eckhoff, 'Lotteries in Allocative Situations' (1989) 28 *Social Science Information* 5–22 at 13–16. Krabbe offers the example of an old Norwegian Gulstings-law (*Gulstingslov*) which stipulated that when a hostelry became overcrowded, lots would be cast to determine who would be required to leave. If those persons randomly chosen to leave refused to do so, they would be fined and, should any other person be injured owing to their refusal to leave, they would also be required to pay compensation to that person's family. See Krabbe (above, n. 12), 171.

[36] See further Elster (above, n. 6), 20–1.

[37] The distinction between social tasks which are and are not suited to financial reward seems to have been overlooked by Goodwin when she suggests that responsibility for 'the cleaning of streets and parks (and, indeed, sewers) . . . and even some kinds of policing' ought to be distributed on either a rotative or a randomized basis and reasons that 'if people can accept conscription . . . they might be persuaded *a fortiori* to see the virtue of spending a day or two every year cleaning up local amenities'. Barbara Goodwin, *Justice by Lottery* (Hemel Hempstead: Harvester Wheatsheaf, 1992), 170–1.

more ambitious speculation that there exists 'less willingness to use lotteries for allocating gains than for allocating losses'.[38] The distinction at the heart of this speculation in fact seems questionable since, as already noted, random allocation of gains also entails random allocation of losses.[39] Unlucky are the majority of those who are chosen where lotteries are used to distribute undesirable social burdens; unlucky are those who are not where lotteries are used to distribute scarce resources. In both instances there comes, with the use of the lottery, bad luck.[40]

There has been presented thus far in this chapter such a dour portrait of the lottery that one might fairly question why anyone might ever want to rely on sortition for the purpose of social decision-making. Perhaps the most basic answer to this question is that one could quite easily invert the argument put forward in the previous paragraph so as to emphasize how lotteries bring good as well as bad luck.[41] Another answer—one which requires considerable elaboration—is that there are to be found buried in this rather gloomy portrait some intriguing, and sometimes rather admirable, features.

Certain of these features might be regarded as either admirable or repugnant, depending upon point of view. Consider, for example, the fact that decision-making by lot will often[42] be a mechanical, anonymous, and impersonal process. This observation can, in at least three ways, be formulated as an objection to such decision-making. First, it might be used to support the assertion that lotteries are blind to talent, need, and desert. When college admissions or places on oversubscribed courses are randomly allocated, for example, it is common for some unsuccessful applicants to complain that the method of selection, being impersonal, unfairly ignores the fact that they have distinct needs or merits which make them especially deserving of selection.[43] Secondly, the observation might be

---

[38] Elster (above, n. 4), 105; and cf. also Hofstee (above, n. 16), 755–60.

[39] In an article proposing the use of a lottery to allocate federal grants, Abert describes random selection not only as a means of determining who should get the good, but also as a means by which 'to distribute disbenefits more fairly'. See James Abert, 'Since Grantsmanship Doesn't Work, Why Not Roulette?', *Saturday Review*, 21 October 1972, pp. 65–6 at 65.

[40] It is worth noting, in this context, Edmond Cahn's discussion of *United States* v. *Holmes* (above, n. 25): according to Cahn, the morally correct action in the shipwreck situation is not to cast lots to determine who should be given a chance of survival, but to surrender hope. '[I]f none sacrifice themselves of free will to spare the others . . . they must all wait and die together. For where all have become congeners, pure and simple, no one can save himself by killing another . . . Under the terms of the moral constitution, it will be *wholly* his self that he kills in his vain effort to preserve himself . . . So, in all humility, I would put aside the talk of casting lots, not only because the crisis involves stakes too high for gambling and responsibilities too deep for destiny, but also because no one can win in such a lottery, no one can survive intact by means of the killing.' Edmond Cahn, *The Moral Decision: Right and Wrong in the Light of American Law* (Bloomington: Indiana University Press, 1956), 71.

[41] See, e.g., Peter C. Fishburn, 'Acceptable Social Choice Lotteries', in Hans W. Gottinger and Werner Leinfellner (eds.), *Decision Theory and Social Ethics: Issues in Social Choice* (Dordrecht: Reidel, 1978), 133–52 at 138.

[42] Though not always, as we shall see when we come to consider the idea of a weighted lottery.

[43] See Robert Klitgaard, *Choosing Elites* (New York: Basic Books, 1985), 58; and David Riesman, 'Educational Reform at Harvard College: Meritocracy and its Adversaries', in Seymour

developed into the claim that decision-making by lot has the potential to disempower. The argument here is that the absence of human agency from lottery decisions means that those who, in one way or another, lose out because of such decisions have no one to blame or to whom to appeal: in short, it is the argument that lotteries are indifferent to losers. Thirdly, the observation might be incorporated into a broader claim that decision-making by lot can have a degrading effect: it is easy to see, whatever one were to make of their feelings, that many people would consider it utterly inappropriate and demeaning to resort to something akin to coin-tossing or dice-throwing in order to determine important and highly emotional issues such as who should fight in a war or be granted public housing or allocated scarce life-saving resources.

These and other objections to decision-making by lot will be considered further in the next chapter. My concern at this point, however, is to emphasize that the observation about the impersonal and mechanistic nature of the lottery can just as easily be used to make a positive case for such decision-making. That lotteries are indifferent to the qualities of the persons in relation to whom a decision is to be reached is not necessarily a drawback. 'The impartiality at the heart of the lottery mechanism is', according to Goodwin, 'its major justification.'[44] 'Random selection', Breger elaborates, 'serves to reduce official discretion (and the danger of abuse of discretion); it prevents stigmatization of those who are denied benefits. In an ironic way, random distribution may affirm human dignity and equality by virtue of ignoring all extraneous characteristics about an individual other than his bare "personhood." '[45] Certainly the impersonality of the lottery means that it may reduce the likelihood of particular individuals being either favoured or disadvantaged within the process of decision-making. As has already been noted, furthermore, the fact that a decision reached through resort to sortition is not attributable to human choice (apart, of course, from the initial choice

---

Martin Lipset and David Riesman, *Education and Politics at Harvard* (New York: McGraw-Hill, 1975), 281–401 at 328–9. While Klitgaard seems to regard student aversion to random selection as a good reason for opposing such selection, Riesman is not entirely convinced: 'I have long contended that places in the Freshman Seminars should be allocated by a lottery where special talents are not required, and that this should also be done with overenrolled undergraduate courses; I have followed this policy in my own seminar and course work' (ibid. 282). In advancing proposals for the reformation of the modern American law school, Kennedy argues in favour of a weighted admissions lottery which combines randomness with affirmative action: 'There should be a test designed to establish minimal skills for legal practice and then a lottery admission to the school; there should be quotas within the lottery for women, minorities and working class students.' Duncan Kennedy, *Legal Education and the Reproduction of Hierarchy: A Polemic Against the System* (Cambridge, Mass.: Afar, 1983), 121–2. In a similar vein, cf. also Robert Paul Wolff, *The Ideal of the University* (Boston: Beacon Press, 1969), 143–4.

[44] Goodwin (above, n. 37), 74; and cf. also John Hart Ely, 'Legislative and Administrative Motivation in Constitutional Law' (1970) 79 *Yale LJ* 1205–1341 at 1234 n. 97.

[45] Marshall J. Breger, 'Legal Issues Raised by Randomized Social Experiments', in Robert F. Boruch, Jerry Ross, and Joe S. Cecil (eds.), *Proceedings and Background Papers: Conference on Ethical and Legal Problems in Applied Social Research* (Evanston, Ill.: Northwestern University Department of Psychology, 1979), pp. 9:1–40 at 9:10.

that the decision be made by lot) means that responsibility for that decision does not fall on a specific individual. Indeed, in so far as random selection possesses the capacity to counteract the impulse to blame, it might be considered useful when decisions have to be taken which perhaps ought not to be laid at the door of any particular person or group. When decisions have to be made 'implying that one person's life is more worth saving than another', Glover notes, '[e]ven deciding by lot must be fairly unpleasant, but it must be much more distressing to decide by making judgements about the value of the lives of different people'.[46] Lotteries, in short, offer a means of selecting when the idea that some individual or group should take responsibility for the selection seems intolerable.[47]

The argument here is not that the blindness of the lottery should be regarded wholly favourably, but that this blindness does not have to be viewed entirely negatively.[48] This is, of course, an argument which can be turned on its head. We need hardly repeat that to nearly every argument in support of decision-making by lot there attach qualifications. Possibly this explains why, when social theorists have argued for more extensive use of lotteries for social decision-making purposes, there has sometimes been a tendency to make a case for randomness by emphasizing the shortcomings of other methods of decision-making. 'In allocative situations,' Greely claims, 'distributions by merit, money, or patience criteria stress goals conflicting with the norm of equality. Random selection is often the best, or least objectionable, alternative method of allocation, and its use as a distributive device should be considered more often.'[49] This argument—that, with regard to some issues, no method of deciding is especially satisfactory and that resort to lot (which at least has respect for equality of opportunity and cost-efficiency on its side) is as good as, if not better than, any other—seems both understandable and reasonable. Indeed, there are points in this study when precisely this defence of lotteries is adopted. The defence hardly works, however, if it is formulated in such a way that one is simply highlighting the problems with other approaches to decision-making in order to take the spotlight off one's own. Advancing a case for decision-making by lot demands recognition of the fact that lotteries can promote impartiality, equality, cost-efficiency, and the like, but that they do not necessarily do so and, indeed, that such qualities cannot be assumed to be unproblematic. Accordingly, while this study offers an argument to the effect that, for social and legal decision-making purposes, lotteries may have advantages which tend to be overlooked, it ought to be stressed that these advantages are never assumed to be unequivocal.

Yet what are the advantages of deciding by lot? And what sorts of qualifications attach to these advantages? Both the advantages and the qualifications are

---

[46] Jonathan Glover, *Causing Death and Saving Lives* (Harmondsworth: Penguin, 1977), 218–19.
[47] See further Greely (above, n. 10), 16–17 (on decision-making by lot as a satisficing method); and Goodwin (above, n. 37), 98–9.
[48] 'The blind element . . . is both the virtue and the shortcoming of the lottery.' Guido Calabresi and Philip Bobbitt, *Tragic Choices* (New York: Norton & Co., 1978), 44.
[49] Greely (above, n. 10), 141.

numerous. A common argument in favour of lotteries is that they offer a highly economical means of decision-making.[50] '[G]iven a context in which there is no identifiably right decision to be made,' Goodwin argues, 'lot-decisions would have as much of a chance of success as decisions made by any other method, and the additional advantage of time-saving.'[51] In certain contexts, this additional advantage might possess considerable appeal. Determining which patients ought to be selected for medical treatment, for example, can be a protracted and time-consuming process.[52] Those concerned with health-care ethics know only too well that to many, if not most, medical decisions there may apply a multitude of criteria—criteria which will compete and often conflict with one another.[53] It is hardly surprising that medical decision-makers will sometimes appear to drag their feet when deciding upon whom to prioritize for treatment. But delay, of course, has its price. Those who are ultimately selected for treatment may suffer considerably before the decision-making process is concluded; there may even be some who die who would otherwise have survived had selection not taken so long. Given such circumstances, it seems understandable that researchers into medical ethics should frequently have been preoccupied with discovering and advancing methods of decision-making which are both fair and quick.[54] Sortition is obviously one such method. 'Randomness as a moral principle deserves serious study', Freund contends, since, 'in a matter of choosing life or death, not involving specific wrongdoing, no one should assume the responsibility of judging comparative worthiness to live on the basis of unfocused criteria of virtue or social usefulness'.[55] Part of the problem with allowing any particular person or group to assume this responsibility is that exercising it is likely to take a considerable amount of effort and time. By stripping away this responsibility, decision-making by lot saves on such effort and time.

Yet the economy of sortition may sometimes be a drawback. While decision-making by lot might hold some appeal where difficult choices need to be made quickly, in other contexts it could serve as a perfect device for the expedient, or even the lazy, adjudicator. In the 1920s, an American judge, Joseph Hutcheson,

---

[50]   See, e.g., John Broome, 'Selecting People Randomly' (1984) 95 *Ethics* 38–55 at 41.

[51]   Goodwin (above, n. 37), 98.

[52]   See Christopher Newdick, *Who* [sic] *Should We Treat? Law, Patients and Resources in the NHS* (Oxford: Clarendon Press, 1995), 20–36.

[53]   There exists a formidable body of literature supporting this point. For three pertinent studies, see Jack G. Copeland *et al.*, 'Selection of Patients for Cardiac Transplantation' (1987) 75 *Circulation* 2–9; Henry K. Beecher, 'Scarce Resources and Medical Advancement' (1969) 98 *Daedalus* 275–313; and Note, 'Patient Selection for Artificial and Transplanted Organs' (1969) 82 *Harvard L. Rev.* 1322–42.

[54]   Consider, for example, Opelz's argument that a fair and efficient allocation of kidneys requires the development of computer programs which ensure optimal match between donors and recipients: see Gerhard Opelz, 'Allocation of Cadaver Kidneys for Transplantation' (1988) 20 *Transplantation Proceedings* 1028–32.

[55]   Paul A. Freund, 'Introduction', in Paul A. Freund (ed.), *Experimentation with Human Subjects* (London: Allen & Unwin, 1972), pp. xii–xviii at xvii. See also Note (above, n. 53), 1329–30.

confessed that he reached decisions in a manner similar to Rabelais's Judge Bridoye.[56] 'I, after canvassing all the available material at my command and duly cogitating upon it, give my imagination play, and brooding over the cause, wait for the feeling, the hunch—that intuitive flash of understanding which makes the jump-spark connection between question and decision'—and, on the basis of this hunch, 'decide the case more or less off hand and by rule of thumb'.[57] In two crucial respects, however, Hutcheson differed from Bridoye. First, he did not adopt Bridoye's practice of deciding cases by throwing dice.[58] Secondly, Hutcheson conceded that his intuitions or hunches would take shape with regard to the relevant precedents or statutory rules.[59] Roman law—in which Rabelais's judge is supposedly well-versed[60]—permitted of certain instances in which disputes might be resolved by recourse to lot.[61] Bridoye, however, resolves all disputes in this way. There is, nevertheless, a little bit more to his judicial method than the mere casting of dice. Although he assumes decision-making by lot to be a common practice among judges, he appreciates that such decision-making is likely to be considered objectionable by those on whom he imposes unwelcome verdicts. Accordingly, he delays communicating the decisions which the dice produce. 'I consider that time ripens all things', Bridoye remarks, and so '[t]hat is why . . . I suspend, delay, and postpone judgement, so that the case . . . may in course of time come to its maturity, and so that the decision by dice . . . may be borne more patiently by the losing party'.[62] The story of Bridoye illustrates how

---

[56] See Rabelais, *The Histories of Gargantua and Pantagruel*, III. 39. In English translations of this work, Bridoye is renamed Bridlegoose. For the significance of the name in both the original and the translations, cf. Theodore Ziolkowski, *The Mirror of Justice: Literary Reflections of Legal Crises* (Princeton: Princeton University Press, 1997), 138.

[57] Joseph C. Hutcheson, Jr., 'The Judgment Intuitive: The Function of the "Hunch" in Judicial Decision' (1929) 14 *Cornell Law Quarterly* 274–88 at 278.

[58] Although Hutcheson did not adopt this practice, he claimed not to be wholly opposed to it: ibid. 282. Adoption of the practice has, on occasions, resulted in judges being censured. See, e.g., United Press, 'Coin-Tossing Judge Censured by Court', *San Francisco Chronicle*, 9 Nov. 1976, § 1, p. 2, col. 1 (municipal judge censured by Louisiana Supreme Court for, *inter alia*, tossing coins to determine guilt or innocence and thereby, according to the press report, 'making the judicial system look ridiculous'); Anon., 'Guilty as Not Charged', *New York Times*, 11 Apr. 1983, § A, p. 24, col. 1 (Manhattan criminal court judge found guilty of misconduct and removed permanently from judicial office for, among other things, 'decid[ing] the length of a defendant's jail sentence by a coin toss'); and also Brian Bix, *Law, Language, and Legal Determinacy* (Oxford: Clarendon Press, 1993), 106; Bernard S. Jackson, *Making Sense in Jurisprudence* (Liverpool: Deborah Charles, 1996), 119–21.

[59] See Hutcheson (above, n. 57), 287; and cf. also Karl N. Llewellyn, 'On Reading and Using the Newer Jurisprudence' (1940) 40 *Columbia L. Rev.* 581–614 at 603–4.

[60] See Theodore Ziolkowski, 'Judge Bridoye's Ursine Litigations' (1995) 92 *Modern Philology* 346–50.

[61] See M. A. Screech, *Rabelais* (London: Duckworth, 1979), 268–72; and also J. Duncan M. Derrett, 'Rabelais' Legal Learning and the Trial of Bridoye' (1963) 25 *Bibliothèque d'Humanisme et Renaissance* 111–71 at 129–30.

[62] *Gargantua and Pantagruel*, III. 40. It is not difficult to justify Bridoye's method of decision, Twining argues, since '[t]hrowing dice ensured that in every case each side had an exactly equal chance of winning. Over the long run it was statistically highly probable that [Bridoye] would get the right result in about half the cases.' The second sentence in this quotation does not follow from the first. The probability that dice-throwing would produce the right result in almost half the cases would

decision-makers might resort to lot and then, not wanting to appear idle or irresponsible, postpone delivery of the decision so as to create or maintain the impression that delivering a judgment requires a considerable amount of work.

Randomization can sometimes generate useful or even welcome incentives (and, for that matter, disincentives). Since random selection will—depending on just how random the method of selection is—either eliminate or reduce the role of human agency in the decision-making process, it will very likely affect the extent to which individuals feel moved to try to influence that process.[63] Indeed, in Chapter 2 we encountered numerous examples of how lotteries or lottery-based systems, particularly when employed for the purpose of selecting political representatives, may diminish incentives to engage in strategic behaviour. Further possibilities might be envisaged here. Where, for instance, conscripts are selected for military service on the basis of age and physical fitness, some of the young and the fit may be tempted to engage, and might well engage, in self-mutilation. Random selection of conscripts, while unlikely to yield the fittest (or the most willing) soldiers, could be expected to reduce this particular temptation.[64] In due course, I shall argue that lotteries may occasionally have powerful positive incentive effects because they are sometimes seen to possess a Solomon-like quality[65]—a quality which explains, in part, why there quite often exists widespread disinclination to use lotteries for social decision-making purposes. For example, multi-member decision-making bodies might (it is important to stress that word) make considerably more effort to reach agreement on an outcome were it to be stipulated that the consequence of not reaching an agreement, or of not doing so within a given time period, would be the determination of the outcome by lot (see Chapter 5, section 3).

Requiring that certain matters be resolved by lot might encourage other forms

only be borne out if roughly 50% of the plaintiffs (or, indeed, the defendants) in these cases deserved to win. See William Twining, *Rethinking Evidence: Exploratory Essays* (Oxford: Blackwell, 1990), 118.

[63] See further Elster (above, n. 4), 39, 109–11. Of course, individuals may still feel moved to try to influence a process—and may be successful in influencing that process—even when it is subject to randomization. When, for example, the US immigration service in 1992 purported randomly to allocate 40,000 non-restrictive immigrant visas to applicants from thirty-six countries, it transpired that 16,000 of these visas had been earmarked for people from the Republic of Ireland and Northern Ireland 'thanks to the highly effective lobbying of politicians by illegal Irish immigrants in the US'. It was claimed at the time that '[t]he disproportionate number of visas granted to Ireland also reflects the clout of the Irish vote in US politics'. Leonard Doyle, 'Advisers Aim to Win with the US Visa Lottery', *Independent*, 4 Aug. 1992, p. 8.

[64] Although a system of selection by lot would not necessarily reduce this temptation. One would expect the temptation to engage in self-mutilation to remain if the relevant lottery was weighted so that, for example, those below a certain age stood a greater chance of being selected. For discussion of how a draft lottery could be weighted along such lines, see Albert A. Blum, 'Soldier or Worker: A Reevaluation of the Selective Service System' (1972) 13 *Midwest Quarterly* 147–67 at 163–6.

[65] See 1 Kings 3: 16–28. The analogy is imperfect, since whereas Solomon makes a threat—or, more accurately, a command—in order to get to the truth, with lotteries the idea is that a threat is made so as to generate improvements in the process of decision-making.

of responsibility. Possibly the introduction of the draft lottery, along with abolition of the right to deferment for most students, increased pressure to end the Vietnam War, as parents in positions of political influence faced the prospect of seeing their children conscripted.[66] Some medical ethicists have argued similarly that the random allocation of scarce life-saving medical resources would probably result in an increased supply of those resources, 'because the holders of economic and political power would make certain that they would not be excluded by a random selection procedure' and so 'would help to redirect public priorities or establish private funding so that life-saving medical treatment would be widely and perhaps universally available'.[67] The general point here is that random distribution of goods and burdens may sometimes have a sobering effect on citizens.[68] Vulnerability—the possibility that one may be unlucky in the draw—might spur those with political and economic power to try, in one way or another, to reduce the amount of bad luck to be spread around. Where individuals have been fortunate to have had the luck of the draw, furthermore, they may be more inclined to demonstrate compassion towards, and offer support for, those who have not been so lucky.[69]

However, the incentives and disincentives which accompany randomization will not always be welcome. Just as lotteries may generate a disincentive to engage in manipulative behaviour, so too they may create a disincentive to act cooperatively. We have noted already that proposals for random selection of political representatives to hold office for a limited duration tend to meet with the objection that office-holders would not only feel little, if any, compulsion to endeavour to acquire political knowledge and skill, but would also have little incentive to try to represent or advance the interests of citizens or to engage in long-term political planning. Furthermore, allocation of resources through use of a lottery system can sometimes—especially when compared with the use of a market system[70]—create a disincentive to be either competitive or productive.

---

[66] See Elster (above, n. 4), 68; Elster (above, n. 6), 165–6.

[67] Childress, 'Who Shall Live When Not All Can Live?' (above, n. 32), 625. For the same argument, cf. Kilner (above, n. 32), 266; and Oberdiek (above, n. 32), 84.

[68] See further Goodwin (above, n. 37), 95–6.

[69] This point echoes the speculation, offered in the previous chapter, that many citizens of 14th-century Florence were disinclined to cause trouble for holders of political office because they sensed the possibility that they themselves could be selected to hold office at some point in the future.

[70] There is, of course, a lottery-like element to markets, to the extent that luck often plays a part in economic success. In so far as markets do bear any resemblance to lotteries, however, they seem to reflect lotteries of the weighted variety, since, within market systems, the value of the resources at one's disposal will often (though not always) have some bearing on the degree to which one is economically successful.

During the 20th century, English courts have on various occasions wound up companies on the basis that their initiatives amounted not to commercial activity but to the operation of a lottery: the classic example of this is the money-spinning venture whereby people are, for a fee, invited to become 'partners' in a company. Those people are then able to recoup some of that fee by persuading others to become partners. These new partners will have the same financial incentive to recruit yet others to become partners. The scheme is a commercial variant on the chain-letter: whether or not

I shall suggest in Chapter 5 that there may occasionally be good arguments in favour of using a combined market-and-lottery system (requiring payment for entry into a lottery pool) where a limited number of commercial rights—such as broadcasting licences or oil-drilling franchises—is to be made available to a larger number of applicants for those rights. A basic problem with allocating these rights in a purely random fashion is that such allocation removes the incentive for competition among applicants.[71] While some economists, moreover, have argued that particular randomized allocations—such as randomized distributions of land,[72] or even tax burdens[73]—may, in certain circumstances, generate utility gains, one might expect lottery distributions in general to be allocatively inefficient, with rights being granted to applicants who would not, had market arrangements prevailed, have valued those rights sufficiently highly (that is, have been prepared to pay an appropriate price) to have been accorded them.

Use of lotteries to distribute rights which are customarily allocated through the mechanism of the market might also militate against productive efficiency. There is, after all, no point in working hard to receive a reward which will be distributed randomly. The broader problem here, of course, is not only that lotteries do not guarantee benefits for the deserving, but also that they do not guarantee withholding of benefits from the undeserving. The lottery can simultaneously ignore social worth and reward vice.[74]

The capacity for random allocation to diminish the incentive to behave prudently becomes very clear if we consider Harris's case for the so-called 'survival lottery'. Imagine that a super-Benthamite scheme[75] were proposed

---

A recoups her initial outlay will depend upon her recruiting *B* and *C* to the scheme; whether *A* actually profits from this venture will depend upon the ability of *B* and *C* to recruit others to the scheme, and so on. The extent to which each party profits—should he or she profit at all—will depend upon how many people can be said to have joined the company as a result of that party being in the chain. For the argument that schemes of this type are lotteries rather than genuine commercial ventures, see *R.* v. *Registrar of Companies,* ex parte *More* [1931] 2 KB 197; *Director of Public Prosecutions* v. *Phillips* [1935] 1 KB 391; *In re Senator Hanseatische Verwaltungsgesellschaft mbH* [1997] 1 WLR 515; and *In re Vanilla Accumulation Ltd., The Times,* 24 Feb. 1998, p. 46.

[71] Goodwin (above, n. 37), 169 states that, in such circumstances, 'it seems that a lottery distribution would not be incompatible with the notion of perfect competition, since all the competing firms would have to be—or become—as competitive as possible in their operations'. However, as she implicitly concedes, it would be the imposition of standards—requiring, for example, 'that all companies competing were sufficiently solvent . . . or sufficiently competent to undertake to exploit properly whatever franchise was being distributed'—rather than the use of the lottery that would encourage competition here.

[72] See J. A. Mirrlees, 'The Optimum Town' (1972) 74 *Swedish Journal of Economics* 114–35.

[73] See Joseph E. Stiglitz, 'Utilitarianism and Horizontal Equity: The Case for Random Taxation' (1982) 18 *Journal of Public Economics* 1–33.

[74] See Leo Shatin, 'Medical Care and the Social Worth of a Man' (1966) 36 *American Journal of Orthopsychiatry* 96–101 at 100; and cf. also Leiman (above, n. 25), 9 (arguing that a lottery can 'make equals out of a group of unequals').

[75] Harris himself does not call the survival lottery super-Benthamite. Nevertheless, the description seems to capture his argument well. On super-Benthamism, see Hilary Putnam, *Reason, Truth and History* (Cambridge: Cambridge University Press, 1981), 139–41. Although Ryan also does not

whereby everyone is 'given a sort of lottery number' and, where two or more lives could be saved except that no suitable organs have become available, a computer randomly selects the number of a suitable donor who is then killed and his or her organs used to save those lives.[76] Harris concedes that such a scheme will no doubt meet with numerous objections. Yet rejection of the scheme carries a high price. Utilitarians, if no one else, he believes, ought to endorse it.[77] For '[w]ith the refinement of transplant procedures such a scheme could offer the chance of saving large numbers of lives that are now lost'.[78]

use the term, he notes that the essentially super-Benthamite implications of Harris's scheme most likely explain why it is generally considered to be objectionable: see Alan Ryan, 'Two Kinds of Morality: Causalism or Taboo' (1975) 5 *Hastings Center Report* 5–7 at 6–7.

[76] Harris, 'Survival Lottery' (above, n. 34), 83. Harris develops the proposal on the assumption that medical technology has advanced to the point where organ transplantation can be carried out with certainty of success (ibid. 81). It is also essential to the proposal that no moral distinction is made between killing and letting die (see ibid. 81–2, 84–5). For arguments to the effect that refusal to make this distinction is objectionable, cf. J. G. Hanink, 'On the Survival Lottery' (1976) 51 *Philosophy* 223–5 at 223–4; Sid Z. Leiman, 'Therapeutic Homicide: A Philosophic and Halakhik Critique of Harris' "Survival Lottery" ' (1983) 8 *Journal of Medicine and Philosophy* 257–67 at 259; and, more generally, Margaret Brazier, *Medicine, Patients and the Law* (2nd edn., London: Penguin, 1992), 35–8.

[77] Harris, 'Survival Lottery' (above, n. 34), 86; and compare Jonathan Glover, 'Life and Death', in Jonathan Glover (ed.), *Utilitarianism and its Critics* (New York: Macmillan, 1990), 119–21 at 120: 'Utilitarians, like other people, show little enthusiasm for this proposal. But there is a question whether their theory gives adequate reasons for opposing it.' That people will not always conceive of medical resourcing in strict utilitarian terms is, of course, a separate matter. Elster (above, n. 6), 182–3, asserts that '[n]obody . . . was outraged when Dr Starzl's team in Pittsburgh made a quintuple transplantation of heart, lung, liver, kidney, and pancreas to one person, in spite of the fact that these organs might have saved the lives of several other people'. On this occasion, one suspects, any feelings of outrage would have been dwarfed by a sense of awe at what had been achieved. The likelihood of outrage over such multiple transplantations would probably be greater were they quite common.

[78] Harris, 'Survival Lottery' (above, n. 34), 83. Whether the appropriateness of an action ought always to be judged by reference to the number of lives that it saves is, of course, questionable. Consider, in this regard, Thomson's efforts to reconcile the cases of the bystander at the switch (who can divert the trolley so that it kills one instead of five) and the surgeon (who can kill one patient and use his organs to save five others). See Judith Jarvis Thomson, 'The Trolley Problem' (1985) 94 *Yale LJ* 1395–1415. For Thomson, although rights trump utilities, '[a]ny plausible theory of rights must make room for the possibility of waiving a right' (ibid. 1405) and so there may be instances when the right not to be killed should be overridden if the result is an increase in utility. Thomson argues that this right ought to be overridden in the case of the bystander at the switch, but not in the case of the transplant surgeon, because in the former case, unlike in the latter, the threat can be imposed upon or diverted to the one instead of the five without altering the nature of the threat: thus, altering the course of the trolley poses the same threat to the lone workman as it previously did to the five, whereas the surgeon must take the life of a healthy patient in order to save the lives of five others who suffer from life-threatening ailments (see ibid. 1407). For a critical analysis of Thomson's argument, Eric Rakowski, *Equal Justice* (Oxford: Clarendon Press, 1991), 345–7.

For an interesting and powerful argument to the effect that the number of lives that might be saved ought normally to have no bearing on our decision as to the best course of action, see John M. Taurek, 'Should the Numbers Count?' (1977) 6 *Philosophy and Public Affairs* 293–316. Rather than counting or estimating how many lives might be saved, Taurek suggests that we might do better to determine our course of action by flipping a coin (ibid. 303, 310–14). For critiques of Taurek's position, cf. Derek Parfit, 'Innumerate Ethics' (1978) 7 *Philosophy and Public Affairs* 285–301; Gregory S. Kavka, 'The Numbers Should Count' (1979) 36 *Philosophical Studies* 285–94; Frances Myrna

Indeed, generally, 'lives might well be more secure under such a scheme'.[79]

It would nevertheless be unfair, Harris claims, 'to allow people who have brought their misfortune on themselves to benefit from the lottery. There would clearly be something unjust about killing the abstemious B so that W (whose heavy smoking has given him lung cancer) and X (whose drinking has destroyed his liver) should be preserved to over-indulge again.'[80] Behind this claim lies one of the basic difficulties with the so-called survival lottery: that such a scheme, if not somehow weighted so as to discriminate in favour of those who take care of themselves,[81] 'removes the natural disincentive to imprudent action'.[82] The motivation for individuals to eschew a variety of unhealthy practices will very likely be diminished if diseased organs can and always will be replaced.[83] That the survival lottery may reduce incentives to act prudently raises the question of whether such a lottery necessarily ought to be favoured by utilitarians. For whereas one normally takes the pleasure from, and pays the price for, one's imprudence, with the imposition of the survival lottery the pleasure and the price are to some degree separated: the ultimate cost—as opposed to the everyday costs—of my gluttony, excessive drinking, or nicotine habit is borne not by me but by the person who is randomly selected to be my saviour.[84] If the imprudent can expect to have their ultimate losses (meaning expended human organs) covered, the incentive for them to avoid incurrence of those losses will be diminished.[85] The survival lottery might not hold much in the way of utilitarian appeal

Kamm, 'Equal Treatment and Equal Chances' (1985) 14 *Philosophy and Public Affairs* 177–94; and John T. Sanders, 'Why the Numbers Should Sometimes Count' (1988) 17 *Philosophy and Public Affairs* 3–14.

[79] Harris, 'Survival Lottery' (above, n. 34), 84.   [80] Ibid. 83.

[81] Such weighting would be achieved to some degree by Harris's hypothetical 'reconditioning lottery'. If it were the case that people could be randomly selected and killed and their organs extracted and reconditioned, Harris suggests, the providers of those organs would not have to be healthy and so the scheme would not prey upon the prudent. 'Incentives to lead healthy lives and thus avoid a gradual deterioration in the health of society would be built in to this lottery. The imprudent as a class would not prey upon the healthy and all would have a reason to minimise their chance of being selected by the lottery, by minimising the number of times the lottery would have to be called upon to rescue the dying.' Harris, *Violence and Responsibility* (above, n. 34), 82–3.

[82] Peter Singer, 'Utility and the Survival Lottery' (1977) 52 *Philosophy* 218–22 at 219; and see also Rakowski (above, n. 78), 344.

[83] In the real world, of course, the force of this argument is reduced owing to the fact that people cannot be sure that replacement organs would be available should they need them, or that organ transplantation would be successful. That people do engage in imprudent actions which are known to cause organ failure is no doubt attributable in large measure to the fact that they believe that the chances of their suffering from organ failure *and* receiving the necessary transplant *and* that transplant being successful are so small that the disincentive to act imprudently is cancelled out by the pleasure derived from the activity. See Elster (above, n. 6), 126.

[84] Leaving aside imprudence, the survival lottery would also meet with objections from utilitarians if the public anxiety generated by the establishment of such a scheme dwarfed the benefits created by it. See Elster (above, n. 6), 190, 222.

[85] Though not eliminated. While the imprudent in Harris's survival lottery scenario may confidently expect to get the organ transplant which they ultimately need, they will also suffer considerably before this happens. Illness itself will still stand as a disincentive to imprudence.

if, by randomizing loss, it reduces the incentive to avoid loss and so enhances the possibility that total losses will be greater than they would otherwise have been.[86]

One of the great advantages of trying to ensure that as many social decisions as possible are reached through resort to lot, Goodwin argues, is that, '[i]n the long term', such a policy 'would move society towards absolute equality'.[87] One might reasonably wonder why absolute equality should be a desideratum. By promoting this ideal, randomization may diminish the incentive to distinguish oneself from one's peers: indeed, as has already been noted, the use of lotteries to reach decisions might sometimes deter (among other things) altruism, competition, and productivity. To pursue a policy of income-equality, for example, would be to attempt to diminish opportunities to use material rewards as incentives to production. 'Any insistence on carving the pie into equal slices would shrink the size of the pie.'[88] Those who advocate randomization on egalitarian grounds tend to do so, however, not because they regard the lottery primarily as a means of guaranteeing equality of resources—the device offers no such guarantee—but because they believe that it promotes equality of opportunity.[89] Since we are all equally susceptible to chance—so the argument goes—to decide by resort to a (non-weighted) lottery is to accord an equal opportunity to everyone within the pool. Over time (and assuming that the lottery is being consistently applied to the same problem), such decision-making may have an equalizing effect on resource-allocation also, since repeated lottery drawings even out in the long run and so will go some way to equalizing individuals' chances of receiving whatever it is that is being distributed.[90] For those who favour more extensive use of randomization for social decision-making purposes, however, the greatest virtue of the lottery is its capacity to treat people impartially by according them equal chances of success.[91] 'Random selection is the only allocative method

---

[86] See Singer (above, n. 82), 221. While my focus here is obviously on the incentive effects of the hypothetical survival lottery, the discussion raises, I think, a deeper problem with Harris's scheme—a problem which Harris himself acknowledges. The problem is that of determining what constitutes imprudent action. Where lies the distinction between actions which make one responsible and those which do not make one responsible for illness requiring organ transplantation? Even if it should prove possible satisfactorily to make this distinction, furthermore, how might it be applied through law? Indeed, '[e]ven if there were cases where we could be confident that a person had in no way contributed to their illness, could we acquire this confidence in time to save them? The meticulous investigation of the life and work of each citizen would, even if theoretically possible, be hopelessly time-consuming.' Harris, *Violence and Responsibility* (above, n. 34), 79.

[87] Goodwin (above, n. 37), 205.

[88] Arthur M. Okun, *Equality and Efficiency: The Big Tradeoff* (Washington, DC: The Brookings Institution, 1975), 48.

[89] See Peter Westen, *Speaking of Equality: An Analysis of the Rhetorical Force of 'Equality' in Moral and Legal Discourse* (Princeton: Princeton University Press, 1990), 149.

[90] The likelihood of particular individuals' chances being so equalized will be significantly reduced if there is a constant flow of people in and out of the lottery pool.

[91] See, generally, Goodwin (above, n. 37), 35–40. Brian Barry notes that some legal and political philosophers advocate resort to random selection on both egalitarian and utilitarian grounds without appreciating that the goals of equalizing chances and maximizing utility may conflict: cf. Barry (above, n. 26), 226, 228–30, 238.

which honestly can claim the objective equality of opportunity from which the satisfaction of equality of expectation springs. It is the allocative method which maximizes the goal of equality.'[92]

This contention illustrates, however, not that lotteries generate equality, but that they may promote a conception of equality. That this conception will often warrant promotion is questionable.[93] The argument here is not that the conception of equality encapsulated within randomization is of no value. Where, for example, parties seeking a scarce resource all appear to be equally entitled to it and those entrusted with responsibility for allocating the resource are unable to distinguish potential recipients, random allocation might be considered fair (for want of a better word[94]) because it appears to offer an equal chance of success to candidates who have already been judged to be equally deserving.[95] While the lottery cannot ensure for these candidates equality of outcome, it might give them an equal chance of getting the desired outcome.[96] Resort to lot becomes particularly controversial, however, when decisions are to be made concerning candidates who, through application of other criteria, can be distinguished. For instance, in situations of crisis, examples of which were suggested at the outset of this section, there may be certain people who possess talents—medical skills, the ability to navigate the lifeboat to shore, or whatever—application of which might ensure the survival of others; in such situations, it would probably be considered acceptable and desirable to treat these people unequally by exempting them from random allocations of risks or suffering. According equal opportunities to people may also seem inappropriate when those people are distinguishable on grounds of need. To take a distinction from Dworkin, while lotteries might guarantee equality of treatment among individuals, they cannot ensure that those individuals are treated as equals—that is, that they are treated with equal concern

[92] Greely (above, n. 10), 122.

[93] See Calabresi and Bobbitt (above, n. 48), 49: 'Lotteries deify absolute equality, but in so doing offend other conceptions of egalitarianism and emphasize society's unwillingness to spend enough to treat everyone decently as well as alike.'

[94] See Elster (above, n. 4), 113. For the claim (a claim which is evidently highly generalized and contestable) that randomization is commonly considered to be the fairest method of allocating scarce resources, see Camille M. Wortman and Vita C. Rabinowitz, 'Random Assignment: The Fairest of Them All' in Boruch *et al.* (above, n. 45), 15:1–10. On the malleability of 'fair', see Stanley Fish, *There's No Such Thing as Free Speech and it's a Good Thing, Too* (New York: Oxford University Press, 1994), 4–7, 16–17.

[95] See Broome (above, n. 50), 39–40, 46–52; John Broome, 'Uncertainty and Fairness' (1984) 94 *Economic Journal* 624–32 at 628; John Broome, *Weighing Goods: Equality, Uncertainty and Time* (Oxford: Basil Blackwell, 1991), 193–6; John Broome, 'Fairness' (1990/91) 91 *Proceedings of the Aristotelian Society* 87–102 at 97–100. Broome's argument is that resort to random selection will be justifiable if the claims of the candidates are roughly rather than exactly equal.

[96] Sher offers a definition of a fair lottery which combines requirements of equality and non-interference: namely, that allocation by lot of indivisible goods to which several persons have equal claims will be fair if, and only if, none of those persons has exercised his or her control over the lottery in such a way as to enhance the possibility of his or her desires being satisfied over and above the desires of the other claimants. See George Sher, 'What Makes a Lottery Fair?' (1980) 14 *Noûs* 203–16 at 211–12.

and respect when decisions are made about how resources and opportunities are to be distributed. If I have two children, one of whom is dying from a disease which is making the other uncomfortable, I treat them equally—but not, on this distinction, as equals—if I toss a coin to decide which of them should receive the remaining dose of a drug.[97] Lotteries can accord equality of treatment but, being insensitive to inequalities, imply nothing about equal well-being.[98]

Leaving aside the fact that equality of treatment is by no means an unqualified virtue, the very idea that lotteries necessarily promote this virtue by equalizing individuals' chances of selection might be viewed with suspicion. Many commentators accept without question that where decisions are made by resort to non-weighted lotteries, everyone within the lottery pool must stand an equal chance of being chosen. Yet equiprobability is by no means guaranteed. Even when not explicitly weighted, lotteries can sometimes produce results which are either not entirely random or, even if genuinely random, are not perceived to be so. Consider, first, the matter of perception. Nobody would realistically expect a fairly tossed coin to land only on heads over ninety or so consecutive tosses.[99] We often do, nevertheless, entertain irrational expectations concerning the emergence of particular patterns or sequences within repeated randomized procedures. For example, where chance procedures are performed repetitively, people have a tendency to assume that randomness will be evident not only throughout the entire sequence of performances, but also throughout any particular cluster within the sequence. (In the previous chapter, we detected the presence of this particular cognitive distortion in Callenbach's and Phillips's proposal for a randomly selected House of Representatives.) Thus it is that, in coin-tossing, people generally regard the sequence H-T-H-T-T-H to be more likely than either the sequence H-H-H-T-T-T or the sequence H-H-H-H-T-H, since, unlike the first sequence, neither of the other two sequences appears truly random if viewed as a discrete cluster (even though we are unlikely to doubt the randomness of either cluster when considered as part of a larger sequence).[100] When engaging in coin-tossing, in short, we often have difficulty in accepting that the coin is without memory and so tend either to fail to grasp or to lose sight of the fact that a run of heads is as likely to be followed by a head as by a tail.[101] Faced with a random process, people tend to 'expect that the essential characteristics of the process will be

---

[97] See Ronald Dworkin, *Taking Rights Seriously* (rev. edn., London: Duckworth, 1978 (1977)), 227; and cf. also Alan Parkin, 'Allocating Health Care Resources in an Imperfect World' (1995) 58 *Modern Law Review* 867–78 at 876.

[98] See Douglas Rae, *Equalities* (Cambridge, Mass.: Harvard University Press, 1981), 91.

[99] See Tom Stoppard, *Rosencrantz and Guildenstern are Dead* (London: Faber & Faber, 1967), 9–13.

[100] On this cognitive distortion and others, see Daniel Kahneman and Amos Tversky, 'Subjective Probability: A Judgment of Representativeness' (1972) 3 *Cognitive Psychology* 430–54 esp. at 434–7.

[101] For the argument that our failure to grasp as much perhaps ought not to be construed as an instance of irrationality, cf. L. Jonathan Cohen, 'Can Human Irrationality be Experimentally Demonstrated?' (1981) 4 *Behavioral and Brain Sciences* 317–70 at 327.

represented, not only globally in the entire sequence, but also locally in each of its parts'.[102] When reality confounds this expectation, there will very likely be some who will question whether the random procedure was genuinely random.

A random outcome, then, may sometimes not be accepted as such, even though it is just that. There are other instances where people may assume an outcome to be wholly random even though it is not. That apparently stochastic outcomes may in fact be deterministic will be obvious to anyone who knows how to toss and catch a coin so as to guarantee the same result each time.[103] In literature discussing the history of lottery-use, one quite often encounters instances of decision-making bodies endeavouring to guard against foul-play by requiring that lots be drawn by children—the assumption being that children will either not wish or not possess the ability to interfere with random processes.[104] Rigging provides the most obvious illustration of how supposedly chance procedures may be subject to deliberate human interference. The story is told in *The Histories* of a proposal to choose among competitors for the Persian throne by appointing as king he whose horse neighed first on sunrise. Darius, who was ultimately chosen, rigged the lottery by contriving to ensure that his horse would neigh at the appropriate time.[105] Sometimes, furthermore, with lotteries which depend upon the occurrence of natural events, it may be the case that one person cannot influence the process but has the capacity confidently to predict a random outcome. If two people gamble on whether or not I shall sneeze within the next ten minutes, one of them may have an advantage in knowing that I currently suffer from a cold and

[102] Amos Tversky and Daniel Kahneman, 'Judgment under Uncertainty: Heuristics and Biases' (1974) 185 *Science* 1124–31 at 1125. This probably also explains why, when endeavouring to imitate randomness, people tend to produce sequences which have too many alternations and too few repetitions. On this phenomenon see, e.g., Gustave J. Rath, 'Randomization by Humans' (1966) 79 *American Journal of Psychology* 97–103; and N. Ginsburg and P. Karpiuk, 'Random Generation: Analysis of the Responses' (1994) 79 *Perceptual and Motor Skills* 1059–67. It is, of course, with the development of computers that human beings become more able to simulate natural randomness: cf. Arthur W. Burks, *Chance, Cause, Reason: An Inquiry into the Nature of Scientific Evidence* (Chicago: University of Chicago Press, 1977), 597–603. More generally, on the difficulties of faking randomness, cf. Jon Elster, *Sour Grapes: Studies in the Subversion of Rationality* (Cambridge: Cambridge University Press, 1983), 75.

[103] On the capacity for coin-tossing to be rendered predictable, see Ivars Peterson, *The Jungles of Randomness: A Mathematical Safari* (Harmondsworth: Penguin, 1998), pp. x, 4; and also Joseph Ford, 'How Random is a Coin Toss?' (1983) 36 *Physics Today* 40–7 at 44–6. According to Vulović and Prange, 'true coins have no intrinsic randomness . . . [W]hat is relevant is the relationship of the (initial) parameters of the coin to the precision of the coin tosser . . . [T]he toss of a coin, by a continuous, realizable change of parameters, could become as obviously nonrandom as switching on or off a light.' Vladimir Ž. Vulović and Richard E. Prange, 'Randomness of a True Coin Toss' (1986) 33 *Physical Review (Ser. A)* 576–82 at 576 (emphasis omitted).

[104] The assumption is obviously questionable. Krabbe (above, n. 12), 171–2, provides examples from Danish and Norwegian courts of the 17th cent. whereby inheritance matters were resolved by resort to sortition and the courts required that the lottery be conducted by a child. See also Stephen M. Stigler, 'Stochastic Simulation in the Nineteenth Century' (1991) 6 *Statistical Science* 89–97 at 89.

[105] Herodotus offers two accounts of how this might have been ensured: see Herodotus, *The Histories* 3. 84–7.

have been sneezing regularly all day. In this instance, inequality stems not from absence of randomness but from asymmetry of information.

In certain instances, it may be difficult to determine whether a purportedly random procedure has been compromised owing to deliberate interference, or whether something more subtle has occurred. In the trial of Dr Benjamin Spock in the late 1960s,[106] for example, it was most likely not the case that anyone, at any one point in the trial, deliberately set out to exclude women from the jury panel. Yet the procedure which was followed for selecting jurors, for all that it was supposed to be random, systematically conspired against the selection of women. In the Spock trial, only nine women appeared among the hundred names selected by the clerk from the court's jury box. How could women be so seriously underrepresented? The process of random selection was in fact compromised on three occasions. First, when the clerk of the court drew names from the police list to fill the court's jury box, he displayed a bias against drawing women.[107] Although women constituted 56 per cent of the police list, only 29 per cent were selected for the jury box. This percentage was then reduced still further—to 9 per cent—when the clerk drew venires from the jury box. Finally, with such a small percentage of women in the venire of the trial judge, prosecution was able to exercise its power of peremptory challenge so as to ensure that no women would sit on the jury. 'The reduction in the number of jurors in the venires of the trial judge thus assumed conclusive dimensions, for it was the key step in the elimination of *all* women jurors at the easy option of the prosecution or, for that matter, of the defense.'[108]

In the Spock trial, it may well have been the case that systematic bias against the selection of women jurors was coupled with an intention on the part of some person, or persons, to obstruct such selection. In other instances, the biases which make their way into ostensibly randomized processes are better characterized as accidental. Consider, first of all, the 1970 draft lottery. A Harvard Study Group— which included, among others, Thomas Schelling, John Rawls, and Charles Fried—concluded in 1967 that only through the use of a lottery could men be conscripted in a 'fair and nondiscriminatory' fashion.[109] In the United States at the beginning of the 1970s, several suits were filed in federal court seeking to void the 1970 draft lottery on the ground that it was not genuinely random and was therefore discriminatory.[110] The point of this lottery was to conscript men

---

[106] Spock and his associates were tried for conspiring to violate the Military Service Act 1967: see *United States* v. *Spock* (1st Cir. 1969) 416 F.2d 165.

[107] Hans Zeisel, 'Dr Spock and the Case of the Vanishing Women Jurors' (1969) 37 *Univ. Chicago L. Rev.* 1–18 at 9: 'The conclusion . . . is virtually inescapable that the clerk must have drawn the venires for the trial judge from the central jury box in a fashion that somehow *systematically* reduced the proportion of women jurors.'   [108] Ibid. 10.

[109] Harvard Study Group, 'On the Draft' (1967) 9 *The Public Interest* 93–9 at 95.

[110] See Stephen E. Fienberg, 'Randomization and Social Affairs: The 1970 Draft Lottery' (1971) 171 *Science* 255–61 at 261; and cf. also Lola L. Lopes, 'Doing the Impossible: A Note on Induction and the Experience of Randomness' (1982) 8 *Journal of Experimental Psychology: Learning, Memory and Cognition* 626–36 at 631.

according to their birth-dates, which were to be ranked by way of random selection. One of the arguments presented against the lottery draw of December 1969 was that it was biased towards the early selection of men with birthdays falling late in the year.

The lottery apparently proceeded as follows:[111] 366 capsules were taken and into each was placed a slip of paper containing a date. Those responsible for conducting the lottery would count out thirty-one capsules and insert into each a January date-slip. These capsules were then placed into a large square box and pushed to one side with a cardboard divider, thereby leaving part of the box empty. The same would then be done for February: twenty-nine capsules were counted out, a date of the month inserted in each, and then the capsules would be placed into the empty part of the box. The divider would then be used to merge the February dates with the January dates. This process was repeated for each month, and each time another set of capsules was placed into the box the months would merge and the dates would, to some degree, mix. But the degree of mixing would differ for each month: while, for example, the January capsules were merged with the other capsules eleven times, the December ones were merged only once. Further mixing would occur when the last date had been included: the box was, at that point, closed and shaken several times. Its contents were then poured into a large bowl and it was from this that the capsules were drawn. The capsules were not stirred in the bowl and it is reported that the selectors, rather than delving below the surface, would generally pick capsules from the top.[112] If the contents of the box were poured from the end where the capsules containing the early dates had been repeatedly shoved, one might expect—assuming that adequate mixing had not taken place—that these capsules would fall to the bottom of the bowl (one would, of course, expect the converse if the capsules were poured from the other end of the box). There is certainly some evidence to suggest that adequate mixing of the capsules did not occur and that the contents of the box were poured from the end where the early dates had been pushed.[113] In the 1970 draft lottery, sixteen December dates—as compared with six for January—appeared in the first hundred draws.[114]

Thus it is that the genuine randomness of the 1970 draft lottery came to be questioned. In 1972, the United States Court of Appeals for the Ninth Circuit

---

[111] The details which follow are taken from David E. Rosenbaum, 'Statisticians Charge Draft Lottery Was Not Random', *New York Times*, 4 Jan. 1970, p. 66. See also Fienberg (above, n. 110), 257–8.　　　　　　[112] See Rosenbaum (above, n. 111), 66.

[113] Presumably, the process would have been considered less objectionable had the months been entered into the box randomly rather than in calendrial sequence, although those with birth-dates falling in the months entered last might still have complained that, owing to insufficient mixing, the process was biased towards their early selection. A more rigorous procedure was adopted for the 1971 draft lottery: see Joan R. Rosenblatt and James J. Filliben, 'Randomization and the Draft Lottery' (1971) 171 *Science* 306–8.

[114] For further details, see Fienberg (above, n. 110), 258.

upheld the use of the draft lottery against the equal protection challenge.[115] In *United States* v. *Kotrlik & Gaevert*, decided by the same court in the same year, it was held that since there was no plan behind or pattern to the drawing of the capsules, the draft lottery was—on a commonsense interpretation of the term—random.[116] The randomness of the 1970 draft lottery was also confirmed in *Stodolsky* v. *Hershey*.[117] In that case, however, the federal court for the Western district of Wisconsin accepted that the procedure was not perfectly random. The pattern of the 1970 draft lottery suggested that the selection of any one sequence of the 366 capsules and the selection of any other sequence of the same were not equiprobabilistic: the lottery appeared to be slightly biased towards certain sequences. Although, in *Stodolsky*, this bias was considered too slight to justify the establishment of a new lottery, the acknowledgement of its existence by the court suggests an important insight: that thorough physical mixing is often extremely difficult to achieve—especially where lotteries contain large numbers of potential draws—and that, for this reason, a totally randomized procedure according exact equality of treatment to all of those within the lottery pool may be hard to guarantee.[118]

Further illustration of how random selection might be unintentionally compromised is to be found in the case of *State of New Jersey* v. *Long*.[119] Here, defence counsel successfully contended that the process of jury selection in Atlantic county was insufficiently random to guarantee a representative jury pool.[120] The jury selection process contained two principal flaws.[121] First, the process began with a source list which was comprised of those within the County holding a driving licence and those entered on the electoral register. That these two categories of citizen overlap was not properly taken into account, with the consequence that almost 40 per cent of those listed were entered into the pool twice and so had double the opportunity of being selected for jury duty. Secondly, once jury venires had been drawn, the jury clerk ordered the lists alphabetically by the fifth letter of each juror's last name. A result of this use of alphabetization was that many people on the same jury panel would have the same fifth letter in their last name. When defence counsel studied patterns in the Atlantic County jury panels, they noted that one panel contained an inordinate

---

[115] See *United States* v. *Johnson* (9th Cir. 1972) 473 F.2d 677.

[116] *United States* v. *Kotrlik & Gaevert* (9th Cir. 1972) 5 SSLR 3693.

[117] *Stodolsky* v. *Hershey* (WD Wisc. 1969) 2 SSLR 3527.

[118] This problem was even more acutely obvious in the 1940 draft lottery: see Fienberg (above, n. 110), 257; Elster (above, n. 4), 45.

[119] *State of New Jersey* v. *Long* (NJ Super L. 1985) 499 A.2d 264.

[120] Note the connection which is made here between randomness and representativeness. We have already cast some doubt on this connection in Chapter 2 and, in due course, will do so further in relation to jury selection.

[121] See, more generally, Valerie P. Hans and Neil Vidmar, *Judging the Jury* (New York: Plenum Press, 1986), 56–7.

number of people with apparently Jewish names, another panel with a large proportion of Italian names.[122] That this should have happened was, according to the mathematical expert called by the defence, attributable to the peculiar ordering of the jury lists: 'the fifth-letter alphabetization', Hans and Vidmar elaborate, 'explained how some panels had large numbers of Jewish names (e.g., Wise*m*an, Feld*m*an) or Italian names (e.g., Fera*rr*o, Dina*rd*o)'.[123]

I have been trying to demonstrate that the procedures adopted for the purpose of random selection are sometimes insufficiently rigorous to guarantee a genuinely random, and therefore equiprobabilistic, outcome. Yet a lottery outcome might, in some instances, be considered fair even if it is not equiprobabilistic. Kornhauser and Sager contend that a non-equiprobabilistic lottery outcome might be deemed fair if it is impersonal. In the case of an impersonal lottery outcome, while the statistical odds of those within the lottery pool may not be equal, the attributes or circumstances of successful claimants do not constitute reasons for their having been chosen. 'Suppose, for example, that an allocating agency rolls a 365-sided die, and then allocates a prize among six candidates by awarding it to the candidate whose birthday is closest to but not later than the "date" (the nth day of the year) showing on the die's upturned face.'[124] Assuming that the allocating agency is ignorant of the birth-dates of the candidates, this lottery will be impersonal: the 'birthdates are neutral in the sense that they could not plausibly be expected to be reasons for choice'.[125] While the lottery may be impersonal, however, the stipulation that the successful candidate's birth-date must come closest to *but not later than* that which appears at the top of the dice means that it is not equiprobabilistic. Imagine that the birth-dates of the six candidates are spaced sequentially throughout the year 'and that candidate B was born on 30 April, candidate C on 1 May, and candidate D on 1 September. Candidate

---

[122] In a similar vein, consider the following observation (cited after Elster (above, n. 4), 46 n. 34) offered by Jensen: 'It must be remembered that experience shows that even if the sample is selected according to an absolutely "neutral" criterion, a "coloured" picture may be obtained. In the town of Mannheim, for example, statistics were compiled regarding the number of children in each family. The sample comprised the families whose names had the initial letters A, B and M. It turned out, however, that names with these initials were especially numerous among Jewish families, and as the children of Jewish families were particularly numerous, the enquiry gave a misleading result.' Adolph Jensen, 'The Representative Method in Practice' (1926) 22 *Bulletin de l'Institut International de Statistique* 381–439 at 429–30.

[123] Hans and Vidmar (above, n. 121), 57. In 1982, the German practice of assigning cases to judges alphabetically by reference to the initial letter of the defendant's last name—so that Judge X could end up hearing the cases of all defendants whose last names begin with 'H'—was challenged in the Frankfurt Industrial Court on the basis that the procedure, rather than generating randomness, ensured that large companies frequently involved in litigation would keep encountering the same judge. For details from the relevant case, see Ulrich Mückenberger, 'Im Namen des Volkes! Urteil des Arbeitsgerichts Frankfurt vom 11. 5. 82 (Meinungsfreiheit im Arbeitsverhältnis)' (1983) 16 *Kritische Justiz* 69–85; and, for discussion, cf. Christoph Berglar, 'Politischer Aktionismus in schwarzer Robe: Vom Freiheitsmißbrauch zur Vertrauenkrise' (1984) 17 *Zeitschrift für Rechtspolitik* 4–9.

[124] Lewis A. Kornhauser and Lawrence G. Sager, 'Just Lotteries' (1988) 27 *Social Science Information* 483–516 at 489.   [125] Ibid.

B has 1 chance in 365 of winning the birthdate lottery, while candidate C has 123 chances in 365'.[126] Impersonal lottery outcomes of this type might be considered fair, Kornhauser and Sager contend, because of their 'opacity'.[127] A lottery will be opaque when, owing to its complexity, neither those operating it nor those who are at its mercy have the advantage of being able to 'make reasonably accurate determinations of the probabilities that attach to various outcomes'.[128] Fairness, in such instances, is attributable to lack of transparency and uncertainty rather than to equality of chances: 'impersonality depends on ignorance rather than an objective state of the world like equiprobability'.[129]

That equiprobability of outcomes is not an essential characteristic of a fair lottery is also suggested by the fact that it is not always the quality that people seek from a lottery. We have already, at various points throughout this study, referred to weighted lotteries—that is, to lotteries with an explicitly in-built bias. Such lotteries are occasionally proposed, and indeed used. The proposal for a system of lottery voting, which was considered in the previous chapter, involves resort to a weighted lottery. Other proposals include building into a draft lottery a bias towards the selection of younger men and a lottery for organ transplantations which is weighted in favour of recipients most likely to benefit.[130] An explicit bias was built into the randomized system of land distribution introduced in the state of Georgia at the beginning of the nineteenth century. Any citizen of the state could register to be entered into the lottery 'if they met certain minimal requirements. Each citizen was entitled to one chance, unless he belonged to a favored group—orphans, Revolutionary War veterans, head of a family and the like—in which case he was given two chances'.[131] In the Netherlands during the 1970s, an admissions policy was introduced for (among other subjects) medicine, dentistry, and veterinary science which accorded all applicants a chance of being selected, but a greater chance to those with higher grades.[132]

The principal value of such weighted lotteries is that they can reflect the special needs, claims, or status of particular participants without ignoring the voices of weaker claimants. While the incorporation of bias means that the lottery no longer accords equal chances, there is a greater likelihood that it will, in the Dworkinian sense, accord equal concern and respect. Simply to allocate a

---

[126] Ibid. 489–90.   [127] Ibid. 490.   [128] Ibid.

[129] Ibid. For further exploration of the idea that the fairness of lotteries stems from uncertainty rather than from equiprobability, see David Wasserman, 'Let Them Eat Chances: Probability and Distributive Justice' (1996) 12 *Economics and Philosophy* 29–49.

[130] See Blum (above, n. 64), 163–6; and Dan W. Brock, 'Ethical Issues in Recipient Selection for Organ Transplantation', in Deborah Mathieu (ed.), *Organ Substitution Technology: Ethical, Legal, and Public Policy Issues* (Boulder, Co.: Westview Press, 1988), 86–99 at 93–6.

[131] Wilms (above, n. 9), 54. The Oklahoma land lottery of 1901, by contrast, was not weighted: see Dale (above, n. 9), 7: 'Each person could register only once and for only one district.'

[132] Hofstee terms this scheme a compromise model which 'fills the gap between straight lottery selection and comparative selection'. Under the scheme, 'an applicant's chances of being admitted— that is, the number of lottery tickets he or she receives—is a monotonically increasing function of his or her [academic] score'. Hofstee (above, n. 19), 112.

resource to the applicant with the strongest claim is to attribute no weight to the reasons which may be adduced in support of assigning that resource to one or another person with a weaker claim. As compared with outright allocation to the strongest claimant, the weighted lottery accords concern and respect to claimants offering weaker reasons by allowing them some chance of receiving the resource. The weaker claimant is not treated equally; nor, however, is he overlooked.

Where a weighted lottery accords concern and respect to weaker claimants in this way, the strongest claimant might question whether appropriate concern and respect is being accorded to him. Consider, here, Brock's argument in favour of a weighted lottery for organ transplants. One of the objections which is sometimes raised against using lotteries for purposes of social decision-making is that to be alive is to be caught up in a lottery. This lottery, moreover, is weighted: some people fare better in fate's 'natural lottery' than do others. '[W]hen we are at the point when we must choose between one person's death and another's', O'Neil observes, 'we find that there already exists the randomization involved in letting the loss lie where it falls. To introduce another lottery or some other method for choosing at this point is unfair to the winner of the initial "lottery." '[133] Rather than simply letting losses lie where they fall, Brock argues, we should, in some instances at least, be able to predict how someone is likely to fare in the so-called natural lottery and weight our lottery for transplants accordingly.[134] Thus, if we must select between 'an otherwise healthy twenty-five-year-old who is expected to have a normal life span without any significant disability if she receives a transplant' and 'a seventy-year-old patient who is expected to die from unrelated medical conditions within one or two years whatever is done', it ought to be clear in whose favour the transplantation lottery ought to be weighted.[135] Yet, leaving aside problems concerning inter-personal comparisons of well-being, it is important to question what a weighted lottery achieves here. If, say, the 25 year old is given a 75 per cent chance in the lottery and the 70 year old 25 per cent, in what sense does the lottery accord equal concern and respect if the latter is then selected? Weighted lotteries accord to the most successful or needy or whomever the greater prospect of receiving whatever it is that is being distributed. But the question which must always be asked with regard to such lotteries is: why is giving a better chance to receive a good (or bad), rather than simply allocating it outright to those who are considered most deserving, the appropriate strategy to adopt?

There is at least one answer to this question. The lottery is a very useful device for handling indeterminacies. Deciding outcomes sometimes requires numerous criteria to be taken into account. Determining the relative importance of each of these criteria, and resolving what to do when relevant criteria conflict, may prove extremely difficult, especially where responsibility for reaching a decision lies

---

[133]   Richard O'Neil, 'Killing, Letting Die, and Justice' (1978) 38 *Analysis* 124–5 at 125.
[134]   Brock (above, n. 130), 95.   [135]   Ibid. 94.

with a number of people who find themselves in disagreement. When required to grapple with an abundance of information within a limited period of time, decision-makers are likely to become all too aware of the bounded nature of rationality and ethics. They are unlikely, in such instances, to be able to prevent arbitrariness from seeping into the decisions which they reach. It is in circumstances such as these that the use of a lottery may begin to look appealing.[136] Usually, the problem will be that an excess of information has rendered decision-makers incapable of distinguishing between (say) potential recipients, and so a non-weighted lottery is instituted in order to accord what is assumed to be an equal chance to all. A primary virtue in resorting to lotteries in such circumstances, it is commonly said, is candour: when decision-makers cannot find within themselves anything which enables them satisfactorily to resolve matters involving incommensurability, the most honest and practical thing to do is to admit as much and let chance decide.[137] The argument that the lottery can help decision-makers to cope with indeterminacies is an important one which will feature more prominently later on in this book (see Chapter 4, section 4). The point to be made at this juncture is simply that, while this argument tends to be developed in order to justify proposals for resort to non-weighted lotteries—that is, to justify proposals to the effect that such lotteries ought to be used where decision-makers cannot satisfactorily distinguish candidates—it might also, on occasions, explain why weighted lotteries are considered appropriate. For decision-makers may sometimes believe that, say, one particular candidate deserves the better chance of being selected, but not that this candidate deserves the only chance. In other words, the information at the disposal of those making the decision may lead them to believe that there are distinctions to be made among candidates, but that this information is not sufficiently compelling to convince them that these distinctions ought to be treated as conclusive. In such circumstances, the relevant distinctions might be built into a lottery so as to accord not equal but what are considered to be fair chances of selection.[138]

That a lottery might be weighted is evidence of the adaptability of the device. When one encounters objections to the use of lotteries for decision-making purposes, it is very often the case that this adaptability is overlooked and that what is being objected to is a rather basic and misleading idea of what a lottery must

---

[136] See Daniel C. Dennett, *Darwin's Dangerous Idea: Evolution and the Meanings of Life* (Harmondsworth: Penguin, 1995), 494–510.

[137] See Elster (above, n. 4), 122; Goodwin (above, n. 37), 99.

[138] Weighted lotteries can sometimes be used to combat negative incentive effects. In the USA it used to be the case that the basketball team which performed poorest throughout a season would be given the first choice in drafting eligible players for the following season (the second worst team being given second choice, and so on). The National Basketball Association decided that this 'worst picks first' system generated too much of an incentive for poor play near the end of the season and so replaced it with an inversely weighted lottery whereby the weakest teams are accorded the best chance—but no guarantee—of having the first choice of players (the second weakest having the second best chance, and so on).

entail. The point of initiating a lottery does not have to be to achieve an equiprobabilistic outcome, just as randomization does not have to operate as a discrete decision-making method. I shall have more to say about the flexibility of lotteries in Chapter 5. My present objective is to examine why it might ever be considered advantageous to decide by lot. So far, I have argued that it will sometimes be appropriate and beneficial to resort to a lottery for social decision-making purposes where an unavoidable risk or misfortune has to be allocated (especially where it seems unfair to place responsibility for that allocation on the shoulders of any particular person or group), where there is a requirement for a decision-making procedure which can be guaranteed to ignore the voices of claimants, where a cost-effective method of decision-making is required, where resort to randomization might generate welcome incentive effects, where decision-makers are looking to provide equality of opportunity, and—this last observation being one to which we shall return—where decision-makers struggle with indeterminacies. Before concluding this chapter, there are three further potentially advantageous features of randomized social decision-making which I wish to consider.

2. INDIVISIBILITY, REPRESENTATION, AND REGULATION

It may sometimes be the case that more than one person claims to be entitled to a particular object but that this object either cannot be apportioned among claimants or cannot be apportioned without losing its value to those claimants. Where scarce goods are incapable of division or where they cannot be divided without loss of value—I shall, for shorthand, term both these types of good 'indivisible'—the sensible course of action will sometimes be to allocate by lot.[139] Many of the instances of random allocation which have thus far been referred to in this book fall into one of these two categories. Randomization is by no means the only, or even necessarily the preferred, method of assigning such goods.[140] But assignment by lot does possess an advantage in such instances. In short, random allocation of scarce indivisible goods promotes what we might call a second-best equity.[141] Guaranteeing equality of outcome

---

[139] See John 19: 23–4; and cf. also John Rawls, *A Theory of Justice* (Oxford: Oxford University Press, 1972), 374.

[140] On methods of assigning indivisible goods, see H. Peyton Young, *Equity: In Theory and Practice* (Princeton: Princeton University Press, 1994), 20–3. Young argues that the best—i.e. the most consistent and impartial—way in which to allocate scarce indivisible goods among claimants is to rank those claimants in terms of priority (see ibid. 40–1, 163–4). In developing this argument, he requires that '[w]e do not assume that the claimants should be treated equally' (ibid. 31). The argument for resorting to lotteries in order to allocate scarce indivisible goods is, of course, that they come into their own when there exists an assumption that claimants should be treated equally.

[141] See further Stephen Demko and Theodore P. Hill, 'Equitable Distribution of Indivisible Objects' (1988) 16 *Mathematical Social Sciences* 145–58 at 148–57; and Klemens Szaniawski, 'On Fair Distribution of Indivisible Goods', in Peter Geach (ed.), *Logic and Ethics* (Dordrecht: Kluwer, 1991), 275–88 at 281–8.

will not be possible, since not every claimant can receive the good in question. What the lottery offers claimants—assuming genuine randomness, of course— is an equal chance to receive the particular good. To be given this chance, Broome suggests, 'is a sort of surrogate satisfaction of the claim' when 'there is not enough of an indivisible commodity to go round everyone who has a claim'.[142] Since division of the good in question is either impossible or destroys its value, the likelihood is that many claimants would welcome the chance to be a winner who takes all.

Of course, not all claimants would welcome this chance. In the type of instance described, becoming a 'winner' is a matter of good luck.[143] Whatever their reasons, some claimants may not consider themselves to be blessed with such luck. For all that such self-perceptions will often seem irrational, they are nevertheless very real; indeed, not only do some people regard themselves as generally unlucky, but others view them likewise (consider, for example, how the Kennedy family is commonly portrayed and, indeed, seen as being blighted by bad luck).[144]

That claimants will sometimes feel ambivalent about relying on luck becomes clearer if we invest the discussion with a legal dimension. As a general rule, disputes are resolved in Anglo-American law so that winner takes all. '[U]nder our system', Coons writes apropos of the United States, 'with rare exceptions, one party loses and one party wins'.[145] Even where a compromise or a division of goods between or among litigants is feasible, courts are more often than not

---

[142] Broome, *Weighing Goods* (above, n. 95), 196. On randomization and equity, cf. also Ann Oakley, 'Living in Two Worlds' (1998) 316 *British Medical Journal* 482–3.

[143] One problem with using lotteries to distribute scarce indivisible goods, Brams and Taylor contend, is that they generate allocations which are unlikely to be 'envy-free': claimants who lose will probably be envious of those who win. See Steven J. Brams and Alan D. Taylor, *Fair Division: From Cake-Cutting to Dispute Resolution* (Cambridge: Cambridge University Press, 1996), 2, 241, 145–6 n. 7.

[144] On the ambivalence of winners to winnings and losers to losses, see Philip Brickman, Dan Coates, and Ronnie Janoff-Bulman, 'Lottery Winners and Accident Victims: Is Happiness Relative?' (1978) 36 *Journal of Personality and Social Psychology* 917–27; and, more generally, Daniel Kahneman and Carol Varey, 'Notes on the Psychology of Utility', in Jon Elster and John E. Roemer (eds.), *Interpersonal Comparisons of Well-Being* (Cambridge: Cambridge University Press, 1991), 127–63.

[145] John E. Coons, 'Approaches to Court Imposed Compromise: The Uses of Doubt and Reason' (1964) 58 *Northwestern University L. Rev.* 750–94 at 752. In relation to the American preponderance-of-the-evidence (what the English tend to refer to as the balance of probabilities) standard, winner-takes-all has been defended on the ground that it will, more often than not, maximize expected utility: see David Kaye, 'The Limits of the Preponderance of the Evidence Standard: Justifiably Naked Statistical Evidence and Multiple Causation' [1982] *American Bar Foundation Research Journal* 487–516. Some doubt is cast on Kaye's thesis by Neil Orloff and Jery Stedinger, 'A Framework for Evaluating the Preponderance-of-the-Evidence Standard' (1983) 131 *Univ. Pennsylvania L. Rev.* 1159–74. For a similar argument relating to compromise judgments—namely, that division of entitlements can, under certain circumstances, generate efficiency gains—see Ian Ayres and Eric Talley, 'Solomonic Bargaining: Dividing a Legal Entitlement to Facilitate a Coasean Trade' (1995) 104 *Yale LJ* 1027–1103.

reluctant to pursue this path.[146] Yet even though courts tend to prefer winner-take-all to compromise judgments, judges are strongly disinclined to resort to lot in order to determine who the winner shall be. Just why there exists this belief that lotteries and adjudication go together like oil and water is discussed and explored in section 4 of the next chapter. At this point, however, at least this much needs to be said: few people are likely to feel at ease with the idea that, in litigation, one should lose—or, for that matter win—by luck. Of course, it may well be—and no doubt many litigants know—that luck will often play a part, if only implicitly, in the determination of outcomes. But the idea that luck should explicitly determine outcomes—that whether or not one receives what one considers to be justice should depend wholly and patently on one's luck—would probably be considered repugnant by most people. As Coons has noted elsewhere, '[p]eople resist having their noses rubbed in the randomness of the system . . . Randomness may be inevitable, but it must express itself indirectly and even covertly at that point in the [judicial] process where the human decider is selected. It should not simply replace him.'[147] As we shall see in due course, this is not the only reason that might be offered for preferring adjudication to random selection; for present purposes, nevertheless, it is the one which ought to be stressed. A system of legal decision-making by lot would result in hollow victories and intolerable defeats: many winners and most losers would, one suspects, find it very difficult to accept such decisions.

Having said all this, I shall still suggest in Chapter 5 that there has been a tendency to underestimate the potential for the use of lotteries within legal systems. It should be clear from what has been discussed so far, furthermore, that it would be incorrect to claim that legal systems never embrace lotteries. Indeed, I wish to conclude this chapter by focusing on what are probably the two primary uses of randomization in law.

The first, and I expect most obvious, of these is random jury selection. The point of random jury selection is not to decide outcomes by lottery, but to use a lottery to determine who should decide outcomes. It is perhaps because jury selection procedure decrees only that the agents of decisions, rather than the decisions themselves, are randomly selected that the use of a lottery is deemed accept-

---

[146] See Ronald Dworkin, *Law's Empire* (London: Fontana, 1986), 178–84 (on reluctance to develop compromised, or 'checkerboard', schemes of justice). Coons bemoans this reluctance and argues that judges ought to be more ready to impose compromises on disputing parties (see Coons (above, n. 145), 751, 756–64). Jaconelli has demonstrated, however, that within the American and (especially) the English common law systems, compromise judgments are not quite so rare as Coons suggests and, furthermore, that where such judgments are eschewed in favour of winner-take-all, there are often good reasons justifying the preference: cf. Joseph Jaconelli, 'Solomonic Justice and the Common Law' (1992) 12 *Oxford Journal of Legal Studies* 480–506; and, for a fairly recent example of such a judgment, see *B* v. *B* [1997] 1 FLR 139 (Court of Appeal upholding first-instance decision whereby, in a dispute over custody, the judge decided that the mother should have custody of one child and the father custody of the other).

[147] John E. Coons, 'Consistency' (1987) 75 *California L. Rev.* 59–113 at 110.

able in this legal context whereas it is not in others. Certainly random jury selection has a long history.[148] The practice can be traced back to classical Athens[149] and numerous arguments might be offered in support of it. Three such arguments are offered here, although the third of these arguments turns out to be deeply problematic.

Assuming, first of all, that the process of selection is genuinely random—an assumption which, considering our earlier discussion of how randomness can be compromised, perhaps ought not to be made lightly—every citizen, subject to qualifications concerning age, citizenship, occupation, criminal history, literacy, and residency, is accorded an equal chance to serve on a jury. Random selection, according to Abramson, respects 'the noble principle . . . that every citizen is equally competent to do justice'.[150] There is no doubt, of course, that many people would consider being selected for jury service to be a thorough inconvenience. My suspicion, none the less, is that even those who would not welcome being selected would by and large have some sympathy with the principle that citizens ought to be accorded equal chances of selection.

Secondly, random selection of jurors should reduce opportunities for manipulation within the legal process.[151] Since those responsible for delivering a verdict are not identifiable in advance of the trial, the potential for parties to the particular case to engage in bribery or threatening behaviour is reduced. The likelihood of manipulation might also be diminished to the extent that a randomly selected jury will be composed of people who are not professional participants in the criminal justice system and who are therefore unlikely to be as susceptible to institutional pressures and political influence as those who do work within the system.[152]

Thirdly, random selection is intended to provide defendants and litigants with the opportunity to be tried by a representative cross-section of the population. The idea here is that fair and democratic social arrangements require that people be accorded the chance to be tried by juries drawn from a cross-sectionally representative pool.[153] That a randomly selected jury will provide the opportunity to be tried by a representative cross-section of the population is, however, by no means guaranteed. Ensuring genuine randomness is obviously one difficulty. Even if randomness in selection is guaranteed in any particular instance, furthermore, a

---

[148] Although in England it is only during the latter half of this century that the virtues of randomization for purposes of jury selection have been explicitly acknowledged: see Maurice Pope, 'Upon the Country: Juries and the Principle of Random Selection' (1989) 28 *Social Science Information* 265–89 at 273–4.

[149] See Douglas M. MacDowell, *The Law in Classical Athens* (Ithaca, NY: Cornell University Press, 1978), 33–5, 252–4.

[150] Jeffrey Abramson, *We, the Jury: The Jury System and the Ideal of Democracy* (New York: Basic Books, 1994), 2.   [151] See Elster (above, n. 4), 95.

[152] See further John Jackson and Sean Doran, *Judge Without Jury: Diplock Trials in the Adversary System* (Oxford: Clarendon Press, 1995), 3–4.

[153] See Abramson (above, n. 150), 99.

representative selection does not necessarily follow: 'a normal distribution, or a perfectly representative sample, is the average ideal of many random samples of a population and is not to be expected in any particular randomly drawn sample— or on any particular petit jury'.[154] Perhaps most importantly of all, even if random selection were to yield a jury perfectly representative of the population, the appropriateness of this outcome might still be contested.

The issue is whether juries ought ideally to be cross-sectionally or proportionally representative—whether, that is, fairness requires that all citizens be equally eligible for jury duty or that there should be demographic balance on the jury rolls.[155] Random selection is better at promoting the former rather than the latter ideal, a consequence of which is that minority groups tend to be underrepresented on jury panels thus selected.[156] It is not surprising, then, to find that in countries and communities where minority representation is high on the political agenda, the random selection of jurors is usually accompanied by the application of 'filters'—such as the use of peremptory challenge—so as to ensure that some influence is exercised over jury composition. In the United States—where jury selection has, at times, been elevated to the status of a 'science'[157]—it is sometimes argued that randomness has been excessively compromised. 'The goal of jury selection these days,' a *Wall Street Journal* commentator observed rather sarcastically a few years ago, seems to be 'to make sure that a panel in no way reflects the views and expertise that might be found in a random cross-section of the population'.[158] Indeed, in some quarters in the United States, it has been argued that the process of random selection ought either to be supplemented or replaced by a selection policy which guarantees the inclusion of specific minorities (proportionate to their presence in the community) on juries—or at least on jury panels.[159]

Random selection of jurors is unlikely to hold much appeal for anyone who takes the view that juries ought to be proportionally representative. Recent history, especially in the United States, has shown that minority groups will sometimes be unconvinced by what they consider to be unfavourable verdicts if those verdicts were delivered by juries on which they were not, or were not sufficiently, represented.[160] Yet it is easy to make too much of proportional representation. Jurors are

---

[154] Marianne Constable, *The Law of the Other: The Mixed Jury and Changing Conceptions of Citizenship, Law, and Knowledge* (Chicago: University of Chicago Press, 1994), 32. If the size of the jury is reduced, the likelihood of representativeness is diminished still further: see Hans Zeisel, '. . . And Then There Were None: The Diminution of the Federal Jury' (1971) 38 *Univ. Chicago L. Rev.* 710–24 at 716, 721.   [155] See Abramson (above, n. 150), 102–3.

[156] Ibid. 130–1.

[157] See Hans and Vidmar (above, n. 121), 63–94; Abramson (above, n. 150), 143–76.

[158] Walter Olson, 'The Jury-Selection Ordeal', *Wall Street Journal*, 7 Dec. 1994, at § A, p. 19.

[159] See, e.g., Note, 'The Case for Black Juries' (1970) 79 *Yale LJ* 531–50; Sheri Lynn Johnson, 'Black Innocence and the White Jury' (1985) 83 *Michigan L. Rev.* 1611–1708; and Albert W. Alschuler, 'Racial Quotas and the Jury' (1995) 44 *Duke LJ* 704–43.

[160] See James Gobert, *Justice, Democracy and the Jury* (Aldershot: Dartmouth, 1997), 139.

not, after all, expected to vote in accordance with their particular group loyalties, but to deliberate their way to a verdict.[161] While, during the past decade, various infamous American cases have prompted a good deal of cynicism about jury composition and deliberation, research indicates that jurors of different ethnic backgrounds normally do deliberate and find grounds for agreement.[162] Failure to cross group lines and reach a unanimous verdict would appear to be the exception rather than the rule.[163]

It has recently been suggested that a system of random jury selection could be devised which might go some way to satisfying the concerns of those who argue for proportional representation. According to Lichtman, the basic problems with a system which requires that twelve-person juries deliver unanimous verdicts are that marginal votes are ignored and that votes cast by individual jurors are weighted inappropriately. 'A unanimous-rule jury split 11-to-1 in favor of conviction is considered to be no different from one split 7-to-5 in favor or even one split 3-to-9 against.'[164] This also means, of course, that 'the single juror dissenting from an 11-to-1 jury wields the same power as five 7-to-5 jurors and nine 3-to-9 panelists'.[165] If jurors' votes carried their proportional weight—rather than the capacity to veto—juries could be made larger (and thereby potentially more representative) without the worry that unanimous verdicts would be more difficult to reach, counsel would have less reason to engage in protracted and often aggressive jury-filtering tactics, and the nature and quality of jury deliberation would probably improve.[166]

Lichtman's proposal for enhancing proportionality is quite radical. He

---

[161] According to Abramson (above, n. 150, 102), the American courts 'have begun to sever the connection between the deliberative and representative features of the jury and to justify the cross-sectional jury in terms borrowed from the world of interest group politics . . . Such a description of the representation we expect from jurors might explain why we call the jury a democratic institution. But it is a vision of democracy so tied to different groups voting their different interests that it cannot inspire confidence in the jury as an institution of justice.' For an attempt to defend this view of the jury, see Vikram David Amar, 'Jury Service as Political Participation Akin to Voting' (1995) 80 *Cornell L. Rev.* 203–59.

[162] See Johnson (above, n. 159), 1629; and Note, 'Out of the Frying Pan or into the Fire? Race and Choice of Venue After Rodney King' (1993) 106 *Harvard L. Rev.* 705–22 at 709.

[163] See Abramson (above, n. 150), 104.

[164] Douglas Gary Lichtman, 'The Deliberative Lottery: A Thought Experiment in Jury Reform' (1996) 34 *American Criminal L. Rev.* 133–61 at 135. It should be noted that Lichtman develops his critique of unanimity purely in relation to American law. In English law, 10-to-2 is 'sufficient to convict: Juries Act 1974, s. 17(1).

[165] Lichtman, 'Deliberative Lottery', 135.

[166] Ibid. 135–6. The last of these three claims seems puzzling. According to Lichtman, '[u]nder a proportional scheme, a growing majority always has strong incentives to engage dissenters in meaningful debate' (ibid.). Surely there will be an equally strong, possibly an even stronger, incentive to engage a potentially dissenting juror in debate when that juror can use his or her vote to veto the majority. The contention—offered in support of the proportionality scheme—that '[n]o juror can be costlessly ignored, outvoted, or marginalized by majority viewpoint jurors' (ibid. 135) seems to hold equally for the unanimous verdict system. On the first of Lichtman's three claims, furthermore, the question of whether or not increasing the size of the jury would increase the number of hung juries (as compared, that is, with the number of juries that are declared hung under the unanimity rule) will depend on just how many jurors are required to agree in order to render a verdict.

suggests that twenty-four jurors should be randomly selected from an unfiltered pool. These jurors should be presented with the relevant evidence and encouraged to debate it. Once they have completed their deliberations, twelve of these jurors should be randomly selected to comprise a second, 'small' jury. These jurors will be asked to vote for their preferred verdict: if ten or more of them agree, their verdict should be rendered; if not, the jury should be declared hung.[167]

There are two significant features to Lichtman's proposal. The first is that it departs from the customary (American) requirement of unanimity. The second is that, for any particular case, two juries are randomly selected. What is the point of this second recommendation? A two-stage jury process, Lichtman believes, will encourage jurors to deliberate rather than merely to vote, for at the point in time when deliberation takes place each juror knows only that he or she will have a 50 per cent chance of being selected to vote. Since, at deliberation stage, none of the jurors knows whether or not he or she personally will be able to vote on the outcome, all of the jurors have an incentive to try to present their own opinions as persuasively as possible. Under this scheme, a 'juror's strongest weapon is a convincing point. Her opportunity to vote is not guaranteed; but her opportunity to influence the jurors who *will* vote is.'[168] The point of introducing an extra layer of randomness is to separate debate from decision; and the purpose of separating debate from decision is to increase the significance of debate.

Lichtman's study appears to be inspired by Amar's argument in favour of lottery voting (see Chapter 2).[169] Like Amar, Lichtman describes his proposal as a 'thought experiment' and no doubt appreciates that it is unlikely to be favourably received, not least because its implementation would demand radical revision of a cherished institution of democracy. The reservations which might be expressed regarding Lichtman's suggestion seem, however, to involve more than just a distrust of radicalism. Perhaps the most significant factor to be considered here is the potential cost of introducing a two-tier jury process. Lichtman is rather dismissive of this concern. His proposal would, he says, 'save[] juror resources in other ways', particularly by reducing the amount of time and money spent on jury-filtering; the removal of the unanimity requirement, furthermore, would 'mean[] fewer hung juries and fewer (costly) re-trials'.[170] That reduction of the number of hung juries would generate significant economic savings within the legal system is, certainly in the United States, highly unlikely.[171] Furthermore, Lichtman's

---

[167] Lichtman, 'Deliberative Lottery', 136. Lichtman concedes that since, with such a large jury panel, deliberations will sometimes be inconclusive, it may on occasions be necessary to impose a time limit on discussion: ibid. 154.

[168] Ibid. 156. On the creation of incentives for juror deliberation, see further Akhil Reed Amar, 'Reinventing Juries: Ten Suggested Reforms' (1995) 28 *Univ. California at Davis L. Rev.* 1169–94 at 1191.   [169] See Lichtman (above, n. 164), 133–4.   [170] Ibid. 155.

[171] Van Dyke points out that, in the USA, jury trials are such a small percentage of total criminal dispositions that a reduction in the number of hung juries would have little impact on the overall efficiency of the criminal justice system in resolving cases. See John M. Van Dyke, *Jury Selection Procedures: Our Uncertain Commitment to Representative Panels* (Cambridge, Mass.: Ballinger, 1977), 209.

response seems not to take account of the fact that, for many people, selection for jury service involves considerable personal sacrifice. His proposal would double the number of jurors required. Some jurors—in particular, one imagines, a certain number of those who are unhappy at having been selected for service—may still be disinclined to do much more than vote for a verdict. One can, moreover, envisage the disgruntlement of many jurors who do devote considerable amounts of time to deliberation only to be told not that they will vote on the verdict but that they have had the opportunity to influence those who will be permitted to vote.[172]

As compared with their American counterparts, English lawyers appear to have been less troubled by the potential perils of random jury selection.[173] The English philosophy, Lord Denning asserted in 1980, 'is that the jury should be selected at random—from a panel of persons who are nominated at random. We believe that 12 persons selected at random are likely to be a cross-section of the people as a whole—and thus represent the views of the common man . . . The parties must take them as they come.'[174] Opportunities to interfere with the process of jury selection are minimal, particularly since the defence in English criminal trials no longer has the right of peremptory challenge.[175] In general, 'little concern is evident that random selection from the available pool of jurors is unlikely to produce a representative jury'.[176] In 1989, the Court of Appeal held that a trial judge was right to refuse an application by defence counsel for a multi-racial jury to be empanelled and that random selection remains the best way to achieve an impartial body of jurors.[177] This coupling of randomness and

---

[172] It may be possible to stave off disgruntlement by allowing all twenty-four jurors to vote, but then to select randomly twelve of those votes to determine the verdict (see Lichtman (above, n. 164), 156 n. 87). While this strategy may diminish disgruntlement, it will not reduce other costs.

[173] See Abramson (above, n. 150), 146 n.*

[174] *R.* v. *Sheffield Crown Court*, ex parte *Brownlow* (1980) 71 Cr. App. R. 19, 25.

[175] Criminal Justice Act 1988, s. 118. More generally, see James J. Gobert, 'The Peremptory Challenge: An Obituary' [1989] *Criminal L. Rev.* 528–38. For the argument that American law would do well to follow the English example, see Morris B. Hoffman, 'Peremptory Challenges Should Be Abolished: A Trial Judge's Perspective' (1997) 64 *Univ. Chicago L. Rev.* 809–71. In England, jury vetting by the Crown is now only permitted in terrorism and national security cases: see, e.g., *McCann, Cullen and Shanahan* (1990) 92 Cr. App. R. 239 (jury vetting in case involving allegations of terrorist activity; Court of Appeal rejected the defence's argument that vetting was unconstitutional). The Crown also continues to hold a limited right to 'stand by' jurors, particularly where a person about to be sworn as a juror is manifestly unsuitable and both the defence and the prosecution agree that the exercise of this right would be appropriate: see *Attorney-General's Guidelines. Juries: The Exercise by the Crown of its Right of Stand By* (1989) 88 Cr. App. R. 123.

[176] Andrew Sanders and Richard Young, *Criminal Justice* (2nd edn., London: Butterworths, 1998), 358.

[177] *R.* v. *Ford* [1989] 3 All ER 445. Whereas, in *Ford*, the Court of Appeal's affirmation of random jury selection might be considered to have disadvantaged the defendant, it is of course, on occasions, equally possible that judicial affirmation of random selection of jurors will serve to protect defendants. In the more recent case of *Tarrant*, the Court of Appeal held that a trial judge had deprived the appellant of the protection of a randomly selected jury by endeavouring to ensure that the jury should not include anyone whose address included the letter 'E' in their postcode (the trial judge considered it important that no one with an East London address be allowed to sit on the jury which would hear the appellant's case). See *R.* v. *Tarrant*, unpublished transcript (Smith Bernal), Court of Appeal (Criminal Division), 18 Dec. 1997; abridged report in *The Times*, 29 Dec. 1997, p. 41.

neutrality has, on occasions, been questioned by researchers into the English jury system.[178] In its report of 1993, furthermore, the Royal Commission on Criminal Justice expressed concern 'that everything possible should be done to ensure that people from the ethnic minority communities are represented on juries in relation to their numbers in the local community'.[179] To this end, the Royal Commission considered a proposal from the Commission for Racial Equality (CRE) that, where a defendant believes (and the judge is persuaded) that he or she will not receive a fair trial from an all-white jury, the jury which is chosen ought to contain up to three randomly selected members of ethnic minority communities. 'If the judge grants the application, it would be for the jury bailiff to continue to draw names randomly selected from the available pool until three such people were drawn.'[180] The Royal Commission stressed that this proposal ought only to be entertained in cases with 'unusual and special features',[181] the meaning of which seems to be that the defendant's ethnic identity must be appurtenant to the alleged wrongdoing. 'Thus, a black defendant charged with burglary would be unlikely to succeed in such an application. But black people accused of violence against a member of an extremist organisation who they said had been making racial taunts against them and their friends might well succeed.'[182]

Few English cases are likely, on this definition, to be deemed by trial judges to be 'unusual and special', which possibly explains why the CRE's proposal remains just that. The Royal Commission confessed to being reluctant to interfere with the current jury selection process; and indeed, in English law, the dominant view of random jury selection appears still to be that which is expressed in the opening paragraph of this chapter. It is worth noting, however, that jury selection is perceived somewhat differently in relation to Northern Ireland: there, the right of peremptory challenge still exists. The Commission which recommended retention of this right referred to the 'special circumstances' in Northern Ireland, and noted 'the importance, which cannot be over emphasised in a divided society, of maintaining confidence in the administration of justice'.[183] The argument is similar to that which underlies the uneasiness which some commentators express concerning the use of random jury selection in the United States: namely, that it

---

[178] In general, see Michael Bohlander, ' ". . . By a Jury of His Peers": The Issue of Multi-racial Juries in a Poly-ethnic Society' (1992) 14 *Liverpool L. Rev.* 67–81.

[179] *Royal Commission* (above, n. 1), 133.   [180] Ibid.

[181] Ibid.

[182] Ibid. 133–4. It has also been proposed recently in the UK that the normal procedure for randomly selecting jurors might sensibly be qualified where juries are to be presented with highly technical evidence relating to serious fraud trials. The essence of the proposed qualification is that, in such trials, random selections should be made from pools of previously screened potential jurors who have shown themselves to possess a certain level of education or training. For details of the proposal, see the Home Office Consultation Document, *Juries in Serious Fraud Trials* (London: Home Office, Feb. 1998), §§ 4.6–24.

[183] The Draft Juries (Northern Ireland) Order 1994, in *Standing Advisory Commission on Human Rights, Report for 1994–95* (London: HMSO, 1995), 78–81 at 81.

is especially unwise to equate randomness with representativeness where deep social divisions exist and where particular communities or groups are numerically dominant.

Jury selection is probably the best example of how a lottery can be put to consistent use within a legal system. Another important, if rather less noted, application of chance for legal ends is regulation by use of a lottery mechanism, the purpose of which is to determine whom or what to inspect. It has already been noted that the neo-classical economic theory of punishment postulates that randomization may sometimes be used to reduce the cost of effective monitoring.[184] In certain instances, that is, the most cost-efficient means of inspection will be to monitor randomly and infrequently but to impose harsh penalties if monitoring reveals undesirable activity.[185] In terms of practical application of lotteries for monitoring purposes, it is important to note that the use of randomized inspection schemes in order to maintain, or to try to maintain, legally established standards has a long history.[186] In modern times, of course, there exists a variety of examples of regulation through resort to spot checks: revenue services sometimes choose people randomly for tax inspection; police are, in some countries, permitted to stop motorists randomly in order to test for intoxication; food and hygiene inspectors may be permitted to inspect the premises of restaurateurs on a random basis; athletes are often subject to random drug tests, and so on. One

[184] See the discussion contained, and the materials cited, in n. 31, above. Arguments concerning cost-effectiveness are sometimes cited in favour of the use of randomized telephone surveys: see, e.g., Alfred J. Tuchfarber and William R. Klecka, *Random Digit Dialing: Lowering the Cost of Victimization Surveys* (Cincinnati: Police Foundation, 1976). Tuchfarber and Klecka argue that, as compared with other survey techniques (such as personal interviews and questionnaires sent by mail), randomized telephone surveys are particularly cost-effective. The efficiency gains which they identify are attributable mainly to the use of the telephone rather than to randomization, although the use of random sampling will usually have some cost-lowering effect (see ibid. 18–19). Cf. also Verling C. Troldahl and Roy E. Carter, 'Random Selection of Respondents Within Households in Phone Surveys' (1964) 1 *Journal of Marketing Research* 71–6.

[185] Consider a somewhat fantastical illustration of this point. In trying to ensure that colleagues are available during their designated office hours, the dean of a faculty (of, say, twenty-five academics) could keep a list of everyone's office hours, check each week to see that all colleagues are available when they are supposed to be, and fine colleagues £1 on each occasion that they fail, without good reason, to keep to their hours. Since such a strategy would, among other things, be very time-consuming for the dean, what he or she might do instead is randomly monitor fewer colleagues but increase the penalty for non-compliance. If the dean were randomly to select only one colleague for inspection each week but leave the fine unchanged, the weekly cost to colleagues of missing office hours will have been reduced to 4 pence. In order to maintain the original level of deterrence, the dean would have to increase the penalty for non-compliance to £25. While the deterrence level will have been maintained, the cost of monitoring will have been reduced. If monitoring is carried out in a genuinely random fashion, the dean might also claim that the system is non-discriminatory—though one envisages that at least some colleagues will view it as playing into the hands of those who are not especially risk-averse (although this objection might be met by altering the ratio of colleagues monitored to size of faculty).

[186] Traditionally, for example, a randomized inspection scheme has been used to check that coinage issued by the Royal Mint meets the Crown's specifications. See Stephen M. Stigler, 'Eight Centuries of Sampling Inspection: The Trial of the Pyx' (1977) 72 *Journal of the American Statistical Association* 493–500.

advantage of spot checks is that they are likely—if they are perceived to be genuinely random—to be considered non-discriminatory, since those who might be subject to any such check will probably, if only implicitly, accept that their chances of being targeted are equal. But perhaps the primary attraction of spot checks, from a regulatory perspective, rests in the fact that random targeting generates unpredictability: it is often desirable that regulatory strategies entail an element of surprise, for when inspections are signalled in advance regulatees may be able temporarily to modify their conduct so as to satisfy the regulators.[187]

It might sometimes make good sense, from a regulatory point of view, to randomize processes other than inspection. For example, in so far as regulatory agencies might be vulnerable to 'capture'—that is, to the possibility of their staff being bribed or otherwise manipulated by regulatees[188]—it may be desirable to assign (and, periodically, to reassign) regulatory responsibilities on a random basis rather than to enable regulators to choose the fields in which they work.[189] Where such choice is allowed, regulators will most likely opt to oversee areas in which they possess expertise. While there may be a good deal of sense in having regulators who are highly knowledgeable about the matters which they are required to oversee, the dangers of capture are fairly obvious. On occasions, for example, there may be some interchange of employees between, say, a regulatory agency and a regulated industry, a consequence of which might be that enforcement officers do not wish to tread on the toes of an old employer or, for that matter, a prospective future one: hence the argument for random assignment of regulators to agencies.[190] A similar argument might be developed in support of randomization as a method of institutional self-regulation.[191] While corruption may grow within organizations owing to the presence of uncertainty, the introduction of random elements into bureaucratic procedures may occasionally combat corrupt activities by making opportunities to profit from wrongs more

---

[187] See Bentham, *Constitutional Code (Volume I)*, IX. 9. A8. Spot checks will sometimes not be considered appropriate because they can, in certain contexts, be impracticable. Consider, for example, Kaufman's study of the activities and regulation of forest rangers. When 'Ranger districts' are to be inspected, he observes, '[t]here are no surprise visits', for 'unless advance notice is given to the units to be visited, there is a chance that the entire staff will be out working when the inspectors arrive, and the inspectors will lose valuable time'. Herbert Kaufman, *The Forest Ranger: A Study in Administrative Behavior* (Baltimore: Johns Hopkins University Press, 1960), 142–3.

[188] On regulatory capture, see Anthony I. Ogus, *Regulation: Legal Form and Economic Theory* (Oxford: Clarendon Press, 1994), 57–8, 94–5, 106–7; and Morton J. Horwitz, *The Transformation of American Law, 1870–1960: The Crisis of Legal Orthodoxy* (New York: Oxford University Press, 1992), 241.

[189] For an argument to this effect, see William A. Niskanen, Jr., *Bureaucracy and Representative Government* (Chicago: Aldine, 1971), 219–23.

[190] Note that this argument bears comparison with that which Thaler presents in favour of random assignment of members of US Congress to congressional committees, as discussed in Chapter 2.

[191] Although instances in which randomization is used for this purpose appear to be rare: see Christopher Hood and Oliver James, 'The Central Executive', in Patrick Dunleavy *et al.* (eds.), *Developments in British Politics 5* (Basingstoke: Macmillan, 1997), 177–204 at 200–2.

difficult to identify in advance.[192] For example, in a police force where some officers are honest and others corrupt, opportunities for dishonest police to take bribes or practise extortion may be reduced if beat patrol is randomized so that they cannot anticipate with whom they will be on duty or whether they will be working alone or in pairs.[193]

Randomization, then, may sometimes offer an effective means of deterrence. An extreme illustration of this point—one which concerns the strategic use of uncertainty rather than randomized decision-making—is Schelling's discussion of threats which leave something to chance. Coupling threats with chance is often bad strategy. 'To say that one *may* act is to say that one *may not* . . . Furthermore, if . . . the opponent fails to heed the threat, and the threatener chooses not to carry it out, he only confirms his opponent's belief that when he has a clear choice to act or to abstain he will choose to abstain.'[194] However, in one type of situation— namely, that in which the final outcome is not chosen but is attributable to chance—this form of threat can be peculiarly effective. To adapt an example that will be familiar to anyone who has sat through westerns, while it is likely that you will not be too impressed by the threat that I *might* shoot you if you do not hand over all of your money, were I to make this threat and then draw a gun and shoot in your direction—so creating the possibility that a bullet might just hit you—the likelihood is that you will take my threat rather more seriously. The threat will probably be taken still more seriously if I endanger myself as much as I do my adversary. Should I tell you that, if you do not row, I may rock the boat so that it tips over and drowns us both, you may well not believe me. But if I say this and then rock the boat in such a way as to put it in jeopardy, you will probably think differently. In each of these instances, I make my threat compelling by engaging in an action which is likely to convince my adversary that the ultimate outcome is not altogether within my control.

The capacity for this type of threat to deter becomes clear, Schelling suggests, if we consider it in relation to military brinkmanship. A war is as likely to be started by chance—because of an accident, say, or a false alarm or misapprehension—as it is to be started deliberately.[195] Successful military deterrence is all about increasing the chances of war occurring—to the point, indeed, where one's opponents back down—without this actually happening.[196] Such a strategy will inevitably involve bluff-calling, and there will be a very real risk that war will break out. But then that risk has to be present if military threats are to possess the capacity to deter. 'Brinkmanship is thus the deliberate creation of a recognizable risk of war, a risk that one does not completely control. It is the

---

[192] See Susan Rose-Ackerman, *Corruption: A Study in Political Economy* (New York: Academic Press, 1978), 184–5.

[193] See Christopher Hood, 'Control Over Bureaucracy: Cultural Theory and Institutional Variety' (1995) 15 *Journal of Public Policy* 207–30 at 214.

[194] Thomas C. Schelling, *The Strategy of Conflict* (New York: Oxford University Press, 1963), 187.   [195] Ibid. 188, 191.   [196] Ibid. 192.

tactic of deliberately letting the situation get somewhat out of hand, just because its being out of hand may be intolerable to the other party and force his accommodation.'[197]

CONCLUSION

The basic point of this chapter has been to try to identify the primary advantages of randomization for social decision-making purposes. Not all of these advantages have been drawn out; there are certainly others discussion of which I wish to defer until the next chapter. Even in so far as I have focused on the advantages of randomized decision-making, my discussion has at times been rather ambivalent. The reason for this was intimated early on in this chapter: the arguments which might be adduced in favour of randomized decision-making tend not to be unequivocal. Accordingly, while I have endeavoured here to paint a fairly positive picture of social decision-making by lot, it has been impossible not to introduce a down-side into the discussion.

Yet I have tried to keep criticisms of randomized decision-making to a minimum, for the simple reason that my discussion would have lost what little structure it has if I had resolved to deal with both the advantages and drawbacks of social decision-making by lot within the space of a single chapter. In the next chapter, we shall devote more specific attention to the down-side. One of the things that will become clear fairly quickly is that, just as many of the advantageous features of randomized decision-making can be qualified, so too can certain of the criticisms. Rather ironically, indeed, by considering the principal disadvantages of randomization we might acquire a better appreciation of the virtues of the lottery as a social decision-making device. Furthermore, an examination of one particular disadvantage—the indifference of lotteries to reason— ought to reveal why the phenomenon of randomized social decision-making has considerable jurisprudential significance.

[197] Schelling, *The Strategy of Conflict*, 200.

4

Dicing with Justice

It has been stated already that an objective of this book is to suggest that lotteries might be used more extensively than they currently are for purposes of political and legal decision-making. Given this objective, it might be considered a matter for concern that the arguments advanced so far in support of randomization have, by and large, been subject to qualification. Some modest suggestions for the more extensive use of randomization within decision-making frameworks will be put forward in the next chapter. In this chapter, we consider the principal drawbacks which can attach to decision-making by lot. While the disadvantages of deciding by lot are numerous, they can be categorized in terms of four themes: lotteries are blind, are constructed, create uncertainty, and eschew reason. These four categories provide the structure for this chapter.

This chapter does not simply examine the drawbacks of randomized social decision-making. Although the principal disadvantages of randomization provide the framework for discussion, I do not present the lottery decision in a wholly, or even in a particularly, unfavourable light. Just as we have seen that the advantages of randomized social decision-making tend to be subject to qualification, so too we will see that an examination of the disadvantages of such decision-making often enables us to appreciate more fully the favourable attributes of lotteries. Indeed, in this chapter, certain of the negative features of randomized social decision-making are used as starting-points for discussions which turn out to depict such decision-making either neutrally or positively. By engaging with the primary disadvantages of social decision-making by lot, I hope to be able to draw out or reiterate certain of the more intriguing or desirable features of this form of decision-making. My main argument, which is to be found in section 4, is that the lottery may provide valuable insights into the nature of, and our assumptions concerning, legal decision-making precisely because we generally consider the notion of a randomized legal decision to be invidious.

I. BLIND, MINDLESS CHANCE

It has already been noted in this study that non-weighted lotteries are blind and mindless. In the last chapter, I attempted to demonstrate that these attributes may, in some circumstances, be emphasized in order to bring out certain positive features of randomized social decision-making. It was also observed, however, that these attributes can just as easily be highlighted so as to capture some of the disadvantages of social decision-making by lot. At this point, we ought to develop this observation.

Since non-weighted lotteries ignore human qualities—since they do not take account of different needs, desires, talents, and entitlements—they are unlikely to be considered satisfactory for purposes of social decision-making whenever there exists an expectation that candidates be distinguished. Deciding by resort to a non-weighted lottery is likely to be considered a satisfactory strategy only if the objective is to accord equal chances of selection. More often than not, however, both those making and those subject to decisions will prefer a decision-making process which accommodates dissimilarities. One of the basic objections to the implementation of draft lotteries, for example, is that randomized conscription will neither identify nor guarantee the selection of those with the desire and the talent to be soldiers. ('The "dove" who is a highly educated musician may be sent to war, while the "hawk" who is a crack shot may remain at home.')[1] Similarly, random allocation of scarce resources will not ensure that they are received by those who are most deserving or in need. In endeavouring to make a positive case for randomized social decision-making, one might argue that the capacity of the non-weighted lottery to generate odd or absurd outcomes illustrates its primary virtue as a political device: namely, that since the lottery is blind and mindless, it is also incorruptible.[2] Indeed, an argument similar to this was advanced in the last chapter. It is also possible to mount a defence of lottery decisions not by stressing the advantageous features of a decision-mechanism which is indifferent to qualities such as merit, talent, and need, but by focusing on the problems which can emerge when decision-making methods do take account of such qualities. Certain advocates of social decision-making by lot emphasize, for example, the types of incommensurability problem which tend to arise when decision-makers consider particular human attributes.[3] The message at the heart of this argument is that there will be a price to pay for not deciding randomly. Sometimes, that price might not be worth paying. While, for instance, several candidates for a scarce good may satisfy all of the criteria which must be met in order to qualify for that good, decision-makers will on occasions be reluctant to try to distinguish those candidates by assessing and comparing the merits of each case because the

---

[1] Guido Calabresi and Philip Bobbitt, *Tragic Choices* (New York: Norton & Co., 1978), 42.

[2] For a development of this line of argument, see Fred Hapgood, 'Chances of a Lifetime' (1975) 3 *Working Papers for a New Society* 37–42. Since '[l]otteries are cheap, equitable, and incorruptible (or can be made so with little effort)', Hapgood asserts, they 'might be useful in contexts that do not involve predictive assessments of success' such as 'juggling claims to desirable apartments in rent-controlled areas, providing access to overburdened national parks, distributing so-called "access minutes" on [North American] local television, and so on' (pp. 39–40). See also J. A. Mirrlees, 'The Economic Uses of Utilitarianism', in Amartya Sen and Bernard Williams (eds.), *Utilitarianism and Beyond* (Cambridge: Cambridge University Press, 1982), 63–84 at 82.

[3] See, e.g., Barbara Goodwin, *Justice by Lottery* (Hemel Hempstead: Harvester Wheatsheaf, 1992), 64–5; Jon Elster, *Solomonic Judgements: Studies in the Limitations of Rationality* (Cambridge: Cambridge University Press, 1989), 74; and Hank Greely, 'The Equality of Allocation by Lot' (1977) 12 *Harvard Civil Rights-Civil Liberties L. Rev.* 113–41 at 140.

costs of engaging in such an exercise may be considered excessive.[4] Thus it is that employers sometimes consider it too costly to make the sorts of finely calibrated distinctions necessary to differentiate job applicants and so randomly select employees, or at least compile shortlists, from a pool of appropriately qualified candidates. In this instance, the appeal of randomization rests in the fact that it is considered to be both impartial and cost-effective.[5]

In the majority of instances, however, those who are concerned with, or responsible for, social decision-making will consider the price of not deciding randomly to be worth paying, because randomness comes at a still higher price. Indeed, owing to the fact that they accord no attention to attributes and preferences, decisions reached by resort to a non-weighted lottery will, in a variety of contexts, meet with a number of objections. These objections seem to fall into six broad categories.

First, non-weighted lottery decisions may offend against commonplace conceptions of justice. That a lottery proceeds fairly does not mean that it is fair to resort to that lottery since, as Finnis observes, 'a perfectly *fair* lottery does not necessarily produce a *just* result'.[6] With a system of allocation by lot, candidates who are generally perceived to be the most deserving might not be selected to benefit. Where there are scarce medical resources to be allocated, a 'fundamental assumption' behind resort to lot, according to Mavrodes, is 'that there are no morally relevant distinctions among the "candidates" for th[ose] resources'.[7] If, therefore, there exists a widespread belief that 'some people really do deserve lifesaving facilities more than others do, then we should not look for a *random*

---

[4] See John Broome, 'Selecting People Randomly' (1984) 95 *Ethics* 38–55 at 41.

[5] This point is acknowledged, for example, in a document produced jointly by the Equal Opportunities Commission for Northern Ireland and the Fair Employment Commission for Northern Ireland, entitled *Random Sampling in the Recruitment Process: Notes for Guidance* (Belfast: EOC (NI)/FEC (NI), Dec. 1997). Random sampling, according to the authors of the document, offers 'a means of reducing applicant numbers to acceptable or manageable numbers' (p. 2) which, when 'correctly carried out, does not in itself discriminate either directly or indirectly against an applicant' (p. 1). There is also cited in the document a case in which an employer decided randomly to select for interview eight of the fourteen applicants who met the requirements for the post of superintendent at a neighbourhood office. One of the applicants who was not selected for interview contested the appropriateness of the method of selection for interview. The industrial tribunal found that random selection is intrinsically non-discriminatory in instances where all those within the pool from which the shortlist is drawn meet the requirements for the job: *Bright* v. *(1) London Borough of Islington (2) Jim Beecher (3) Mary Corbishley*, London North Industrial Tribunal, 28 Nov. 1990, cited in *Random Sampling in the Recruitment Process*, annex B, p. 12. See also *Isonor* v. *Dept. of Social Security* (18. iv. 94, EAT 965/93), summarized at (Nov. 1994) 508 *Industrial Relations Law Bulletin* 14–15. It is worth noting that when arguments in favour of randomized recruitment practices are advanced or accepted, it is almost invariably in relation to low-grade posts which require that employees possess no special skills. Rarely is it argued that shortlists should be determined randomly where there exists an excess of suitably qualified candidates for skilled or professional occupations— though, for an exception, cf. Thomas M. Divine, 'Women in the Academy: Sex Discrimination in University Faculty Hiring and Promotion' (1976) 5 *Journal of Law and Education* 429–51 at 443–4.

[6] John Finnis, *Natural Law and Natural Rights* (Oxford: Clarendon Press, 1980), 161.

[7] George I. Mavrodes, 'Choice and Chance in the Allocation of Medical Resources: A Response to Kilner' (1984) 12 *Journal of Religious Ethics* 97–115 at 99 (emphasis omitted).

method of allocating medical resources. We should look for some value-sensitive procedure which will take such deserts into account'.[8] This view seems to inform the not unrelated argument that decision-makers might be justified in resorting to lot when they find themselves unable to discern relevant distinctions between candidates (which is not to say that such distinctions are therefore non-existent).[9]

Secondly, lottery outcomes might sometimes be considered objectionable because they can force people into making selections or prioritizations which run counter to their intuitions. This observation needs to be distinguished from the previous one. Our intuitions will often, but not always, coincide with what we consider to be the morally appropriate course of action. My gut reaction may be to allocate scarce life-saving medical resources to A and B rather than to Y and Z—even though I acknowledge that, if one considers criteria such as life-expectancy, potential social contribution, severity of illness, or whatever, the latter pair appear to be more deserving than the former—for the simple reason that A and B are closely related to me. The point here is that, just as a lottery decision might prove objectionable because it will generate an outcome which takes no account of (and which, in many instances, will stand little chance of reflecting) considerations of justice, so too the decision might be considered objectionable because it does not take into account, and probably will not reflect, one's instincts.[10]

Owing to the fact that they are blind to attributes and preferences, thirdly, non-weighted lotteries cannot ensure selection of the most suitable or best qualified candidates. Perhaps this insight goes some way to explaining the appeal of the lottery as a tie-breaking device: that is, determining an outcome by lottery might begin to seem both attractive and acceptable to decision-makers when they have tried and failed to distinguish candidates on grounds of suitability to task, qualifications, or other criteria.[11] It is, in fact, only rarely that decision-makers will proceed in this fashion. Courts and other decision-making bodies are invariably reluctant to declare themselves unable to reach a decision—even though some of the judgments which they render might be supported by only the slenderest of majorities or distinctions.[12] Where, furthermore, burdens are particularly unpleasant or goods are scarce and highly prized, those who are randomly

---

[8] Mavrodes, 'Choice and Chance', 102.   [9] See Broome (above, n. 4), 45–8.

[10] The argument here, I should stress, is not that a lottery outcome will necessarily *be* objectionable where it fails to reflect such instincts. Indeed, it is sometimes the case that we engage in randomized decision-making precisely because the lottery does not cater to emotionally skewed preferences.

[11] See George Sher, 'What Makes a Lottery Fair?' (1980) 14 *Noûs* 203–16 at 203.

[12] See Otto Neurath, 'The Lost Wanderers of Descartes and the Auxiliary Motive (On the Psychology of Decision)' (1913), in Robert S. Cohen and Marie Neurath (eds. and trans.), *Otto Neurath: Philosophical Papers, 1913–1946* (Dordrecht: Reidel, 1983), 1–12 at 8–9: 'But woe to the statesman who behaved like this publicly. If, in a concrete case, he came to the insight that he could not decide between two alternatives and therefore wanted to decide by lot, he would expose himself to the reproach of frivolity or cynicism. Popular feeling would be deeply hurt.'

assigned burdens or denied goods because an excess of candidates cannot be distinguished are likely to object that decision-makers have been insensitive to distinctions which ought to have been made. Such objections might, in fact, be more widespread. '[M]ost people reject random admission on the grounds [*sic*] that students do differ', notes Klitgaard in relation to a proposal for the introduction of an admissions lottery at Harvard University. 'Most of us believe that we can distinguish, even among those who can do the work at Harvard.'[13] The fact that students, principally through grading, tend to be distinguished further once admitted to college lends support to this claim.

Fourthly, since non-weighted random selections provide no guarantee of quality, they may—as was noted in the previous two chapters—have deleterious effects on people's incentives. When discussing the costs and the unreliability of peer review, it is sometimes the case that academics will propose that research grants ought instead to be allocated randomly.[14] Such proposals seem generally to be premissed on the assumption that the pool of applicants would remain unchanged were one to move from a system of allocation based on peer review to a system of allocation by lot.[15] Yet it is highly unlikely that this would be the case, for peer review—whether or not it always performs the function satisfactorily— is by and large regarded as a quality-screening device. Removal of the device would be likely to create an incentive for more or less anyone with a research proposal—no matter how inadequate—to apply for funding.[16] Since random selection will not discriminate between different standards of application, those applicants with more deserving proposals who are not chosen will have little, if any, incentive (professional pride apart) to formulate proposals of a similar standard in the future.

It was noted in the previous chapter that random selection may promote a so-called second-best equity. That is, where guaranteeing equality of outcome is either impossible or undesirable—since the resource to be allocated is indivisible or, once divided, loses its value to those who want it—randomization offers the next-best option of according candidates an equal chance of receiving that resource. Equalization of opportunities may create the type of negative incentive problem just suggested. Such equalization, however, does not necessarily lead to

---

[13] Robert Klitgaard, *Choosing Elites* (New York: Basic Books, 1985), 58.

[14] See, for example, the comments attributed to Les Allen in 'Peer Review: Democracy, Sausages and Lotteries', *Times Higher Education Supplement*, 6 Feb. 1998, p. 14 ('I suggest that the [Engineering and Physical Science Research Council] throw out the panels, throw out the referees and have a lottery for all the available funds. Such a system would be fairer than the present one and would also be better at supporting truly original research. Pure chance must give me more hope than the opinions of a subset of my peers.')   [15] See Elster (above, n. 3), 111.

[16] With the 'announcement of lotteries as a means of allocating rewards', Cole observes, '[m]any individuals who would not consider themselves qualified for jobs, grants or awards, would apply nonetheless because of the "chance" to be selected'. Jonathan R. Cole, 'The Paradox of Individual Particularism and Institutional Universalism' (1989) 28 *Social Science Information* 51–76 at 73.

this problem.[17] Furthermore, perceived difficulties with equalizing opportunities—and with the use of lotteries to equalize opportunities—will often have little, if anything, to do with incentives. It will sometimes be the case that people distrust resort to randomization because the equality of opportunity which might be generated by the lottery offends against some other, more morally compelling consideration. Dworkin's illustration of the distinction between equal treatment and treatment as equals, discussed in Chapter 3, captures this point. Consider also Fishkin's discussion of a hypothetical lottery system whereby, at birth, babies are randomly assigned to families. Such a system would, Fishkin argues, have the beneficial effect of equalizing life chances. 'Any newborn infant's chance of reaching any highly valued position would be precisely equal to that of any other newborn infant.'[18] Perhaps more importantly, however, such a system would offend against the belief that parents should usually be free to raise their own children. The resort to a lottery in this instance, Fishkin concludes, 'depends on a violation of the autonomy of families . . . While removal of a child from its parents might be justified . . . in some isolated cases of extreme deprivation . . . such a wholesale process of reassignment clearly could not rest on such a basis.'[19]

Fishkin's hypothetical lottery can be related to the fifth objection to be considered here: that the blindness of randomization to attributes means that it can sometimes have what might be termed a demeaning effect. Random allocation of babies to families, according to this argument, entails an inappropriate valuation of both of these entities. This argument is usually developed as a critique of proposals favouring the commodification of what are traditionally perceived to be 'non-market' objects. To treat (among other things) sex, children, the environment, or human tissue and organs as commodities is—so the argument goes—to value these goods inappropriately. Commodification cannot adequately capture or reflect the value of the goods in question; hence the demeaning effect.[20] Randomization, like commodification, might sometimes meet with the same objection. That is, just as commercialized allocation of, say, children available for adoption or scarce life-saving medical resources to patients might be considered to have a demeaning effect, so too might randomized allocation of these goods.

Just how much emphasis ought to be placed on the potentially demeaning effects of lottery decisions is difficult to estimate. Objections to the demeaning effects of markets are, I think, quite often either exaggerated or misdirected.[21] With lotteries, the problem seems largely to revolve around explicitness. Take, for instance, the issue of research grant allocation as just discussed. Chance will

---

[17] See John E. Roemer, *Equality of Opportunity* (Cambridge, Mass.: Harvard University Press, 1998), 33–5.

[18] James S. Fishkin, *Justice, Equal Opportunity, and the Family* (New Haven: Yale University Press, 1983), 57.   [19] Ibid.

[20] See, generally, Elizabeth Anderson, *Value in Ethics and Economics* (Cambridge, Mass.: Harvard University Press, 1993).

[21] See Neil Duxbury, 'Do Markets Degrade?' (1996) 59 *Modern L. Rev.* 331–48.

often play a significant role in the peer review process.[22] That an application for a research grant meets with success, for example, will 'to a significant extent [be] dependent on the applicant's luck in the program director's choice of reviewers'—indeed, research has suggested that 'the fate of a particular grant application is roughly half determined by the characteristics of the proposal and the principal investigator, and about half by apparently random elements which might be characterized as the "luck of the reviewer draw." '[23] Yet for all that chance may, as it were, play a significant part behind the scenes in the grant-allocation process, and for all that many if not most applicants are likely to be aware of this, one expects that those applicants would consider their endeavours as scholars and researchers to have been demeaned were the awarding body explicitly to allocate grants by lot. While we may often be able to accept the implicit role that luck plays within a decision-making process, even when it works to our disadvantage, we will frequently be uncomfortable with proposals openly to import an element of chance into any such process.[24]

Why is this so? One answer is that when we explicitly import an element of chance into a decision-making process, we become responsible for the consequences of randomness in a manner in which we are not when chance is an inevitable, immanent feature of that process. Explicit importation of chance seems also to have the capacity to introduce into decision-making processes the demeaning effect to which we have been referring. That explicitness should introduce this demeaning effect is perhaps best explained in terms of symbolic resonance. Explicit reference to a pricing mechanism sometimes has a similar effect.

Many people, to give an example of a familiar kind, will leave their spouses for a month to do a job they do not like in order to earn some money. And yet they will not agree to leave the spouse for the same month for an offer of money, even a significantly larger sum of money. They will feel indignant that someone supposes that they are willing to trade the company of their spouse for money from a stranger.[25]

With regard to randomization, the problem of explicitness might be made clearer if we consider the issue of child custody adjudication. The notion that the best interests of the child ought to be the foremost consideration in the resolution of child custody disputes is sometimes contested on the ground that the best interests principle is indeterminate. After all, in endeavouring to apply this principle,

[w]hat set of values is a judge to use to determine what is in the child's best interests? Should the judge be concerned with happiness? Or should he or she worry about the child's spiritual goodness or economic productivity? Is stability and security for a child more

---

[22] For an illustrative discussion concerning submission of articles to journals, see Douglas P. Peters and Stephen J. Ceci, 'Peer-Review Practices of Psychological Journals: The Fate of Published Articles, Submitted Again' (1982) 5 *Behavioral and Brain Sciences* 187–255.

[23] Stephen Cole, Jonathan R. Cole, and Gary A. Simon, 'Chance and Consensus in Peer Review' (1981) 214 *Science* 881–6 at 885.   [24] See further Cole (above, n. 16), 73.

[25] Joseph Raz, *The Morality of Freedom* (Oxford: Clarendon Press, 1986), 348–9.

desirable than intellectual stimulation? Should the best interests of the child be viewed from a short-term or a long-term perspective? The conditions that make a person happy at age ten or fifteen may have adverse consequences at age thirty.[26]

Requiring that judges make decisions in the child's best interests is really a requirement that they rely on and impose their own values when deciding what is best for the child. Besides being indeterminate, the best interests principle may also turn out to be self-defeating: the effort to determine which party will be most suited to serving the child's best interests, that is, may lead to protracted litigation which could be detrimental to the welfare of the child.[27]

Might there, then, be a case for replacing a decision-making process which is driven by indeterminacy with one which is driven by randomness? Commenting on the fact that the grading of examinations entails a considerable degree of subjectivity and, in some instances, error, Edgeworth once speculated that border-line cases could just as fairly be resolved by resort to lot.[28] Specifically in rela-tion to child custody disputes, it might be argued that recourse to sortition would mean that 'decisions [would be] reached quickly and the possibility of harm to the child caused by protracted litigation [be] reduced. A randomized selection process also treats each parent equally'.[29] Assuming that both parents deserve to be treated equally—that neither is less fit than the other to take custody—resort to a lottery in such circumstances might be considered to be both fair and cost-effective.[30] Use of a lottery here might even be considered honest. 'Some deci-sions are going to be arbitrary and epistemically random no matter what we do, no matter how hard we try to base them on reasons. Chance will regulate a large part of our lives, no matter how hard we try to avoid it.'[31] As with the peer review process in relation to research grant applications, chance is likely to play a signif-icant role in child custody adjudication. Judges may be assigned randomly to particular child custody cases. Exactly which values are relied upon and imposed for the purpose of determining what, in those cases, is in the child's best interests may be largely a matter of happenstance. Randomly to grant custody, it might be

---

[26] Robert H. Mnookin, 'Foster Care: In Whose Best Interest?' (1973) 43 *Harvard Educational Review* 599–638 at 618.   [27] See Elster (above, n. 3), 146–7.

[28] F. Y. Edgeworth, 'The Statistics of Examinations' (1888) 51 *Journal of the Royal Statistical Society* 599–635 at 626. For a more recent suggestion along the same lines, cf. Conall Boyle, 'Organizations Selecting People: How the Process Could be Made Fairer by the Appropriate Use of Lotteries' (1998) 47 *The Statistician* 291–321 at 298–302; and also David McKie, 'It's a Lottery', *Guardian*, 22 June 1998, p. 17. Edgeworth ('Statistics', 626) proceeds to dismiss the proposal on the basis that it is inappropriate to introduce more chance into a system which is already over-reliant on chance. Indeed, in a later essay he offers a number of suggestions concerning how the element of chance within the grading process might be neutralized: see F. Y. Edgeworth, 'The Element of Chance in Competitive Examinations' (1890) 53 *Journal of the Royal Statistical Society* 644–63 at 658–62.

[29] Katherine Hunt Federle, 'Looking for Rights in All the Wrong Places: Resolving Custody Disputes in Divorce Proceedings' (1994) 15 *Cardozo L. Rev.* 1523–66 at 1546–7. It ought to be mentioned that Federle presents these arguments in order to knock them down.

[30] See Elster (above, n. 3), 172.   [31] Ibid. 121.

argued, simply renders explicit something which is likely to occur implicitly within the adjudicative process anyway.

The arguments suggested in the previous paragraph can be countered with various objections. It goes without saying, indeed, that plenty of criticisms might be levelled at the proposition that it may be advantageous to resolve child custody disputes by the toss of a coin.[32] I shall consider some of these criticisms in section 4 of this chapter. Nevertheless, I also argue there that the merits of deciding child custody disputes randomly are not insignificant and that resistance to the idea is indicative of what I termed, at the conclusion of Chapter 1, attraction to reason. At this stage, I wish only to draw attention to the potentially demeaning effect of explicitly random decision-making in this context. Whatever other advantages or drawbacks might attach to determining child custody by the flipping of a coin, there seems to be no doubt that the idea brings with it a rather dubious—some might say horrible—symbolic resonance. 'Deciding a child's future by flipping a coin', one commentator remarks, 'symbolically abdicates government responsibility for the child and symbolically denies the importance of human differences and distinctiveness.'[33] This negative symbolic resonance appears to derive from the fact that the randomness of the decision-making process is rendered explicit (and, having been rendered explicit, is considered to entail an inappropriate valuation of the subject-matter of the decision).

The blindness of randomness to attributes—and here we encounter our sixth objection—means that decisions reached by lottery sometimes seem too clear-cut. The basic idea here seems to be that '[l]otteries . . . make it all too clear that some are chosen and others are rejected'.[34] Yet what could it mean to say that selection or rejection is made all too clear? There appear to be two possible answers to this question.

The first is that the unequivocality of decision-making by lot might lead people within the lottery pool—or even those responsible for administering the lottery[35]—to feel uncomfortable about their lack of ability to influence the

---

[32] For a discussion of drawbacks and advantages, see generally Jon Elster, 'Custody by the Toss of a Coin?' (1988) 27 *Social Science Information* 517–35.

[33] Robert H. Mnookin, 'Child Custody Adjudication: Judicial Functions in the Face of Indeterminacy' (1975) 39 *Law and Contemporary Problems* 226–93 at 290.

[34] Jon Elster, *Local Justice: How Institutions Allocate Scarce Goods and Necessary Burdens* (Cambridge: Cambridge University Press, 1992), 136.

[35] Oakley offers the example of a research project which she directed concerning the random allocation of social support to women during pregnancy. Just over 500 women agreed to participate in the study and, over a fifteen-month period, four midwives were enlisted to provide social support. In agreeing to participate in the study, each woman was accorded a 50% chance of receiving social support. Oakley reports that one of the primary grievances over the randomized allocation of social support was 'that the women themselves could not choose their fates'. This complaint, however, was expressed not by the women in the study, but by the midwives. Indeed, Oakley reports that all four midwives 'tried various ploys to control the randomization process'. Ann Oakley, 'Who's Afraid of the Randomized Controlled Trial? Some Dilemmas of the Scientific Method and "Good" Research Practice', in Helen Roberts (ed.), *Women's Health Counts* (London: Routledge, 1990), 167–94 at 176–8.

outcome. If the lottery is genuinely random and is not susceptible to manipulation, the outcomes which it generates ought to be treated as final. The only point
of appealing against such an outcome would be to contest the initial decision to
resort to lot. Many of us, as children, have encountered something similar to this
problem when, in arguing about some choice or other with a friend or sibling, it
is proposed that the matter be settled by the toss of a coin. Usually, the child who
loses the toss will then either declare the lottery invalid or demand that it be
altered (by, for example, insisting that the winner should be the person who gets
the best of three or five or some other number of tosses). The capacity of lotteries to generate an uneasy sense of impotence comes across especially clearly in
Boyes's and Happel's discussion of a proposal for the random assignment of
rooms to Faculty members. When their Faculty was relocated to a new building,
Boyes and Happel note, an acceptable method had to be found for allocating
rooms (some of which were more desirable than others) to staff. Various allocative methods were suggested, including use of a lottery. This suggestion 'was
initially met with excitement since everyone would start with an equal chance for
the best offices. However, grumbling soon developed as those with the better
offices in the old building began to fear a welfare loss through no fault of their
own and with no way to offset the loss.'[36] The proposed use of a lottery was eventually rejected because those who saw themselves as potential losers recognized
that they were unable to exert control over this particular method of decision-
making.

Recognition of the indifference of lotteries to losers points us to a second answer
to the question of why random decisions might be considered too clear-cut: the
peremptory nature of the lottery outcome might generate or exacerbate loss of self-
esteem. Randomization may sometimes appeal because it produces decisions which
are not seen to be a matter of human judgement. In relation to the allocation of scarce
medical resources, for example, it has been questioned whether 'a chance procedure
would make rejection easier and would reduce emotional stress and anxiety for the
patient and those close to him more than other selection procedures'.[37] The basic
argument in support of such a proposition would appear to be that 'people are better
able to accept and reconcile themselves to certain kinds of decisions when made by
fate, rather than through the application of principles they dislike or of limited human
reason'.[38] But this argument can be easily overstated. Given that non-weighted
lotteries take no account of desert, it is perhaps ironic that people should often interpret undesirable lottery outcomes as a sign of being undeserving. Bad luck is quite
frequently regarded as punishment for something—even, and sometimes particu-

---

[36] William J. Boyes and Stephen K. Happel, 'Auctions as an Allocation Mechanism in
Academia: The Case of Faculty Offices' (1989) 3 *Journal of Economic Perspectives* 37–40 at 38.

[37] L. Duane Willard, 'Scarce Medical Resources and the Right to Refuse Selection by Artificial
Chance' (1980) 5 *Journal of Medicine and Philosophy* 225–9 at 226. As with the quotation from
Federle (above, n. 29), Willard himself is not supporting this argument but merely using it for the
purpose of focusing critique.   [38] Greely (above, n. 3), 123.

larly, by those who suffer bad luck.[39] Within a sample of participants in the 1971 American draft lottery, '[t]here was a tendency for the self-esteem of subjects who were less fortunate than most of their fellow group members [that is, those whose birth-dates were selected early] to fall and for the self-esteem of subjects who were more fortunate than most of their fellows to rise'.[40] Subjects tended to interpret 'the falls and cuts of arbitrary fate . . . as the workings of a metaphysical justice'.[41]

Even if one acknowledges that randomized decisions may generate or aggravate loss of self-esteem, one might question to what degree peremptoriness contributes to this process. It would be no great surprise, for example, to discover that, when people equate luck with desert, they tend to do so because they cannot help but believe that chance must have its cause: *suam habet fortuna rationem*, to steal the words of the Roman satirist, Gaius Petronius.[42] Randomness, pure and simple, is a phenomenon which people often find peculiarly difficult to accept.[43] Accordingly, the conclusion which people quite regularly draw from the fact that they have been beset by bad luck is that their predicament must indicate that they have caused offence to *something* out there.[44] That these people will very

[39] See, e.g., Melvin J. Lerner and Carolyn H. Simmons, 'Observer's Reaction to the "Innocent Victim": Compassion or Rejection?' (1966) 4 *Journal of Personality and Social Psychology* 203–10; and Melvin J. Lerner and Dale T. Miller, 'Just World Research and the Attribution Process: Looking Back and Ahead' (1978) 85 *Psychological Bulletin* 1030–51. Lerner and his associates produced many of these so-called 'just world' studies. The basic thesis of these studies is that, when people assume the world to be essentially just, they are likely also to assume that those who suffer bad luck must somehow deserve their fates.

[40] Zick Rubin and Anne Peplau, 'Belief in a Just World and Reactions to Another's Lot: A Study of Participants in the National Draft Lottery' (1973) 29 *Journal of Social Issues* 73–93 at 84–5.

[41] Ibid. 85.

[42] For the 19th-cent. probability theorist, Poincaré, '[e]very phenomenon, however minute, has a cause; and a mind infinitely powerful, infinitely well-informed about the laws of nature, could have foreseen it from the beginning of the centuries . . . Chance is only the measure of our ignorance. Fortuitous phenomena are, by definition, those laws which we do not know.' Henri Poincaré, 'Chance' (n.d.), in James R. Newman (ed.), *The World of Mathematics: A Small Library of the Literature of Mathematics from A'h-mosé the Scribe to Einstein* (4 vols., Redmond, Wash.: Tempus, 1988 (1956)), ii. 1359–72 at 1359; and compare Richard Dawkins, *The Selfish Gene* (Oxford: Oxford University Press, orig. publ. 1976, new edn. 1989), 218. Consider also, from the 1730s, the following lines from Alexander Pope's 'Essay on Man' (I. x. 289–91): 'All nature is but art, unknown to thee / All change, direction, which thou canst not see; / All discord, harmony not understood'. On the meaningfulness of chance occurrences, see generally C. G. Jung, *Synchronicity: An Acausal Connecting Principle* (Eng. trans. R. F. C. Hull, London: Routledge & Kegan Paul, 1972 (1952)).

[43] For the idea that human beings are fundamentally disposed to believing that order, design, regularity, patterns, or whatever must reside within random or chaotic occurrences, see generally Ivars Peterson, *The Jungles of Randomness: A Mathematical Safari* (Harmondsworth: Penguin, 1998). Weather-forecasting provides a fairly obvious illustration of this disposition: see, e.g., Ronald A. Fisher, 'On the Random Sequence' (1926) 52 *Quarterly Journal of the Royal Meteorological Society* 250 (correspondence).

[44] There are those, as Aristotle remarked, who 'believe that chance is a cause, but that it is inscrutable to human intelligence, as being a divine thing and full of mystery'. *Physics* 2. 4 (196^{b} 5–7). On the notion of chance as hidden cause, cf. generally Deborah J. Bennett, *Randomness* (Cambridge, Mass.: Harvard University Press, 1998), 83–108. Conversely, for the argument that cause conceals chance—or, more precisely, that causality is probabilistic rather than deterministic in character—see Patrick Suppes, *Probabilistic Metaphysics* (Oxford: Blackwell, 1984), 35–70.

frequently profess not to know what it is that they have offended or how they might have caused offence—that they have most likely not offended anything— is immaterial. The point is that, on suffering bad luck, people sometimes begin to conceive of themselves as potentially culpable. Is it not this feeling—the feeling that one's bad luck might be a measure of one's badness—which explains why lottery outcomes can generate loss of self-esteem?

While conceding this point, I would argue that peremptoriness is also a significant factor when we consider the capacity of lotteries to diminish self-esteem. Lotteries, after all, reject without providing reasons—or rather, without providing any reason other than that one was unlucky in the draw. It will sometimes be the case—especially where the issue to be determined is of major importance to the candidates—that those who fail to benefit from, or who are condemned to suffer because of, a lottery will have difficulty in accepting the terseness and finality of the decision once it has been reached. That people struggle to come to terms with the decisiveness of lottery outcomes seems clear from the types of dissatisfaction which are sometimes expressed after the event. Lottery losers—once they have discovered that luck was not on their side—will sometimes complain that they were never really in favour of, or comfortable with, the use of random selection. The decisiveness of the outcome may even cause them to complain, as is the case in Shirley Jackson's eerie story, that the lottery was not conducted fairly.[45] It often seems, furthermore, that the starkness of lottery outcomes causes the unlucky to lose sight of their *ex ante* perspectives. According equal chances to two parties by deciding with the toss of a coin may seem acceptable to both sides right up until the coin lands. It is after the coin has landed that the losing party is likely to complain that his case was not heard fairly.[46]

2. THE LOTTERY AS CONSTRUCT

The capacity of lotteries to generate or exacerbate loss of self-esteem is obviously not wholly or even primarily attributable to the unequivocality of random outcomes. Another factor to take into account when considering the demoralizing potential of randomized decisions is the construction of the lottery. What are the terms of the lottery? What chances does it accord to those who are within the pool? How does it proceed?

Lotteries possess considerable capacity for cognitive distortion, not least because our intuitions concerning the occurrence of events are often out of line with the actual probability of those events occurring. One of the reasons for this

---

[45] See Shirley Jackson, 'The Lottery' (1948), in Richard Ford (ed.), *The Granta Book of the American Short Story* (London: Granta, 1992), 62–70. Part of the eeriness of this story derives from the fact that one is never sure whether the lottery was conducted fairly.

[46] See Elster (above, n. 3), 117–18; and also Peter L. Bernstein, *Against the Gods: The Remarkable Story of Risk* (New York: Wiley, 1996), 103–4.

dissonance between intuition and probability rests in our tendency to anthropomorphize chance—to assume, that is, that chance must have a mind of its own and will therefore correct itself (as we might correct ourselves were we trying to decide randomly) when it has produced too many repetitious outcomes.[47] In one way or another, our mind will often play tricks on us when we endeavour to assess chances.[48] One common cognitive error in this context is what we might term the tendency to subjectivize probability. One sometimes sees colleagues or classmates express surprise that they have the same birthday as one of their peers.[49] Yet, among a group of twenty-five or more persons, the chance of two or more people sharing a birthday is greater than 50 per cent. We tend to treat such coincidences as remarkable because we are prone to focusing on a specific birthday— invariably our own—and wondering what the probability would be of that being shared by one or more of the other people in the group. Once probability has been subjectivized, the coincidence does become fairly remarkable: the chance of one or more of the other twenty-four people in the group sharing my birthday is less than 7 per cent.

A more extreme illustration of this point is the double lottery winner. When a woman won the New Jersey state lottery twice within four months, the probability of this occurrence was assumed to be around one in seventeen trillion.[50] Yet, out of the many millions of Americans who regularly purchase lottery tickets, it is not especially surprising that some person should, at some point in time, win twice. Indeed, statisticians have calculated 'that it is better than even odds to have a double [lottery] winner in seven years someplace in the United States' and that '[i]t is better than 1 in 30 that there is a double winner in a four-month

---

[47] Piaget and Inhelder observe that children sometimes conceive of chance in this way: cf. Jean Piaget and Bärbel Inhelder, *The Origin of the Idea of Chance in Children* (Eng. trans. L. Leake, Jr., P. Burrell, and H. D. Fishbein, London: Routledge & Kegan Paul, 1975 (1951)), 63–6. The phenomenon of the so-called 'gambler's fallacy', however, indicates that the tendency is by no means confined to children. 'After observing a long run of red on the roulette wheel, for example, most people erroneously believe that black is now due, presumably because the occurrence of black will result in a more representative sequence than the occurrence of an additional red. Chance is commonly viewed as a self-correcting process in which a deviation in one direction induces a deviation in the opposite direction to restore the equilibrium. In fact, deviations are not "corrected" as a chance process unfolds, they are merely diluted.' Amos Tversky and Daniel Kahneman, 'Judgment under Uncertainty: Heuristics and Biases' (1974) 185 *Science* 1124–31 at 1125.

[48] For an illustrative discussion, see Bennett (above, n. 44), 174–88. For examples of erroneous assessments of chances in legal contexts, see Roger G. Noll and James E. Krier, 'Some Implications of Cognitive Psychology for Risk Regulation' (1990) 19 *Journal of Legal Studies* 747–79; and also Heidi Li Feldman, 'Science, Reason, and Tort Law: Looking for the Reasonable Person' in Helen Reece (ed.), *Law and Science: Current Legal Issues 1998,* i (Oxford: Oxford University Press, 1998), 35–54. Cf. also *Reay* v. *British Nuclear Fuels* [1994] 5 Med. LR 1, 12; and Christopher E. Miller, 'Radiological Risk and Civil Liability: A Review of Recent Developments in the United Kingdom', in Robert Baldwin (ed.), *Law and Uncertainty: Risks and Legal Processes* (London: Kluwer, 1997), 273–91 at 278–88.

[49] This example is taken from Bennett (above, n. 44), 174–5.

[50] See Gina Kolata, '1-in-a-Trillion Coincidence, You Say? Not Really, Experts Find', *New York Times,* 27 Feb. 1990, § C, pp. 1–2.

period'.[51] What we encounter here is the law of large—or rather, very large—numbers: events which are rare per person occur frequently in the presence of large numbers of people. The essence of the law of very large numbers is captured by the so-called 'blade-of-grass paradox':[52] were I to stand in a large field and stoop to pull up a blade of grass, the likelihood of my selecting any particular blade will be extremely remote; yet one blade or another has to be selected. In the case of the double lottery winner, it is again the subjectivization of probability—what are the chances of *my* being a double lottery winner?—that makes the occurrence appear ludicrously improbable.[53]

It is all very well, of course, to treat as a cognitive deficiency the tendency for human beings to subjectivize, and consequently to misrepresent, probabilities. But the fact is that this tendency is common to the majority of us. What is significant here is that the way in which a lottery proceeds or is constructed may have a bearing on how probability is subjectivized. Where a lottery accords equality of chances, Hume asserted, one ought to be indifferent as to the lot which one draws: it would not matter which ticket, ball, straw, or whatever one takes, since such a lottery determines that 'no one chance can possibly be superior to another'.[54] If everybody within the lottery has an equal chance, everybody should be indifferent about the chance which they have. While this indifference might be in evidence *ex ante*, however, the situation changes on completion of the draw. At this point, chance is subjectivized—is translated into good and bad fortune—and so participants are no longer likely to be indifferent to their lot. Depending on the nature of the lottery, participants might even abandon indifference before the draw is completed: it may already have become clear that I have drawn a very short straw or that nobody else will get a lower number on casting the dice.[55]

Furthermore, the way in which one perceives one's fate—whether losses are accepted philosophically or taken personally, for example—may depend on the terms of the lottery. Let us say that I have a spare copy of a rare book and that two of my colleagues would very much appreciate receiving that book as a gift. Being unsure as to whom I should donate the book, I decide to settle the matter randomly. My initial impulse is to flip a coin; instead, however, I resolve to give the book to whichever of the two colleagues I first encounter around the Faculty.

[51] Persi Diaconis and Frederick Mosteller, 'Methods for Studying Coincidences' (1989) 84 *Journal of the American Statistical Association* 853–61 at 859 citing (without source) the calculations of Stephen Samuels and George McCabe of the Department of Statistics at Purdue University.

[52] See Kolata (above, n. 50), 2.

[53] In relation to the New Jersey lottery case, Diaconis and Mosteller (above, n. 51), 859, remark that '[t]he 1 in 17 trillion number is the correct answer to a not-very-relevant question. If you buy one ticket for exactly two New Jersey state lotteries, this is the chance both would be winners.'

[54] Hume, *A Treatise of Human Nature*, I. iii. 11.

[55] Note that this observation points to a distinction between lotteries in which each lot is spent, as it were, upon selection, and lotteries which allow for multiple selections of the same lot. Drawing straws is an illustration of the first type of lottery; an example of the second is the British national lottery, which allows participants to select as they wish among the available numbers (thus ensuring that many selections will be replicated).

Having seen one of the colleagues on my corridor and having handed over the book, I subsequently discover that the other colleague is away from the Faculty for the week. Not only do I now consider my mode of selection to be regrettable, but this second colleague would probably feel the same were she to learn of what I had done. Her objection would, one suspects, be not that I had resolved the dilemma by resort to a lottery, but that I should not have resorted to a lottery the basic condition of which put her at a disadvantage.

Our estimation of a lottery will depend to a large degree on the probability of its outcome being the one which we prefer: even minor changes to the odds may significantly alter our assessment of the risks involved in being a participant.[56] It could even be the case that two or more lotteries offer the same odds and yet, owing to the distinctness of the terms of each lottery, perceptions of the outcomes which each generates differ significantly. Imagine that a thousand people, including myself, face death.[57] Only one of these people can be rescued and that person is to be selected randomly. Should I be selected, I will feel very lucky but will not consider my luck to require explanation—I will simply be of the view that somebody had to be lucky, and that it may as well have been me as anyone else. Imagine, however, a different lottery: I have been sentenced to death, but the sentence will be remitted if my gaoler draws the longest of a thousand straws. If my gaoler picks this straw, there would be something to be explained. It would be strange simply to conclude that this outcome was as likely as any other. In both lotteries, the chance that my life will be saved is the same. Yet the lotteries are clearly different. In the first, nothing special happens: whatever the result, somebody would be rescued. In the second, however, the outcome is special: of the thousand possible results, only one would save a life. That this particular possible result turns out to be the actual result seems to require an explanation—an explanation, furthermore, which does not merely attribute the result to coincidence. For all that the outcome might be explained in terms of the blade-of-grass paradox,[58] most people—including the person whose sentence has been remitted—are likely to wonder whether this second lottery was, in fact, rigged. The terms of the lottery have a bearing on how the outcome is subjectivized.

It has already been noted in this study that a principal advantage of a non-weighted lottery is that it will—so long as randomness has not been somehow compromised—accord equal chances to those within the pool. Where lotteries guarantee equiprobable outcomes to candidates, those candidates are treated in an impartial manner. Accordingly, should it be the case that candidates have been

---

[56] See further David Gauthier, 'Resolute Choice and Rational Deliberation: A Critique and a Defense' (1997) 31 *Noûs* 1–25 at 5–12.

[57] The example which follows is taken from Derek Parfit, 'Why Anything? Why This?', *London Review of Books*, 22 Jan. 1998, pp. 24–7 at 24. (For the concluding instalment of this essay, cf. *London Review of Books*, 5 Feb. 1998, pp. 22–5.)

[58] See further Haim Gaifman, 'Why the "LRB"? Why Anything?', *London Review of Books*, 16 Apr. 1998, p. 4 (correspondence).

judged to be equal—that they all, say, meet the stipulated criteria of eligibility—there is likely to be a compelling argument for resorting to lot in order to determine which of them should receive the scarce indivisible resource which they all seek. This line of reasoning might be met with a number of objections. Certain of these objections—such as that human beings may struggle to construct, and might sometimes not even recognize, a genuinely random lottery—were raised in the previous chapter. There is, however, one specific objection which has thus far been skirted and which needs to be developed.

The objection, in essence, is that a non-weighted lottery according equality of chances may turn out to operate in a discriminatory fashion. This objection might, at first glance, seem rather puzzling. Certainly we have seen already in this study that the fact that a lottery does not guarantee equiprobability of outcomes does not mean that such a lottery must be unfair.[59] A lottery which is intended, and yet which fails, to accord statistically equal odds to all candidates may still be fair if nobody either knew or believed that it favoured any particular candidate.[60] If, for example, the point of the 1970 draft lottery in the United States had been to select not all possible birth-dates but only one, then the accidental failure to ensure adequate mixing of all the capsules 'would not make the drawing unfair, since neither the allocator nor the potential conscripts would have any idea of who was (dis)favored, and there could be no distributional objection to the choice of one individual rather than another'.[61] Of course, repeated drawings from this lottery may—as, indeed, it was argued before certain courts at the time—have a disproportionate impact on identifiable groups. But this disproportionality could have been yielded even if the capsules had been adequately mixed. A lottery which accords equality of chances to all candidates may still produce outcomes which look biased.

That an outcome arrived at by virtue of a randomized procedure looks biased does not, of course, mean that it is biased. Indeed, one reason for using non-weighted lotteries in order to make allocations is that the outcome will be randomly as opposed to arbitrarily determined: selections, in such instances, are attributable to luck rather than to human preference. It is quite often the case that randomization is relied upon actually to combat arbitrariness or guard against bias. Application of random methods for these purposes is a common feature of scientific experimentation.[62] Consider the use of randomization in clinical trials.

[59]   See Sher (above, n. 11), *passim*; Lewis A. Kornhauser and Lawrence G. Sager, 'Just Lotteries' (1988) 27 *Social Science Information* 483–516; and David Wasserman, 'Let Them Eat Chances: Probability and Distributive Justice' (1996) 12 *Economics and Philosophy* 29–49.

[60]   Conversely, a lottery which successfully accords statistically equal odds might, in certain circumstances, be unfair. Consider, for example, Broome's observation (above, n. 4), 51–2, that an equiprobable randomized procedure for assigning scarce life-saving medical resources treats claimants of different ages unequally in so far as it does not treat a year saved by the younger claimant as having the same value as a year saved by the older claimant.

[61]   Wasserman (above, n. 59), 41.

[62]   On randomization as the most effective way to eliminate bias in scientific experiments, see Sir Ronald A. Fisher, *The Design of Experiments* (8th edn., Edinburgh: Oliver and Boyd, 1966), 17–21, 41–4. For a critique of Fisher's own applications of randomizing techniques in agricultural

Randomized clinical trials are quite frequently considered to be ethically problematic, not least because entering patients into such trials—although valuable as a means of trying to determine medical advancement—will not always be in their best interests.[63] Thus it is that there has emerged in this area a large literature dealing with the issue of informed consent.[64] By and large, however, medical practitioners appear to regard the randomized clinical trial as something akin to a necessary evil. '[T]he only rigorous method' of comparing treatments, it has been suggested, 'remains the properly randomized experiment. Its use cannot be avoided.'[65]

The primary argument in favour of randomized clinical trials is that they reduce the possibility of bias in experimentation. In order to test the impact of a new medication on a particular condition, for example, a clinical researcher might randomly divide a set of patients into two groups and allocate the new medication to one group while providing a dummy treatment or placebo for the other group. By randomizing the allocation of treatments, the patient ought not to know which one he or she is receiving. Indeed, the trial may be set up so as to ensure 'double blinding', so that the relevant information about treatments is concealed from both patient and doctor. Double blinding may be considered a valuable strategy where there exists concern that the person responsible for allocating patients to treatment-groups will, unwittingly or otherwise, demonstrate bias. Randomization 'does not ensure blinding, but it is difficult to arrange any form of blinding without randomization'.[66] By endeavouring to keep patients, or both patients and doctors, blind, clinical researchers ought to be able to acquire an accurate impression of the effectiveness or otherwise of new medication. The randomized experiment, in short, performs a distortion-stripping, truth-detecting role in clinical research. The use of

field experiments, cf. Isaac Levi, 'Direct Inference and Randomization', in Peter D. Asquith and Thomas Nickles (eds.), *PSA 1982: Proceedings of the 1982 Biennial Meeting of the Philosophy of Science Association* (2 vols., East Lansing, Mich.: Philosophy of Science Association, 1983), ii. 447–63. The idea that randomizing techniques might profitably be used in the design of experiments appears to have emerged during the latter half of the 19th cent.: see Ian Hacking, 'Telepathy: Origins of Randomization in Experimental Design' (1988) 79 *Isis* 427–51.

[63] See Arthur Schafer, 'The Ethics of the Randomized Clinical Trial' (1982) 307 *New England Journal of Medicine* 719–24. On the advantages and drawbacks of such trials, cf. generally the special issue of the *British Medical Journal* on 'The Randomised Controlled Trial at 50' (1998) 317 *BMJ* 1167–1248.

[64] For an overview, see Sophie Botros, 'Equipoise, Consent and the Ethics of Randomised Clinical Trials', in Peter Byrne (ed.), *Ethics and Law in Health Care and Research* (Chichester: Wiley, 1990), 9–24.

[65] Daniel Schwartz, Robert Flamant, and Joseph Lellouch, *Clinical Trials* (Eng. trans. M. J. R. Healy, London: Academic Press, 1980 (1970)), 15. For another illustration of the argument that randomization in this context is a necessary evil, see Michael Baum, 'The Ethics of Clinical Research', in Byrne (above, n. 64), 1–7.

[66] Aviva Petrie, 'Why Randomization is Essential and How to Do It', in Niels Tygstrup, John M. Lachin and Erik Juhl (eds.), *The Randomized Clinical Trial and Therapeutic Decisions* (New York: Marcel Dekker, 1982), 105–16 at 106; and cf. also *Guidelines on the Practice of Ethics Committees in Medical Research Involving Human Subjects* (3rd edn., London: Royal College of Physicians, Aug. 1996), § 6. 28.

randomization in clinical trials, that is, ought to reduce the likelihood that results will be contaminated by bias.

Yet it is possible—and this, for our purposes, is the important point—for a randomized clinical trial to conceal bias. Those responsible for setting up the trial may have 'a natural inclination to bias the design toward obtaining favorable results'.[67] Before patients are randomly allocated to treatments, for example, clinicians may introduce a degree of bias in determining which patients ought to be asked to participate in the trial. Clinicians are often, and understandably, inclined to approach those patients who appear most likely to consent.[68] Perhaps of greater concern is the fact that clinicians will sometimes prefer to approach healthier patients who, being likely to respond well to treatment, may place the drug on trial in an unduly flattering light.[69]

The general point being developed here might be expressed thus: to construct a lottery is not only to ascertain who should be eligible for entry into the pool, but also to determine who should be excluded. Entry into a lottery will often require that one meets certain requirements. Someone seeking entry into a lottery pool who fails to satisfy the criteria for admission might be minded to question the appropriateness of those criteria. Although the lottery might accord equal treatment to those within the pool, the determination of how people become eligible to enter that pool requires discrimination.[70]

This discrimination may or may not be difficult to justify. Consider, for example, the possibility of a lottery being biased in favour of those with relevant knowledge. With some lotteries, this bias will not arise. If the pool of eligibles is selected without there being any need to apply to be considered—as would normally be the case, for instance, with a draft lottery—knowledge-based bias will not be a problem. With other lotteries, the possibility of this bias arising will be so minimal as to be uncontroversial. Where the number of potential applicants is small, for example, and all of those potential applicants ought to have no difficulty in discovering that they are eligible to enter the lottery pool, it is unlikely that anyone will contend that they were disadvantaged owing to a lack of knowledge. The situation will probably be different, however, if information concerning eligibility for a lottery pool is poorly disseminated or difficult to comprehend.

---

[67] Patrick Suppes, 'Arguments for Randomizing', in Asquith and Nickles (above, n. 62), ii. 464–75 at 469.

[68] See Marvin Zelen, 'A New Design for Randomized Clinical Trials' (1979) 300 *New England Journal of Medicine* 1242–5 at 1245.

[69] See further David L. Sackett, 'The Competing Objectives of Randomized Trials' (1980) 303 *New England Journal of Medicine* 1059–60 at 1059.

[70] In certain instances, a lottery might be considered to be biased because of its failure sufficiently to discriminate among candidates. For example, it may sometimes be the case—one could envisage this sort of problem arising in relation to tax inspection, say, or baggage inspection at airports—that a strictly random inspections procedure will be seen to be biased in favour of offenders, owing to the fact that those carrying out inspections will not be relying on their instincts in determining who to inspect. Randomization, in short, will not target those who are more likely to be guilty.

The introduction of a poorly advertised or complicated applications process operates as an allocative filter, since not all potential applicants will have the knowledge or other resources necessary in order to follow through the bureaucratic procedures which stand between them and their entitlements.[71] It is important to stress that knowledge is not the only barrier which might be erected. Similar issues arise when people are required to buy their way into (or, for that matter, out of) a lottery pool. Problems concerning bias occur, moreover, not only with lotteries but with any allocative mechanism which requires prospective candidates to satisfy criteria of eligibility.[72]

There is another way in which non-weighted lotteries can incorporate bias. '[O]perating a lottery', Elster observes, 'requires procedural decisions with considerable scope for choice.'[73] Instituting a lottery may demand that a variety of procedurally oriented decisions be reached. Precisely what sort of lottery do we want? Ought we to practise double-sortition? Are there other ways in which we might safeguard randomization? The operation of a lottery may minimize, but it does not eliminate, human choice and agency. That this is so becomes even clearer if we turn our attention away from procedure and towards outcomes. Although lotteries may allow for a potentially limitless number of outcomes, the range of conceivable outcomes offered by any particular lottery will often be quite narrow.

In so far as there is a problem here, it is not with the phenomenon of randomization but with the bounded nature of human imagination. A species which is fundamentally inclined to seek explanations for, and establish connections

---

[71] See Calabresi and Bobbitt (above, n. 1), 96; and Elster (above, n. 34), 115.

[72] Non-weighted lotteries might also be considered biased for the reason that they do not challenge current distributions of resources. A fairly recent in-house document prepared on behalf of the Equal Opportunities Commission for Northern Ireland notes, for example, that one of the drawbacks of using random selection in order to recruit employees is that this mode of selection does not address underlying inequalities among those within the applicant pool: see Janet Trewsdale, *An Assessment of Random Selection Procedures* (Belfast: EOC (NI), [1998]), §12. 2. Those familiar with the economic analysis of law will know that the neo-classical perspective is often criticized for reinforcing the *status quo* (and so favouring those who already possess considerable wealth) by accepting the existing distribution of entitlements among citizens: for two classic developments of this criticism, see C. Edwin Baker, 'The Ideology of the Economic Analysis of Law' (1975) 5 *Philosophy and Public Affairs* 3–48; and Lucian A. Bebchuk, 'The Pursuit of a Bigger Pie: Can Everyone Expect a Bigger Slice?' (1980) 8 *Hofstra L. Rev.* 671–709. A similar observation might be made in relation to randomized resource-allocation: i.e. as allocative devices, non-weighted lotteries cannot in themselves guarantee the redress of biased resource-distributions. Thus we find Hapgood, in a study which by and large shows him to be very much in favour of more extensive resort to randomized social decision-making, concluding (above, n. 2) that the 'strongest objection' to the use of lotteries for allocative purposes is that they 'do nothing about inequalities in the present distribution of power and money' (p. 42). To claim that lotteries do nothing about such inequalities is an overstatement. They may well redress inequalities—but whether or not they do will be a matter of chance. Whereas markets, being (to a large degree) driven by human preferences, have the capacity to alter distributions of economic entitlements, non-weighted lotteries are not similarly responsive: there is, in short, no comparable invisible hand of chance.

[73] Elster (above, n. 34), 64.

among, events will almost inevitably struggle to grasp randomness.[74] During the twentieth century, and particularly during its second half, the ability of human beings to generate and utilize randomness has advanced remarkably.[75] The reason for this is not that human beings have in themselves become better randomizers— we have not[76]—but that massive strides have been made in computer technology and programming.[77] Generation of random numbers by computer became feasible only in the late 1940s.[78] Prior to that, the systematic generation of random numbers was considered, in the main, to be an odd idea.[79] The mathematician, von Neumann, remarked as late in the day as 1951 that '[a]ny one who considers arithmetical methods of producing random digits is, of course, in a state of sin'.[80] Yet this remark came precisely during the era in which scientific attitudes concerning the generation of randomness by deterministic formulae, and through computer programming, were undergoing radical revision.[81] 'The generation of random numbers', Gardner remarked during the 1970s, has become 'too important to be left to chance'.[82] 'Today, random numbers are needed for economic

[74] On the elusiveness of randomness, see William A. Dembski, *The Design Inference: Eliminating Chance Through Small Probabilities* (Cambridge: Cambridge University Press, 1998), 32–5, 138–45, 167–74; Aaldert Compagner, 'Definitions of Randomness' (1991) 59 *American Journal of Physics* 700–5; Ricardo Aguayo, Geoff Simms, and P. B. Siegel, 'Throwing Nature's Dice' (1996) 64 *American Journal of Physics* 752–8; and Mark Kac, 'What is Random?' (1983) 71 *American Scientist* 405–6. Kac (ibid. 405) observes that '[i]f pressed for a definition of randomness, most people will fall back on such formulations as "lack of regularity" or "unpredictability." But they are then faced with the equally difficult task of defining "regularity" or "predictability," and soon find themselves immersed in metaphysics.'

[75] See, generally, Alfred M. Bork, 'Randomness and the Twentieth Century' (1967) 27 *Antioch Review* 40–61.

[76] See, generally, W. A. Wagenaar, 'Generation of Random Sequences by Human Subjects: A Critical Survey of Literature' (1972) 77 *Psychological Bulletin* 65–72.

[77] See, e.g., George Marsaglia and Arif Zaman, 'A New Class of Random Number Generators' (1991) 1 *Annals of Applied Probability* 462–80.

[78] Much of the pioneering work in this area was undertaken at the University of Manchester by the mathematician, Alan Turing. By the autumn of 1949, Turing and his associates had developed a random number generator which exploited the noise created by the random movement of electrons within electronic circuitry: see Andrew Hodges, *Alan Turing: The Enigma of Intelligence* (London: Unwin, 1983), 402. That Turing's system 'produced truly random numbers', as Hodges claims (ibid.), is in fact questionable: cf. Martin Campbell-Kelly, 'Programming the Mark I: Early Programming Activity at the University of Manchester' (1980) 2 *Annals of the History of Computing* 130–68 at 136 ('At the request of Turing an instruction to generate a random number from a noise source was provided. Unfortunately, the numbers turned out to be not particularly random, and debugging was difficult because programmes were not repeatable; consequently, the instruction eventually fell into disuse.')

[79] '[B]efore the twentieth-century no one would even have thought of the *possibility* of producing a book [of random digits]; no one would have seen any use for it. A rational nineteenth-century man would have thought it the height of folly to produce [such] a book.' Bork (above, n. 75), 40.

[80] John von Neumann, 'Various Techniques Used in Connection with Random Digits' (1951) 3 *Journal of Research of the National Bureau of Standards (Applied Mathematics Ser.)* 36–8 at 36.

[81] With regard to both mathematically and computer-generated randomness, indeed, von Neumann would himself soon become an apostate: see Herman H. Goldstine, *The Computer from Pascal to von Neumann* (Princeton: Princeton University Press, 1972), 295–7; and Bennett (above, n. 44), 141–2.

[82] Martin Gardner, *Mathematical Carnival* (London: Allen & Unwin, 1976), 169.

models (predicting when the bond market will decline and by how much) and traffic models (predicting when a car will reach an intersection or when a car will run a red light). Computer models that simulate molecular movement or the behavior of galaxies require vast quantities of random numbers.'[83] Not only has computer power made us more able to generate vast quantities of random digits, but we have also had little difficulty in making such digits an important feature of modern life.[84]

Yet our increased ability to generate and utilize random digits reveals primarily the limits, rather than an advancement, of our cognitive capacities. For the fact of the matter is that, in social and legal decision-making contexts, we almost invariably will not want—indeed, will lack the capacity to use—complex lotteries which can provide an abundance of random numbers. Even the most visionary of decision-makers will usually be able to think of only a very limited number of desirable possible outcomes.[85] In Luke Rhinehart's novel, *The Dice Man*, the protagonist supposedly becomes more liberated by abandoning free will and allowing his behaviour and the majority of his actions to be determined by the fall of the dice. 'Create the options. Shake the dice. All else is nonsense.'[86] While, however, the protagonist has no difficulty at all with shaking the dice, he is constantly struggling to think up new options. Hence, living by the dice turns out to be more oppressive than liberating.[87] Human beings will surely always be condemned thus. A random device will offer a number of possible draws. We are obviously able to increase the number of possible draws as our capability for generating random digits improves. Decision-makers, however, must marry possible draws to desirable outcomes. While most random devices offer a plethora of draws, our ability to devise a broad range of feasible social choices is, by comparison, markedly limited.

One might object that the point being made here concerns not bias but incapability: there are limits to what humans can do with randomness, since random outcomes have to be vested with significance. In relation to social decision-making,

---

[83] Bennett (above, n. 44), 150–1.

[84] See Robert Matthews, 'It's a Lottery' (1995) 147 *New Scientist* 38–42 at 39 (arguing that 'the need to conjure . . . up [randomness] on demand has never been greater'). While the discussion here hinges upon the use of computers to generate random digits, it is of course possible for computers to generate other random phenomena (for a mildly irreverent—Sokalesque—illustration, cf. <http://www.cs.monash.edu.au/links/postmodern.html> visited 11 Nov. 1998).

[85] See, more generally, Christopher Cherniak, *Minimal Rationality* (Cambridge, Mass.: MIT Press, 1986).

[86] Luke Rhinehart, *The Dice Man* (London: HarperCollins, 1994 (1972)), 541. For an intriguing comparison, cf. Paul Feyerabend, *Against Method: Outline of an Anarchistic Theory of Knowledge* (London: Verso, 1978 (1975)), 215–20 esp. at 218–19: 'Remove the principles, admit the possibility of many different forms of life, and such ["rationalist"] phenomena will disappear like a bad dream.' Unlike Rhinehart's protagonist, Feyerabend urges liberation through anarchism or Dadaism rather than through dice-casting.

[87] See Rhinehart (above, n. 86), 195–6; and also Pierre Moessinger, *Irrationalité individuelle et ordre social* (Geneva: Droz, 1996), 172–6.

none the less, the issue of bias arises because, when we formulate our repertoire of options, we have to make judgements concerning what are and what are not desirable outcomes. The lottery, it could be said, is rather like an empty vessel. Biases emerge when we decide what ought to be put into that vessel. Although a lottery might be considered to be procedurally fair because it demonstrates no favouritism towards any particular candidate (or candidates), the outcomes which have been connected with possible draws may not only be limited but also appear insufficient. The point, in essence, is that it is possible to select in an unbiased fashion from a range of options which is restricted to the extent that it betrays bias.

3. UNCERTAINTY

As a tool of social decision-making, the lottery tends to be either used or recommended for the purpose of negotiating uncertainty. We resort, or might be inclined to resort, to randomization when we find ourselves unable to make either satisfactory differentiations or convincing comparisons: sometimes, we may consider people or objects to be so alike as to be indistinguishable or so distinct as to be incommensurable.[88]

The problem of indistinguishability, Buridan's ass notwithstanding,[89] rarely troubles us deeply. It sometimes appears that we pick at random when there is little, if any, point in making the effort to do otherwise. While I cannot be certain that there are no differences among the apparently identical boxes of Kleenex tissues which fill the supermarket shelf—for all I know, the contents may vary slightly from one box to the next—I have neither the inclination nor the capacity to distinguish them, and so I devote hardly any thought to my mode of selection. Even when goods can be distinguished, shoppers will still, on occasions, appear to pick at random because they will consider deliberation over alternatives to be too time-consuming.

Whether people really are picking at random in such instances is often questionable. It is probably the case that we are generally better at choosing than we are at picking: that, even when faced with what appear to be identical alternatives, we will often have some reason—unconscious of it though we may be—for selecting one alternative as opposed to any of the others.[90] This is not to assert that human beings are incapable of making random selections—we select in this manner when we open a book at no particular page or (to return to an earlier image) stoop to pick a blade of grass from a field. The

---

[88]   See Elster (above, n. 3), 107–9.

[89]   See, generally, Nicholas Rescher, 'Choice Without Preference: A Study of the History and of the Logic of the Problem of "Buridan's Ass" ' (1959–60) 51 *Kant Studien* 142–75.

[90]   On the distinction between selecting with and selecting without preference, see Edna Ullmann-Margalit and Sidney Morgenbesser, 'Picking and Choosing' (1977) 44 *Social Research* 757–85.

human capacity to randomize seems, however, to be markedly limited. With most selections, we discern distinctions—trivial or strange though these distinctions may often be—among the alternatives. Should it be the case that we cannot distinguish among alternatives, that we cannot make a choice, we might decide to employ a randomizing device which can, as it were, pick on our behalf.[91]

A greater problem of uncertainty is likely to be posed not when we are unable to detect differences but when those differences are so vast that we cannot compare them and use them as a basis for choosing among alternatives. The differences which we perceive among choices will sometimes, in one way or another, overwhelm us. Rather than choose in such a situation, we might decide not to choose and so delegate, as it were, the power of selection to a randomizing device.[92] It is important to emphasize, however, that resort to a lottery here may enable us to deal with, but will not eradicate, uncertainty: although the lottery may select an alternative on our behalf, it will not render the alternatives commensurable.[93]

Recourse to sortition may create new uncertainties. If one decides an issue by resort to lot, one cannot say anything—beyond reference to the fact that this is how one decided—to explain the outcome: one is uncertain of why the matter was decided thus. No reasons or justification can be offered, other than that this is what chance dictated. Those awaiting a decision which is to be arrived at by lot will, moreover, probably consider their prospects of getting a favourable outcome to be no more certain—very likely more uncertain—than would be the case were any other decision-making method to be adopted. If a lottery is instituted for the purpose of assigning undesirable burdens among candidates who are considered to be indistinguishable, the fact that this lottery will generate an outcome which is uncertain could, prior to the draw, cause candidates to feel demoralized. With regard to institutions, furthermore, the uncertainty of lottery-generated outcomes might rule out the possibility of long-term planning—indeed, it was noted in Chapter 2 that this is one of the principal arguments against random selection of political representatives.

Lotteries, then, can generate, just as they might quell, uncertainty. Yet uncertainty,

---

[91] Should it ever be the case that people are absolutely indifferent as between alternatives, one might question why they should wish to use a lottery, as opposed to any other decision-making device, to execute the task of picking. In the event of indifference, after all, would it not be the case that one decision-making method would be as good as another? I suspect that the answer to this question is that it will all depend on the nature of the decision. Although the decision-makers might express indifference, and so have no reason to prefer a lottery over any other decision-mechanism, they may still be concerned about justifying the decision to those whom it affects. Depending upon context, resort to some decision-mechanisms may be easier to justify than resort to others.

[92] See Cass R. Sunstein and Edna Ullmann-Margalit, *Second-Order Decisions* (John M. Olin Law and Economics Working Paper, 2nd ser. 57, Law School, University of Chicago, June 1998), 12.

[93] See Calabresi and Bobbitt (above, n. 1), 41–2.

worrisome though it may be, can be put to constructive uses.[94] The uncertainty generated by lotteries is of especial value when, for one reason or another, elimination of predictability is a desideratum. It is better, we have noted already, that the assignment of certain social tasks be unpredictable: jurors selected well in advance of trial might be more susceptible to bribes and threats, and the incentive for conscripts to engage in self-mutilation is likely to be all the greater when they can confidently anticipate being selected for service. Similarly with regard to the assignment of scarce social resources: if potential recipients are made aware of the criteria of eligibility for public housing, say, or certain forms of medical treatment, then in certain instances they may engage in actions which not only ensure that they satisfy those criteria but also entail considerable cost for themselves and possibly others. In contexts such as these, the uncertainty created by randomization seems to perform a socially useful function. Uncertainty generated by randomized inspections functions similarly: it may be difficult temporarily to modify behaviour in preparation for inspections which have not been signalled in advance.

There are other ways in which uncertainty created through randomization might eliminate complacency and prove motivational. In various contexts, it is conceivable that the employment of randomizing techniques, while capable of generating negative organizational 'atmosphere' among those affected,[95] might promote desirable institutional goals. One can envisage, for example, that organizations concerned about homogeneity and lack of dynamism among personnel might derive some benefit from randomly moving goalposts, as it were, so that, from one promotional round to the next, candidates—not knowing which criteria for promotion will be prioritized—will lack an incentive to conform to the traditional organizational type. To offer another example—which, for some, may be fairly close to home—when universities accept greater numbers of students, one likely consequence is an escalation in staff marking-loads. Faculties may want to counter this escalation without adopting a mode of assessment which allows students to pass by studying only a small portion of the course. One strategy which faculties might adopt in order to keep marking-loads at reasonable levels,

[94] See, in general, Robyn M. Dawes, *Rational Choice in an Uncertain World* (San Diego: Harcourt Brace Jovanovich, 1988), 256–73; and also, with regard to the specific idea that 'unpredictability is power', Albert O. Hirschman, *The Passions and the Interests: Political Arguments for Capitalism before its Triumph* (Princeton: Princeton University Press, 1977), 50. To draw attention to but one discipline, it is possible to discover throughout the literature of political theory numerous arguments to the effect that the creation of states of uncertainty possesses the capacity to liberate, enlighten, or otherwise bring out the best in people: see, e.g., John Rawls, *A Theory of Justice* (Oxford: Oxford University Press, 1972), 136–42; and Roberto Mangabeira Unger, *False Necessity: Anti-Necessitarian Social Theory in the Service of Radical Democracy (Part I of Politics, a Work in Constructive Social Theory)* (Cambridge: Cambridge University Press, 1987), 35–6, 530–5.

[95] On 'atmosphere' within institutional settings, cf. Oliver E. Williamson, *Markets and Hierarchies: Analysis and Antitrust Implications* (New York: Free Press, 1975), 37–40, 79–80. Michelman is concerned with much the same phenomenon when he develops the idea of 'demoralization costs': see Frank I. Michelman, 'Property, Utility, and Fairness: Comments on the Ethical Foundations of "Just Compensation" Law' (1967) 80 *Harvard L. Rev.* 1165–1258 at 1214–15.

while ensuring that most students take courses seriously, would be, within any particular course, to set, say, four compulsory written assignments throughout the academic session and to inform students that two of their four essays will be selected at random and marked in order to determine their degree classification in that course.

The notion that randomized decisions might be put to strategic uses is prominent within game theory. The central theorem, or solution concept, in game theory is the so-called Nash equilibrium,[96] which stipulates that all games in which players do not cooperate with one another must have an equilibrium point—a point at which, given the different strategies adopted by each player, no participant in the game will be able to improve upon his or her position by adopting a new strategy. In a two-person non-cooperative game—to try to put the point as simply as possible—the strategies of both players will form a Nash equilibrium if the strategy adopted by each player is one which, given the other player's strategy, cannot be bettered. That a set of strategies constitutes a Nash equilibrium within any particular game will be evident from the fact that no player will have an incentive to deviate from his or her strategy (so long as none of the other players deviates from his or her own strategy).

A Nash equilibrium is said to be comprised of pure strategies when there is associated with each player a specific strategy which he or she should adopt. A Nash equilibrium may also consist of mixed strategies whereby, in equilibrium, each player adopts a strategy which randomizes among—or, more precisely, operates as a weighted lottery over—the available pure strategies. The notion of a Nash equilibrium, and the difference between pure and mixed strategies, might seem less abstruse if we consider an illustration[97] (see Figure 1). As a landowner on the side of a river, it may be in my interests to maintain my embankment, but only if my neighbour on the same side of the river maintains his embankment. Let us assume that neither I nor my neighbour is prepared to cooperate with the other and that neither of us is able to find out what the other intends to do. Should neither of us maintain an embankment, we will both suffer damage in the event of a flood. Maintaining an embankment costs £4,000, and a flood brings damages of £6,000: if we both maintain an embankment (at a cost of £4,000 each), there will be no flooding; if neither of us maintains an embankment (thus incurring no maintenance costs), we will each suffer flood damage of £6,000. If one of us maintains an embankment and the other fails to maintain, he who maintains will

---

[96] So named after John Nash, who expounded and developed the concept in the early 1950s: for the primary works, see John Nash, 'The Bargaining Problem' (1950) 18 *Econometrica* 155–62; 'Equilibrium Points in N-Person Games' (1950) 36 *Proceedings of the National Academy of Sciences* 48–9; 'Noncooperative Games' (1951) 54 *Annals of Mathematics* 289–95; and 'Two-Person Cooperative Games' (1953) 21 *Econometrica* 128–40. For an account of Nash's bizarre career, see the biography by Sylvia Nasar, *A Beautiful Mind* (London: Faber & Faber, 1998).

[97] This illustration is adapted from Douglas G. Baird, Robert H. Gertner, and Randal C. Picker, *Game Theory and the Law* (Cambridge, Mass.: Harvard University Press, 1994), 35–9.

Landowner 2

	Maintain	Fail to maintain
Maintain	–£4k, –£4k	–£10k, –£6k
Fail to maintain	–£6k, –£10k	–£6k, –£6k

Landowner 1

Fig 1

suffer flood damage of £6,000 and also incur maintenance costs of £4,000, while he who fails to maintain will suffer flood damage of £6,000 but incur no maintenance costs.

In game-theoretic terms, it can be said that a Nash equilibrium is formed in this scenario when each landowner adopts the strategy of maintaining his embankment: if I maintain my embankment, my neighbour's best response is to maintain his embankment also, since this strategy will cost each of us £4,000 as opposed to £6,000. The problem, of course, is that neither of us can be sure that this is the strategy which the other will adopt. The reason for this is that there is, in this scenario, more than one possible Nash equilibrium point. A Nash equilibrium will also be formed if neither of us maintains an embankment: if one of us fails to maintain, the best response of the other is to do likewise, since the decision by one of us not to maintain means that the other will suffer from flooding in any event. If neither of us maintains, we each suffer flood damage of £6,000; should one of us maintain, however, that person will suffer the same amount of flood damage and incur maintenance costs of £4,000. Given that each of us would prefer a loss of £6,000 to a loss of £10,000, an alternative Nash equilibrium will be formed if we both decide on a strategy of non-maintenance.

In this scenario, a Nash equilibrium of the pure-strategy type will be formed if both parties decide to maintain their embankments. The same type of Nash equilibrium will be formed if both parties decide not to maintain their embankments. It is also possible, in this situation, for there to be formed a Nash equilibrium of the mixed-strategy type. A conceivable mixed strategy here would be for one of the landowners to toss a coin in order to determine whether or not he should maintain his embankment. However, this particular strategy—resort to a non-weighted lottery which accords equal chances to the options of maintenance or non-maintenance—is not part of a Nash equilibrium. This much is evident if we consider the best possible response of the other landowner: if I were to toss a coin to determine whether or not I should maintain my embankment, what are my neighbour's expected losses should he either fail to maintain or maintain his embankment? We already know what happens in the event of failure to maintain: for either landowner, the cost of non-maintenance is always flood damage of £6,000. With regard to the alternative, if I were to adopt the mixed strategy of tossing a coin in order to decide whether or not to maintain, my neighbour could expect a loss of £7,000 were he to maintain his embankment (since he incurs a maintenance cost of £4,000 and has a 50 per cent chance of suffering flood damage of £6,000). To put the point mathematically: $(1 \times -4) + (0.5 \times -6) = -7$.[98] Should either landowner decide on the mixed strategy of tossing a coin, accordingly, the other's best response will be not to maintain his embankment. Moreover, should one party decide not to maintain, the other party would do best to adopt the same strategy rather than to toss a coin. For where one landowner has resolved not to maintain, the expected cost for the other landowner of tossing a coin is £8,000 (a 50 per cent chance of incurring a loss of £6,000 and a 50 per cent chance of the loss being £10,000). Again, mathematically: $(0.5 \times -6) + (0.5 \times -10) = -8$.

How, then, might mixed strategies produce Nash equilibria? In the illustration being used here, a landowner ought to be willing to adopt a mixed strategy— ought to be willing, that is, to select randomly between the two pure strategies— only if the cost of adopting either of the two pure strategies is the same. We know that unless I maintain my embankment, my neighbour would do best not to maintain his. Let p_1 be the probability of my maintaining, and $1-p_1$ be the corresponding probability of my not maintaining, my embankment. To determine how much cost my neighbour can expect to incur for maintaining his embankment in relation to any probability that I will or will not maintain my embankment, we must add $-4 \times p_1$ and $-10 \times (1-p_1)$. Whether or not this amount will be greater or less than the cost that my neighbour will definitely incur for not maintaining (£6,000) will depend on the value of p_1. My neighbour's expected cost for maintaining his embankment will be equal to the cost of not maintaining only when p_1 has a value of ⅔—that is, when there is a two-thirds probability that I will maintain my embankment. Unless I am twice as likely to maintain as not, my neighbour will not be willing to incur a certain loss of £6,000 in exchange for the possibility of losing only £4,000 but with a risk of losing £10,000.

If, accordingly, there is a two-thirds probability that I will maintain my embankment, my neighbour ought to be indifferent as between maintaining and not maintaining his embankment: either strategy will cost him the same amount *ex ante*. A Nash equilibrium composed of mixed strategies would arise in this scenario if both my neighbour and I were to select randomly between the two pure strategies (of maintaining or not maintaining) while weighting our lotteries so as to accord a two-thirds probability to the option of maintaining. Where we each adopt a mixed strategy of maintaining with two-thirds probability, we choose a best response given the strategy of the other.

For all that the illustration which has just been developed demonstrates game theory quite simplistically, one might be left with the impression that the enterprise requires considerable intellectual effort and suspension of disbelief in order

---

[98] An alternative relevant calculation would be: $(0.5 \times -4) + (0.5 \times -10) = -7$.

to generate rather meagre insights. One problem with game-theoretic reasoning is that it invariably points not to a best solution, but to a number of equally good solutions.[99] Even in the very simple, two-person illustration which we have been using, it is possible to discern three different Nash equilibria (the two pure strategies of maintaining or not maintaining the embankment, and the mixed strategy of maintaining with two-thirds probability). The problem here is not so much that game theory formalizes ambiguity—that it demonstrates by way of modelling that the best way for a player to proceed will depend on what the other players do—but that, with many games, it will be impossible to identify all conceivable equilibria. Although game theorists have endeavoured to refine the Nash equilibrium concept so as to limit the range of possible equilibria for some games,[100] the fact remains that many games allow for sets of equilibria so large as to ensure that attempts to determine the best solutions for those games will always turn out to be incomplete.[101]

If one leaves aside the problem of multiple equilibria and attempts to apply game theory to real strategic interactions, the difficulties with the approach begin to appear more far-reaching. Even in the illustration which has been used here, contestable assumptions are being made concerning the human capacity to deal with information and exercise rational choice (let alone the artificiality of assuming that flood damage will always amount to £6,000).[102] For any player, a mixed strategy will only ever be rationally prescribed where he can anticipate the course of action that will be adopted by the other player (or players). Choosing a mixed strategy on anything other than an arbitrary basis would require a degree of information which is almost as unlikely to be available in everyday decision-making contexts as it is in hypothetical non-cooperative games. In many real-life interactions, furthermore, the strategies of those with whom one interacts cannot be taken as given: equilibrium points will rarely be stable because 'players' frequently alter their strategies.[103] Even if, within any particular game, there is a

---

[99] There is a fairly large literature on this issue. For an overview, see Ian Ayres, 'Playing Games with the Law' (1990) 42 *Stanford L. Rev.* 1291–1317 at 1310–11.

[100] See Roger B. Myerson, *Game Theory: Analysis of Conflict* (Cambridge, Mass.: Harvard University Press, 1991), 108–14.

[101] The converse difficulty is that some games do not embody any Nash equilibria: for an illustration, see Martin van Hees, *Rights and Decisions: Formal Models of Law and Liberalism* (Dordrecht: Kluwer, 1995), 137–8.

[102] The rationality assumptions underlying game theory are much the same as those underlying neo-classical economics. There is an abundance of critical literature on these assumptions: one of the best examples is Richard H. Thaler, *The Winner's Curse: Paradoxes and Anomalies of Economic Life* (Princeton: Princeton University Press, 1992).

[103] Within game-theoretic literature, the tendency has been to try to develop models within which players will choose not to deviate from their strategies. Harsanyi, for example, has suggested that players might be inclined to stick to their chosen strategies where games are modelled in such a way that losses (or, more precisely, payoffs) are randomly altered so that each player is uncertain of the other players' precise payoffs: see John C. Harsanyi, 'Games with Randomly Disturbed Payoffs: A New Rationale for Mixed-Strategy Equilibrium Points' (1973) 2 *International Journal of Game Theory* 1–23.

stable Nash equilibrium which can be reached, its attainment will not necessarily benefit participants. This much is obvious from that hardy perennial of game theory, the prisoner's dilemma. The scenario is so commonplace that it hardly needs recounting.[104] Two prisoners, each suspected of a crime, are interrogated individually and offered the same deal. Each is told that if he confesses to the crime, and the other prisoner does not confess, he will be a witness for the prosecution and freed without charge; if he does not confess, and the other prisoner does, he will receive a maximum sentence of ten years; if both confess, they will each be convicted of the crime and receive a five-year sentence; and if neither confesses, each will be convicted of a lesser crime carrying a one-year sentence. The only Nash equilibrium for the prisoner's dilemma has both parties confessing. It can be shown for each prisoner that, no matter what the other prisoner does, he is better off confessing than not confessing: if the other does not confess, then no time in jail is better than one year; if the other confesses, then five years in jail is preferable to ten. Yet if the Nash equilibrium is formed and both prisoners confess, they put themselves in a considerably worse position than if they were both not to confess.[105]

It is, of course, possible to progress further with these and other critical observations on game theory, but that would not be appropriate here. My basic objective has been to demonstrate that randomization is sometimes a key strategic feature of game-theoretic reasoning. Although, in endeavouring to demonstrate as much, I have focused on the Nash equilibrium concept, other models lend themselves to essentially the same exercise.[106] What is particularly significant for the purposes of this study is the fact that legal and regulatory theorists have recently begun to consider how the application of lotteries within games may enable us to understand better how legal frameworks might be improved so as to encourage more compliance with rules and dispute resolution. Game-theoretic analyses of compliance tend to focus on the capacity of randomly generated uncertainty to encourage cooperative behaviour.[107] One recent game-theoretic study of the possible applications of lotteries to encourage litigation settlement is rather more intriguing since it postulates that, in relation to dispute resolution, the capacity of the lottery to generate desirable incentives derives not from the fact that it creates uncertainty, but from the fact that it can be used by one litigating party to render

---

[104] See, generally, William Poundstone, *Prisoner's Dilemma: John von Neumann, Game Theory and the Puzzle of the Bomb* (New York: Doubleday, 1992).

[105] See further Brian Skyrms, *Evolution of the Social Contract* (Cambridge: Cambridge University Press, 1996), 48–9, 60–1.

[106] See, e.g., John C. Harsanyi, 'Games with Incomplete Information Played by "Bayesian" Players, I–III' (1967–8) 14 *Management Science* 159–82, 320–34, 486–502.

[107] See, e.g., Ian Ayres and John Braithwaite, *Responsive Regulation: Transcending the Deregulation Debate* (New York: Oxford University Press, 1992), 51–2, 76–7, 98, 165 n. 10, 167 n. 10; and also Neil Duxbury, 'Games and Rules' (1997) 83 *Archiv für Rechts- und Sozialphilosophie* 1–13 at 7–10.

information credible to the other.[108] Asymmetric information can prevent litigating parties from communicating credibly with one another and negotiating a settlement. Let us say, for example, that in the event of a defendant being found liable, the penalty (P) imposed on him will either be high (P-*high*) or low (P-*low*). Assume also, in a particular case, that the defendant has private information which leads him to conclude that $P = P$-*low*. The defendant may be unable to convince the plaintiff of the validity of this information, a consequence of which may be that the parties cannot reach a settlement. To communicate his information in a credible fashion, the defendant might propose that, from the outset, there be built into the dispute-settlement process a lottery element which the defendant himself might only be expected to accept were his information valid. The defendant might propose, for example, that should the parties go to trial and the plaintiff be successful in establishing liability, then if $P < X$ the defendant escapes all liability, whereas if $P \geq X$ the defendant must pay the plaintiff P. The value of X will be set so that P-*low* $< X < P$-*high*. The defendant will benefit from this arrangement if, and only if, $P < X$. If the defendant is willing to pay a large enough sum for this arrangement, the plaintiff might infer that $P = P$-*low* and so decide not to continue with the trial.[109] In this type of situation, the virtue of the lottery is that it can function as a signalling device with the capacity to reduce litigation costs.

4. The Lure of Reason

Generally, we are uncomfortable with decisions from which reason is absent.[110] Especially troublesome is the idea that it might be possible to reach a legal decision which is good even though unreasoned. While academics and judges sometimes disagree over the role of reason in adjudication,[111] a common assumption among both groups is that the alternative to reasoned adjudication is unchecked

---

[108] See James D. Miller, 'Using Lotteries to Expand the Range of Litigation Settlements' (1997) 26 *Journal of Legal Studies* 69–94 at 69–89. Miller's study lends substance to Friedman's and Savage's speculation that '[l]otteries seem to be an extremely fruitful, and much neglected, source of information about reactions of individuals to risk.' Milton Friedman and L. J. Savage, 'The Utility Analysis of Choices Involving Risk' (1948) 56 *Journal of Political Economy* 279–304 at 287.

[109] See also Miller (above, n. 108), 70–1; and Kathryn E. Spier, 'Pretrial Bargaining and the Design of Fee-Shifting Rules' (1994) 25 *RAND Journal of Economics* 197–214 at 204.

[110] '[W]e are', Calabresi and Bobbitt assert with regard to lottery decisions (above, n. 1), 49, 'born to reason and any attempt to keep someone from pointing out the unchosen choices that are being made is bound to fail.'

[111] Judges, for example, are quite often of the opinion that academic lawyers are prone to adopting too idealistic a view of the place and function of reason in adjudication: see, for example, Richard A. Posner, *The Problems of Jurisprudence* (Cambridge, Mass.: Harvard University Press, 1990), 21–3. For the argument that judges and legal theorists of necessity conceive of the role of reason (or, more specifically, principles) in adjudication in very different ways, cf. also Robert Goff, 'The Search for Principle' (1983) 69 *Proceedings of the British Academy* 169–87.

judicial discretion: if judges do not reason their way to decisions, they must decide on the basis of instinct or caprice. I have endeavoured to show elsewhere that one of the central themes—possibly the central theme—of American jurisprudence over the past century is the notion that the only way to combat arbitrariness in judicial decision-making is to generate faith in reason.[112] 'It is my belief that our society will not survive', Fuller wrote at the outset of the 1940s, 'unless . . . we . . . again come to believe that reason can have something to say concerning legal and social institutions.'[113] During that decade, and particularly in the one which followed, many prominent American academic lawyers became insistent that reasoning was essential to adjudication in a democracy.[114] Even where the outcomes determined by courts were laudable, it was argued, those outcomes would not be satisfactory if insufficiently grounded in reason; for, in the long run, the reasons for a result might prove more significant than the result itself.[115]

Contemporary American academic lawyers tend to regard the faith-in-reason perspective rather as many young Americans might (I surmise) look upon the willingness of an earlier generation to subscribe to flower-power. Although, for some time, the faith-in-reason approach occupied a position of dominance in American legal thought, it is—in that extremely restless and fashion-conscious world that is American legal scholarship—nowadays considered, more often than not, to be naive and *démodé*. While, however, many academic lawyers may now look askance at the specific school of jurisprudential thought which, in the years following the Second World War, was concerned with the promotion of faith in reason, it would be wrong to assume that reason itself has somehow gone out of fashion.[116] One commentator has recently noted that the belief that adjudication cannot be such unless it is grounded in reason remains at the core of American legal thought. According to Schlag, while 'a great number of varied and incompatible beliefs are passed off as if they were the products of reason'[117]—indeed, while 'reason' is rarely 'anything more than a pleasant name for faith, dogma, prejudice, and company'[118]—American legal thinkers are prone to deifying[119] the idea of reason

[112] See Neil Duxbury, *Patterns of American Jurisprudence* (Oxford: Clarendon Press, 1995), 205–99. A more ambitious study would probably have revealed that this so-called faith in reason was a key feature of American legal thought some time before the 20th cent. For the claim that this was the case, see Suzanna Sherry, 'The Sleep of Reason' (1996) 84 *Georgetown LJ* 453–84 at 469–70.

[113] Lon L. Fuller, *The Law in Quest of Itself* (Chicago: The Foundation Press, 1940), 126.

[114] The point is not that American academic lawyers had never offered this sort of argument before—they had (see Duxbury (above, n. 112), 210–23)—but that the argument had never before been presented so consistently.

[115] This argument is famously developed by Herbert Wechsler, 'Toward Neutral Principles of Constitutional Law' (1959) 73 *Harvard L. Rev.* 1–35 at 32–4, in relation to the US Supreme Court decision in *Brown* v. *Board of Education* (1954) 347 US 483.

[116] See Owen M. Fiss, 'Reason in All its Splendor' (1990) 56 *Brooklyn L. Rev.* 789–804.

[117] Pierre Schlag, *The Enchantment of Reason* (Durham, NC: Duke University Press, 1998), 37.

[118] Ibid. 144–5.

[119] The imagery is Schlag's: see ibid. 17; and also, from a continental European perspective, cf. Chaïm Perelman and L. Olbrechts-Tyteca, *The New Rhetoric: A Treatise on Argumentation* (Eng. trans. J. Wilkinson and P. Weaver, Notre Dame: Notre Dame University Press, 1969 (1958)), 28.

and are generally unwilling to consider the possibility of a decision-making scenario in which reason is a spent force which cannot be relied upon to yield and support an outcome. 'From the perspective of the rule-of-law ideal, the exhaustion of reason is tantamount to an admission that legal actors do not know what they are doing—that law is, in a word, lawless.'[120] Decisions which are not supported by reasons could never, on this account, be regarded as genuine legal decisions.

Lost in the Forest

I shall, at the outset of the next chapter, consider Schlag's argument further and, indeed, take issue with it. Before so doing, however, I want to try to build upon his basic observation that reason is commonly considered to be essential to legal decision-making. The specific emphasis here on legal decision-making may be something of a red herring. Although, as we shall see, consideration of legal decision-making highlights particularly well the attraction of human beings to reason, there seems in fact to be a tendency for people to seek reasons in all manner of decision-making contexts. We are inclined, Elster has argued, to try to find meaning in all phenomena.[121] We are also inclined to seek reasons for actions and occurrences, and to create reasons for actions and occurrences even when none appears to exist.[122] Faced with uncertainty, Descartes advises, our best response will be to adopt a course of action and pursue it steadfastly. The result of manufacturing reasons to combat uncertainty will be vacillation, for the reasons which we produce will not only be spurious but will tug us in different directions. '[T]ravellers lost in a forest ought not to wander this way and that, still less stand in one place, but should proceed constantly in as straight a line as possible, never changing direction for minor reasons, even though at the outset it may have been chance alone which determined the selection; for even if, in this way, they do not exactly reach the point they desire, they will at least ultimately arrive somewhere which will most likely be preferable to the middle of a forest.'[123] Since we have what appears to be 'a deep-rooted desire that the proximate causes of our decisions be reasons',[124] this advice is rarely reflected in our actions.

That this is the case is very well argued by Neurath. In an essay inspired by Descartes's parable of the travellers lost in the forest, Neurath begins with the proposition that '[i]n order to make progress one very often finds oneself in the position of having to choose one of several hypotheses of equal probability'.[125]

[120] Schlag (above, n. 117), 21.
[121] See Jon Elster, *Sour Grapes: Studies in the Subversion of Rationality* (Cambridge: Cambridge University Press, 1983), 101–8.   [122] See Elster (above, n. 3), 55–8.
[123] Descartes, *Discours de la méthode*, III. 24–5.   [124] Elster (above, n. 3), 90.
[125] Neurath (above, n. 12), 3; and cf. also John Barth, *The End of the Road* (London: Secker & Warburg, 1962 (1958)), 99 ('If the alternatives are side by side, choose the one on the left; if they're consecutive in time, choose the earlier. If neither of these applies, choose the alternative whose name begins with the earlier letter of the alphabet. These are the principles of Sinistrality, Antecedence, and Alphabetical Priority—there are others, and they're arbitrary, but useful.')

In such situations, where insight is lacking, what is one to do? According to Neurath, one might decide by instinct,[126] by reference to 'oracles, omens, prophecies and the like',[127] or by formulating reasons on which to base one's decision.[128] While the latter option is usually considered to be the most appropriate, Neurath contends, it is in fact, in instances of indeterminacy, every bit as irrational a strategy as is reliance on instinct or omens. By appealing to reason in such instances, after all, one is 'carefully consider[ing] all eventualities, weigh[ing] all arguments and counter-arguments and [reaching a decision] on the basis of inadequate premises of whose deficiencies [one] is unaware'.[129] In essence, Neurath's argument is that sometimes, in the face of indeterminacy, reason becomes exhausted. To persist with reasoning in such situations is to exhibit 'pseudorationalism'.[130]

Neurath believed that the genuinely rational course of action in such instances would be to resort to 'the unloved drawing of lots'.[131] Occasionally, we are indeed inclined to adopt this course of action. Consider, again, randomized clinical trials. One argument which has been elicited in support of such trials is that '[w]hen doctors are able to admit to themselves and their patients uncertainty about the best action . . . it cannot be less ethical to choose a treatment by random allocation within a controlled trial than to choose by what happens to be readily available, hunch, or what a drug company recommends'.[132] Randomization, in this instance, might be considered to be the least insidious method of selecting a treatment. In most instances, however, 'no one dares to cast the die, and to go honestly by the hazard'.[133] Generally, Neurath notes, 'tossing a coin to decide is considered frivolous, and the more frivolous, the more important the matter in question is. Even people who otherwise lack all piety and tradition are usually morally outraged if one suggests to them to decide by lot where insight is at an end.'[134] As Summers observes, human beings are rational animals and so 'generally prefer to order their affairs through reason than through random or arbitrary action'.[135]

Yet a genuine rationalist, Neurath argues, would surely be inclined to cherish the option of the lottery rather than to express wariness about it. After all, if one accepts that '[r]ationalism sees its chief triumph in the clear recognition of the limits of actual insight',[136] one ought to appreciate that, where insight has been exhausted, resort to lot may be the most rational course of action. We must, of course, be careful not to resort to lot too quickly: more often than not, we will be

---

[126] See Neurath (above, n. 12), 5.   [127] Ibid. 6.   [128] Ibid. 7–8.
[129] Ibid. 10.   [130] Ibid. 8.   [131] Ibid. 7.
[132] Michael B. Bracken, 'Clinical Trials and the Acceptance of Uncertainty' (1987) 294 *British Medical Journal* 1111–12 at 1111.
[133] Anthony Trollope, *Phineas Finn: The Irish Member* (ed. Jacques Berthoud, Oxford: Oxford University Press, 1982 (1869)), 204.   [134] Neurath (above, n. 12), 9.
[135] Robert S. Summers, 'Evaluating and Improving Legal Processes: A Plea for "Process Values" ' (1974) 60 *Cornell L. Rev.* 1–52 at 26.   [136] Neurath (above, n. 12), 8.

able reasonably to distinguish options and so will have no need for recourse to sortition.[137] Where, however, we do lack reasons for deciding one way rather than another, our most rational strategy, Neurath believes, is to abandon faith in reason and to assign the task of decision-making to chance. If people are averse to adopting this strategy, then there is a problem not with the strategy but with the people who exhibit this aversion: to uncover the existence of human addiction to reason when faced with uncertainty is to demonstrate the limits of our wisdom rather than the limits of the lottery as a device of social decision-making.[138] '[T]he wise man . . . is conscious of the incompleteness of his insight . . . The man who hesitates to use [the lottery], who refrains from its use, cannot be helped . . . But this is not an objection to [the lottery]; it is not a generally accepted principle that everyone can be helped.'[139]

The central message of Neurath's essay is particularly stark and challenging. His general, rather Weberian thesis[140] seems to be that the more that we aspire to be rational—indeed, the more that rationality triumphs in human affairs—the more we will find ourselves dependent on unreason. To be rational is to recognize that reason has its limits. The decision-maker who wishes to be rational must be prepared to recognize those limits and, in such instances, adopt decision-making strategies which might commonly be considered unreasonable. Thus it is that the rational response to uncertainty will sometimes be to decide by lot. There seems, however, to be a fundamental blind-spot in Neurath's argument. While it may be rational, on occasions, to concede the limits of reason, it is by no means clear why it should be rational to concede as much *and then resort to a lottery*. Neurath concludes that, in certain instances, it will be rational to resort to a lottery because it will not be rational to apply other methods of decision-making. There is here an assumption, but no explanation, of the rationality of proceeding to random selection. Is such a move really rational?

Any answer to this question will obviously depend upon how one defines rationality. It is, I think, possible to argue that deciding by lot may, in some cases, constitute a rational course of action if one conceives of rationality in terms of strategies which minimize economic and emotional costs. If one does conceive of rationality in this manner, however, rational strategies might not seem particularly desirable. This argument can be substantiated if we return the discussion to legal decision-making. In law, as elsewhere, indeterminacy sometimes confounds

[137] Neurath (above, n. 12), 9.
[138] See also Elster (above, n. 3), 116–17; Greely (above, n. 3), 141.
[139] Neurath (above, n. 12), 10.
[140] See Max Weber, 'Science as a Vocation' (Eng. trans. M. John) in Peter Lassman *et al.* (eds.), *Max Weber's 'Science as a Vocation'* (London: Unwin Hyman, 1989; essay orig. publ. 1918), 3–31 at 30–1. In Weber's work, the thesis is considerably more elaborate: cf. W. T. Murphy, *The Oldest Social Science? Configurations of Law and Modernity* (Oxford: Clarendon Press, 1997), 49–50. The implications of the general thesis, furthermore, continue to trouble political philosophers deeply: see Jürgen Habermas, *Between Facts and Norms: Contributions to a Discourse Theory of Law and Democracy* (Eng. trans. W. Rehg, Cambridge: Polity, 1996 (1992)), p. xli.

reason.[141] Should it ever be the case that legal decision-makers cannot agree that there are stronger reasons for choosing one outcome rather than another, then a lottery could—certainly in theory—be resorted to in order to resolve the matter. In such a scenario, the lottery might even be considered a rational option. I shall, presently, endeavour to show why a lottery might be considered thus. I shall also attempt to demonstrate that the conception of rationality being employed in this context emphasizes expediency of outcome in preference to justice in procedure. While, however, it is quite understandable that the lottery should, for legal decision-making purposes, be considered anathema—while aversion to the use of sortition for such purposes provides us with considerable insight into what it is that we do want from legal decision-making—I shall conclude by arguing that the idea of reaching legal decisions by lot ought not to be cursorily dismissed.

It was noted at the outset of this chapter that courts and other legal decision-making bodies are rarely, if ever, in the business of throwing up their hands and declaring themselves unable to decide. It is expected, and it will invariably be the case, that legal decision-makers will practise casuistry, that they will use whatever resources are available to resolve the problem at hand.[142] Yet there may be dishonesty in casuistry. While adjudicators may sometimes be unsure of how to decide an issue, they are nevertheless likely to see their task as being one of finding some reason, or reasons, on which a decision can be based. No doubt adjudicators themselves will usually be convinced by the reasons which they offer. But it would surely be wrong to believe that they will always be so convinced. The reasons which we adduce to support our actions might not sincerely or accurately reflect what we think.[143] This is not to claim that our proffered reasons are, in such instances, unimportant—that one professes reasons insincerely does not mean that those reasons cannot explain one's actions.[144] The point, rather, is that we will sometimes not be sure of what we think but—considering it inappropriate to appear unclear—provide reasons which we hope will disguise our uncertainty. Not knowing how to be principled on an issue, a decision-maker may nevertheless consider it important to appear principled on that issue; for, without appearing principled, the decision-maker may feel that he or she stands little, if any, chance of being considered credible.

[141] See, generally, John A. Eisenberg, *The Limits of Reason: Indeterminacy in Law, Education, and Morality* (New Brunswick, NJ: Transaction, 1992).

[142] See N. E. Simmonds, 'Bluntness and Bricolage', in Hyman Gross and Ross Harrison (eds.), *Jurisprudence: Cambridge Essays* (Oxford: Clarendon Press, 1992), 1–28 at 23–5. On casuistry, cf. Guido Calabresi, *Ideals, Beliefs, Attitudes, and the Law: Private Law Perspectives on a Public Law Problem* (Syracuse, NY: Syracuse University Press, 1985), 120–1 n. 10; and Cass R. Sunstein, *Legal Reasoning and Political Conflict* (New York: Oxford University Press, 1996), 121–35.

[143] See Martin Hollis, *The Cunning of Reason* (Cambridge: Cambridge University Press, 1987), 182–4.

[144] For a compelling demonstration of this point in relation to Bolingbroke's opposition to Walpole, see Quentin Skinner, 'The Principles and Practice of Opposition: The Case of Bolingbroke versus Walpole', in Neil McKendrick (ed.), *Historical Perspectives: Studies in English Thought and Society in Honour of J. H. Plumb* (London: Europa, 1974), 93–128.

That legal decision-makers do well to appear principled is quite often emphasized by academic lawyers. The proper justification of a legal decision requires not only that the decision is grounded in reason, Hellman argues, but that it is made to 'appear so to those to whom it is addressed'.[145] On this account, adjudication resembles a public relations initiative. 'Just as for a teacher to explain is to offer an account that is likely to make sense to students, for a court to justify is to provide reasons that are likely to be acceptable to members of the court's audience.'[146] The production of reasons which will likely be considered acceptable is important because 'public officials have a duty to maintain an appropriate appearance in order to foster the public trust'.[147] The search for reasons is construed here very much as an exercise in dressing to impress: one formulates reasons rather as one might wear a suit and tie for work.[148] A comparable line of analysis is presented by Nesson, who argues that it is far more important that a verdict be acceptable than that it reflects what most probably occurred.

A verdict based on a high probability may be unacceptable if it fails to make a statement about what happened; conversely, a verdict based on a low probability may be acceptable if it makes such a statement. The aim of the factfinding process is not to generate mathematically 'probable' verdicts, but rather to generate acceptable ones; only an acceptable verdict will project the underlying legal rule to society and affirm the rule's behavioral norm.[149]

Perhaps it is only *realpolitik* to assume, as Hellman and Nesson do, that there exists—out there, as it were—an audience upon whom courts must make the right impression. Possibly it would be naive to think otherwise. Yet both the equation of reasoning with packaging and the emphasis on acceptability in preference to probability lend some support to the suggestion that there may sometimes be dishonesty in casuistry. For Hellman and Nesson, what matters most is acceptable appearance. Yet, were a court concerned with reasons primarily for their symbolic or cosmetic value—if the principal point of providing reasons were not to explain decisions but to make those decisions acceptable—the likelihood would be that this court would sooner or later be accused of providing reasons with camouflage rather than enlightenment in mind.

My objective here is not to take issue with the argument that there are benefits

---

[145] Deborah Hellman, 'The Importance of Appearing Principled' (1995) 37 *Arizona L. Rev.* 1107–51 at 1109.   [146] Ibid. 1125.   [147] Ibid. 1126.
[148] Ibid. 1124; and cf. also, for a similar line of argument, Jerald Greenberg, 'Looking Fair vs. Being Fair: Managing Impressions of Organizational Justice', in Barry M. Staw and L. L. Cummings (eds.), *Research in Organizational Behavior*, xii (Greenwich, Conn.: JAI Press, 1990), 111–57.
[149] Charles Nesson, 'The Evidence or the Event? On Judicial Proof and the Acceptability of Verdicts' (1985) 98 *Harvard L. Rev.* 1357–92 at 1359; and see also, in a similar vein, his 'Agent Orange Meets the Blue Bus: Factfinding at the Frontier of Knowledge' (1986) 66 *Boston Univ. L. Rev.* 521–39 at 537–9. For a general critique of Nesson's perspective, cf. Ronald J. Allen, 'Rationality, Mythology, and the "Acceptability of Verdicts" Thesis' (1986) 66 *Boston Univ. L. Rev.* 541–62.

to be derived from creating acceptable appearances.[150] I wish only to emphasize that reasoning can conceal as well as reveal, and that it may turn out to serve the former purpose where decision-makers struggle to distinguish options. Now and again legal decision-makers, like Descartes's travellers, may find themselves lost (metaphorically speaking), and the idea that it will be possible to reason away the disorientation may be pure pseudo-rationalism. That decision-makers might, in such instances, simply resort to a lottery in order to produce an outcome would no doubt be considered by most people to be an objectionable suggestion. Yet the fact that a proposal is likely to meet with widespread opposition is hardly reason for refusing to consider it. '[M]an would not have attained the possible', Weber once remarked, 'unless time and again he had reached out for the impossible.'[151] The very activity of scholarship is likely to be impoverished, and indeed undermined, if academics neglect to develop ideas for fear that they may offend against conventional sensibilities. Consider the case of Chicago law and economics, which was once treated as something of a lunatic fringe in American academic legal circles—which is subjected to vigorous criticism, indeed, to this day. Over the past four decades, its influence on American legal theory and practice has been immense.[152] That neo-classical lawyer-economists adopt rationalistic premises which the majority of their opponents find highly contestable has not diminished this influence; nor, indeed, has this influence waned owing to the fact that neo-classicists sometimes advance proposals which are unlikely ever to be accepted and implemented. Indeed, Chicago law and economics has probably thrived because of these factors rather than in spite of them; for the counter-intuitiveness of the Chicago approach has challenged, focused, and stimulated the minds of those who resist it. This counter-intuitiveness is largely attributable, I think, to the fact that neo-classical lawyer-economists tend to be concerned not with the question of what, in any particular situation, the feasible or acceptable human action might be, but with what would constitute rational action. My primary concern here, similarly, is not with whether the use of lotteries to reach legal decisions might be considered feasible—we shall see in due course that there is rarely much chance of their being considered so—but with whether such use might be deemed rational. Indeed, the question of whether it might be rational to resort to a lottery for legal decision-making purposes would be worth raising if only to draw out a distinction between

---

[150] Not that I embrace the argument. Contriving to impress is usually thoroughly unimpressive, whereas the truly impressive are often naturally unconcerned with how they appear to others. See Paul Veyne, *Le Pain et le cirque: Sociologie historique d'un pluralisme politique* (Paris: Seuil, 1976), 679 ('Seule une expression qui ne cherche pas à faire effet en produit un et fait preuve'). For developments of this theme, cf. Jon Elster, *Political Psychology* (Cambridge: Cambridge University Press, 1993), 51–7, 66–7; Elster (above, n. 121), 44–52, 66–71; and Neil Duxbury, 'When Trying is Failing: Holmes's "Englishness" ' (1997) 63 *Brooklyn L. Rev.* 145–64.

[151] Max Weber, 'Politics as a Vocation' (Eng. trans. H. H. Gerth and C. W. Mills), in H. H. Gerth and C. Wright Mills (eds.), *From Max Weber: Essays in Sociology* (London: Routledge & Kegan Paul, 1948; essay orig. publ. 1918), 77–128 at 128.

[152] See, generally, Duxbury (above, n. 112), 301–419.

rationality and reason and to demonstrate that, in relation to adjudication, the latter quality is generally valued more highly than the former.

Child Custody Adjudication

One might fairly ask, of course, whether legal decision-makers ever really do find themselves in positions comparable with that occupied by Descartes's travellers. Is it ever the case, in legal decision-making contexts, that reason becomes exhausted? Should this ever be the case, furthermore, might resort to a lottery be considered a rational course of action? It was intimated in section 1 of this chapter that one area of legal decision-making where these questions might become relevant is child custody adjudication. Distinguishing parties in terms of fitness for custody and awarding custody on the basis of children's best interests are notoriously hazardous tasks.[153] That one party may be no more obviously fit (or unfit) to take custody than the other party—that it is impossible to say that a child will be better off with either—is a fact which courts quite often concede. Although, in England, there exists a statutory checklist of factors which courts are required to consider in ascertaining how a child's welfare is to be satisfied,[154] judges still, on occasions, fail convincingly to distinguish parties contesting for custody.[155] The problem with regard to many child custody disputes, Lord Fraser once observed, is that 'there is no right answer . . . [T]here are often two or more possible decisions, any one of which might reasonably be thought to be the best, and any one of which therefore a judge may make without being held to be wrong.'[156]

Why might this be so? In England, ever since the enactment of the Guardianship of Infants Act 1925, the primary principle of child care law has been the welfare of the child. 'When a court determines any question with respect to . . . the upbringing of a child . . . the child's welfare shall be the court's paramount consideration.'[157] The articulation of this principle in terms of welfare would, one imagines, intrigue many an economist or rational choice theorist: in according paramount consideration to the child's welfare, it might be asked, is the task of the judge to compare the expected utility for the child of living with his

---

[153]   See Robert H. Mnookin *et al.*, *In the Interest of Children: Advocacy, Law Reform, and Public Policy* (New York: W. H. Freeman & Co., 1985), 16–24; Laura M. Purdy, *In Their Best Interest? The Case Against Equal Rights for Children* (Ithaca, NY: Cornell University Press, 1992), 23–4; and Jane Fortin, *Children's Rights and the Developing Law* (London: Butterworths, 1998), 216–22. Although, here and elsewhere in this book, I write about award of custody, it ought to be noted that, in English law, courts now make 'residence orders' as opposed to custody awards: see Children Act 1989, s. 8(1). Since I am not concerned specifically with English law, I have retained the ecumenically more appropriate 'custody'.   [154]   Children Act 1989, s. 1(3).

[155]   See, e.g., *B* v. *B* [1997] 2 FLR 602 (CA).

[156]   *G* v. *G* [1985] FLR 894, 898 (HL).

[157]   Children Act 1989, s. 1(1). As used in this context, the notion of paramountcy is open to more than one interpretation: see John Eekelaar and Robert Dingwall, *The Reform of Child Care Law: A Practical Guide to the Children Act 1989* (London: Routledge, 1990), 30.

mother with that of living with his father? Furthermore, in attempting either task—and here we repeat an observation made earlier in this chapter—should the judge be concerned with long-term or short-term welfare? Just as the very idea of childhood itself can vary from one culture and era to another,[158] so too the notion of children's welfare is indeterminate. This observation is very often offered by those who profess scepticism over the idea that it might ever be possible to determine what constitute the best interests of the child.[159] 'Because the "best interests of the child" standard is more a vague platitude than a legal or scientific standard,' one such sceptic observes, 'it is subject to abuse both by judges who administer it and parents who use it to further their own interests.'[160]

Observations of this nature can very easily be exaggerated,[161] and it is worth emphasizing that there are those who insist that indeterminacy can, in this context, be combated by the application of relevant rules and requirements (such as those set out in section 1(3) of the Children Act 1989) which render the notion of children's welfare less woolly.[162] Yet those commentators who urge that we should not be too eager to pronounce the indeterminacy of the best interests standard sometimes reveal, in a roundabout way, that there are deeper problems with

[158] See C. John Sommerville, *The Rise and Fall of Childhood* (Beverly Hills, Calif.: Sage, 1982); Philippe Ariès, *Centuries of Childhood* (Eng. trans. R. Baldick, Harmondsworth: Penguin, 1962 (1960)); and M. D. A. Freeman, *The Rights and the Wrongs of Children* (London: Frances Pinter, 1983), 6–31. For a critique of Ariès's thesis, cf. Linda A. Pollock, *Forgotten Children: Parent-Child Relations from 1500 to 1900* (Cambridge: Cambridge University Press, 1983), 1–22, 54–5, 96–7.

[159] See, generally, Mnookin (above, n. 33), 226–82; Robert H. Mnookin, 'Children's Rights: Legal and Ethical Dilemmas' (1978) 41 *The Pharos of Alpha Omega Alpha* 2–7 at 3–4 (repr. (1978) 11 *The Transcript* 5–10 at 5–7); and David L. Chambers, 'Rethinking the Substantive Rules for Custody Disputes in Divorce' (1984) 83 *Michigan L. Rev.* 477–569 at 487–99. In addressing the best interests principle, I am concerned only with arguments concerning its indeterminacy. There are other criticisms of this criterion, such as that its application tends to conceal gender bias: see Sandra S. Berns, 'Living Under the Shadow of Rousseau: The Role of Gender Ideologies in Custody and Access Decisions' (1991) 10 *Univ. Tasmania L. Rev.* 233–55; and also Martha L. Fineman and Anne Opie, 'The Uses of Social Science Data in Legal Policymaking: Custody Determinations at Divorce' [1987] *Wisconsin L. Rev.* 107–58.

[160] Andrea Charlow, 'Awarding Custody: The Best Interests of the Child and Other Fictions' (1987) 5 *Yale Law and Policy Review* 267–90 at 267. For comments in a similar vein, see Arthur G. LeFrancois, 'Children's Representation in Custody Litigation in America and Australia' (1988) 6 *Law in Context* 1–28 at 13–14. In relation to the claim that the best interests principle is platitudinous, it is worth noting the argument—considered by Mnookin (above, n. 33), 268–9, and Elster (above, n. 3), 144—that, were it really the case that the child's welfare is of paramount consideration in custody disputes, courts ought to be permitted and indeed advised to remove children from their biological parents where other parents would be willing and able to provide even more for those children.

[161] Consider, e.g., Michael King, *A Better World for Children? Explorations in Morality and Authority* (London: Routledge, 1997), 61: 'Who knows today what is good or bad for children? How is it possible for institutions designed to promote children's welfare to rely on anything other than a self-generated version of what that welfare consists of?' While there may often be little consensus concerning what constitutes the best interests of children, it does not follow that there exists no consensus concerning what is particularly bad for children: see further Mnookin (above, n. 33), 261.

[162] See, e.g., Stephen Parker, 'The Best Interests of the Child: Principles and Problems', in Philip Alston (ed.), *The Best Interests of the Child: Reconciling Culture and Human Rights* (Oxford: Clarendon Press, 1994), 26–41; and also Carl E. Schneider, 'Discretion, Rules, and Law: Child Custody and the UMDA's Best-Interest Standard' (1991) 89 *Michigan L. Rev.* 2215–98.

that standard when it is applied to resolve custody issues. Take the basic idea that the indeterminacy of the welfare principle might be mitigated if there exist rules which indicate how the principle should be interpreted and applied. A difficulty with introducing such rules is that they may solve some problems but create others.[163] If, for example, in assessing the welfare of children courts are instructed to have regard, *inter alia*, to 'the ascertainable wishes and feelings of the child concerned (considered in the light of his age and understanding)',[164] there may emerge legitimate concern that this exercise might generate information which will not, if treated as valid, advance the child's welfare. It may indeed be the case, as MacCormick claims, that '[c]hildren are not always or even usually the best judges of what is good for them, so much so that even the rights which are most important to their long-term well-being ... they regularly perceive as being the reverse of rights or advantages'.[165] This specific example supports, I think, a more general argument: that the difficulty with tempering discretion through the introduction of rules is that rules can bring their own disadvantages. As Mnookin observes:

the choice between indeterminate standards and more precise rules poses a profound dilemma. The absence of rules removes special burdens of justification and formulation of standards characteristic of adjudication. Unfairness and adverse consequences can result. And yet, rules that relate past events to legal consequences may themselves create substantial difficulties in the custody area. Our inadequate knowledge about human behavior and our inability to generalize confidently about the relationship between past events or conduct and future behavior make the formulation of rules especially problematic. Moreover, the very lack of consensus about values that makes the best-interests standard indeterminate may also make the formulation of rules inappropriate: a legal rule must, after all, reflect some social value or values. An overly ambitious and indeterminate principle may result in fewer decisions that reflect what is known to be desirable. But rules may result in some conspicuously bad decisions that could be avoided by a more discretionary standard. What balance should be struck?[166]

Note that Mnookin begins this passage by referring to a choice, and concludes it by questioning the possibility of striking a balance, between precise rules and discretionary standards. In fact, advantages and disadvantages attach to both rules and discretion, and judges do not typically choose between one or the other but between different mixtures of the two.[167] Specifically in relation to child custody,

---

[163] In relation to s. 1(3) of the Children Act 1989 in particular, see Eekelaar and Dingwall (above, n. 157), 31–2; and Andrew Bainham, *Children: The Modern Law* (2nd edn., Bristol: Family Law, 1998), 35–7.   [164] Children Act 1989, s. 1(3).

[165] Neil MacCormick, *Legal Right and Social Democracy: Essays in Legal and Political Philosophy* (Oxford: Clarendon Press, 1982), 166. On justifications for paternalism, see also Michael D. A. Freeman, 'Taking Children's Rights More Seriously', in Philip Alston, Stephen Parker, and John Seymour (eds.), *Children, Rights, and the Law* (Oxford: Clarendon Press, 1992), 52–71 at 66–9; and Scott Altman, 'Should Child Custody Rules be Fair?' (1996–7) 35 *Univ. Louisville J. of Family Law* 325–54.   [166] Mnookin (above, n. 33), 264.

[167] See Carl E. Schneider, 'Discretion and Rules: A Lawyer's View', in Keith Hawkins (ed.), *The Uses of Discretion* (Oxford: Clarendon Press, 1992), 47–88.

however, the task of achieving a suitable mixture or balance is often likely, as Mnookin observes, to be particularly hazardous. On the one hand, we cannot be certain that resort to rules will satisfactorily remedy the problem of indeterminacy which accompanies the best interests criterion. On the other hand, it would be foolish to ignore the fact that indeterminacy is a problem and that efforts to apply the best interests criterion might do more harm than good.

Just what sorts of harm might be incurred through the application of the best interests standard? There are at least three observations which might be offered in response to this question. The first is that judicial use of the standard may create an incentive to litigate.[168] One of the themes of the next chapter is that uncertainty can sometimes encourage settlement of disputes. It would be unwise, however, not to attach any weight to the counter-proposition: namely, that uncertainty of outcome may persuade parties that they have a strong case. '[T]he use of an inde-terminate standard for adjudication may result in more cases being litigated than would be true if more rule-like standards governed custody disputes',[169] because both parties may be able to convince themselves that the standard being applied favours them. Secondly, the best interests standard could operate as a cloak for expediency. 'Social workers, their supervisors, and juvenile court judges lack the time and energy (given substantial case loads) to make careful individualized determinations of what would be best for a child ... [B]ecause virtually any conclusion can often be justified under the vague rubric of best interests, there is no necessity for these officials to specify ... their value judgments'.[170] The final observation is that 'any delay in determining [a child custody dispute] is likely to prejudice the welfare of the child'.[171] Use of the best interests principle might create delay—not only because the principle may, as already noted, be a spur to litigation, but also because serious efforts to ascertain the best interests of a child could require considerable effort and time.[172]

The argument which is being advanced here is not that it is wrong to apply the best interests standard in custody disputes, only that interpretation and application of the principle will often prove problematic. Best interests is, of course, not the only criterion in town: in resolving child custody disputes, courts have at times been guided by other criteria, such as the presumption of maternal preference, bias towards the primary caretaker, and compromise solutions. But these alternative criteria are accompanied by their own problems: maternal presumption may discriminate against both men and women;[173] the notion of primary caretaking suffers from indeterminacy (as with efforts to determine best interests, attempts to determine which party provided primary care for the children may sometimes lead to protracted litigation[174]); and imposed compromise solutions—the splitting of

---

[168] See Charlow (above, n. 160), 270, 289–90; Elster (above, n. 3), 147.
[169] Mnookin (above, n. 33), 282.   [170] Ibid. 273–4.
[171] Children Act 1989, s. 1(2); and cf. also ss. 11, 32.
[172] See further Elster (above, n. 3), 134, 143, 145–7.
[173] Ibid. 159.   [174] See Chambers (above, n. 159), 527–48.

siblings or sharing of custody—may be psychologically damaging for children and resented by the contesting parties.[175] What we discover, in the field of child custody adjudication, is a selection of flawed decision-making criteria.[176] Small wonder that we should find judges professing that this is an area in which it will sometimes be impossible to say that there exists a best answer.

It is against this backdrop that arguments in favour of randomized resolutions of child custody disputes ought to be considered. The issue is not whether decision-makers would be inclined to resolve such disputes in this way, but whether or not decision-makers act irrationally when, staring indeterminacy in the face, they endeavour to muddle through in the hope that they will somehow reason it into submission. 'Many of our men of speculation,' Burke believed,

instead of exploding general prejudices, employ their sagacity to discover the latent wisdom which prevails in them. If they find what they seek, and they seldom fail, they think it more wise to continue the prejudice, with the reason involved, than to cast away the coat of prejudice, and to leave nothing but the naked reason; because prejudice, with its reason, has a motive to give action to that reason, and an affection which will give it permanence.[177]

A similar manœuvre seems to take place in relation to child custody adjudication. Making reasons fit an outcome may sometimes be largely a matter of prejudice. A different outcome might be supportable by the same, or by equally strong (or possibly stronger), reasons. Having settled on an outcome, however, a legal decision-maker is likely to be wary of conceding as much. To do so may look like an admission of defeat in the face of uncertainty. Thus it is that, come what may, reasons are fitted to some particular outcome. Once an outcome has been chosen and reasons connected to it, there is a likelihood that this outcome will seem like the most reasonable possibility precisely because it has been chosen and reasons have been connected to it.[178] That it might seem so, however, does not mean that it must be so: in deploying reasons to support a particular outcome, a decision-maker may be trying to justify a personal bias towards that outcome, may be acting in ignorance of information which would have made other possible outcomes seem more reasonable (or less unreasonable), or may simply be doing what he or she considers to be the task in hand—getting to a decision. A less positive formulation of the argument that reasons invest decisions with authority is the proposition that the impulse to ground decisions in reason is a sign of insecurity concerning the authoritativeness of those decisions. To provide reasons for decisions may be an indication that those decisions are considered somehow too fragile to stand

---

[175] See Elster (above, n. 3), 162–3.

[176] See, generally, Chambers (above, n. 159), 515–58.

[177] Edmund Burke, *Reflections on the Revolution in France, And on the Proceedings in Certain Societies in London Relative to that Event* (ed. Conor Cruise O'Brien, Harmondsworth: Penguin, 1968 (1790)), 183.

[178] See Brian Bix, *Law, Language, and Legal Determinacy* (Oxford: Clarendon Press, 1993), 104–5.

unaided. Without foundation in reason, those decisions may look no more plausible than other decisions which might have been reached. As the example of child custody adjudication is intended to demonstrate, even when decisions are grounded in reason, the plausibility problem may still persist owing to the indeterminacy of the criteria around which reasoning takes place.

But even if decision-makers sometimes do deploy reasoning in such a way as to mask indeterminacy, does this make their behaviour irrational? Such behaviour can certainly be interpreted as dishonest, and one argument in favour of resort to randomization is that it may represent candour in decision-making.[179] An honest adjudicator might be inclined to resort to lot where he or she recognizes that the matter at hand will otherwise be settled by resort to distinctions which are only artificially supported by reasons. In the child custody context, Mnookin observes, '[w]e would more frankly acknowledge both our ignorance and the presumed equality of the natural parents were we to flip a coin'.[180] In short, recourse to a lottery may be a candid—perhaps, on occasions, a refreshingly candid—method by which to acknowledge one's limitations as a decision-maker. While it is most unlikely that legal problems of considerable social significance will ever be customarily resolved by resort to lot, Katz argues, 'it does not follow that a process which gives the appearance of rationality should always be chosen over one which concedes that rational choice among competing demands is not possible at a given level. It is undoubtedly true . . . that law often has symbolic offices to fill; but it is also true that law must *be* fair as well as *seem* rational.'[181] That resort to lot may sometimes be a decision-maker's most honest option, however, does not necessarily make it the rational option. Indeed, adopting the honest strategy and deciding by lot instead of by reference to reasons may be considered irrational if it has the effect of damaging confidence in, and undermining respect for, the decision-making process.

In what ways, then, might it ever be considered rational to resolve legal problems by recourse to sortition? Most arguments concerning the rationality of randomized legal decision-making can be reduced to the claim that such decision-making is likely to prove cost-beneficial. Consider, first of all, the idea that resolving child custody disputes by the toss of a coin might encourage privately negotiated compromise between parties who would otherwise litigate.[182] The general idea that lotteries might be incorporated into legal frameworks for the purpose of encouraging litigation settlement was considered briefly in the

---

[179] See Elster (above, n. 3), 121. [180] Mnookin (above, n. 33), 289.
[181] Al Katz, 'Process Design for Selection of Hemodialysis and Organ Transplant Recipients' (1973) 22 *Buffalo L. Rev.* 373–418 at 391.
[182] Discussion here proceeds on the assumption that the lottery will accord to each party a 50% chance of being awarded full custody of the children. We ought at least to note, none the less, that randomization offers other options. A lottery might be designed, for example, to provide a third possible outcome of shared custody. It more or less goes without saying that the incentive for parties to negotiate a private solution may depend on, among other things, the range and probability of outcomes offered by the lottery.

conclusion to the last section. In the event that both parties to a child custody dispute are equally fit to assume, and equally eager to be awarded, custody of the children, the possibility that an equiprobabilistic lottery might be used to determine who should get custody rights might encourage the parties to reach a compromise (such as a shared custody arrangement). A significant factor here will be the attitude of each party towards risk.[183] Since the lottery will accord each party a 50 per cent chance of being awarded custody, the expected outcome for each is half-custody; however, we cannot simply assume that each will bargain as if certain that he or she will receive half of the child's time. Attitudes of the parties towards risk may be clarified by asking each to compare the certainty of receiving half of the child's time with a lottery whereby the expected or average outcome is one half of the child's time. To consider these alternatives as equally desirable would be to exhibit risk-neutrality. To accept a certain outcome of less than half-custody so as to avoid the possibility of losing the lottery (and thereby receiving no custody rights) is to exhibit risk aversion. The risk-preferential party would rather enter the lottery and stand a 50 per cent chance of being awarded full custody than accept a certain outcome of split custody. One would expect risk-averse parties, if presented with a choice between reaching a compromise or entering an even-chance lottery, to seek out compromise.

The effectiveness of introducing the threat of resort to a lottery in order to reduce the likelihood of litigation will, in most instances, be undermined by the complexities of the dispute. Litigating parties are likely to have, among other things, different attitudes towards risk and being awarded custody. In relation to divorce proceedings, it has been questioned whether problems arising out of complexity might be minimized or pre-empted if parties were legally required to proceed with the lottery at the time of the marriage. The idea here is that, should the parties have children and subsequently separate (and be in disagreement over custody arrangements), custody would—in the absence of evidence demonstrating unfitness—be awarded to the winner of the lottery.[184] One can only speculate about what sorts of effects such an arrangement might have on people's incentives. Would the requirement that a lottery be conducted weaken incentives to marry and have children? Would those who lose such lottery draws have a stronger commitment than they would otherwise have to remaining married? Might their attachment to their children be weakened? The winner of such a lottery would probably have a significant bargaining advantage in divorce proceedings. But this will only be the case if the lottery can be legally enforced. If it cannot be enforced, the lottery outcome will only prevail if both parties remain committed to it. It is unlikely, however, that both will remain so committed. In custody disputes, it has been suggested, '[a] judicially

---

[183] See Robert H. Mnookin and Lewis Kornhauser, 'Bargaining in the Shadow of the Law: The Case of Divorce' (1979) 88 *Yale LJ* 950–97 at 970–1.

[184] See Mnookin (above, n. 33), 290.

supervised drawing of lots between two acceptable psychological parents might be the most rational and least offensive process for resolving the hard choice'.[185] Whether or not it is rational, the procedure will very likely be considered offensive—to generate what was earlier termed negative symbolic resonance—if it is imposed upon the parties without their consent.[186] Yet even if couples were to consent to the use of a lottery at the time of marriage, the unlucky party may be expected to have little respect for the outcome, and to be opposed to its enforcement, since—as was noted at the end of section 1 of this chapter—the attractiveness of equality *ex ante* tends quickly to evaporate once one has lost the draw.

While, accordingly, one might argue that it is rational to decide—or even simply to introduce the possibility of deciding—by lot if the strategy encourages private settlement and thereby reduces litigation, it is important to note that significant obstacles are likely to hinder efforts actually to pursue such a strategy. This is not, however, to dismiss rationalistic arguments in favour of lottery use. Such arguments might be developed further. Leaving aside the claim that lotteries may diminish incentives to litigate, a more basic contention is that reasoning comes at a price and that randomized decision-making will invariably be relatively cheap and quick. In relation to child custody disputes, such decision-making 'would avoid the pain associated with an adversary proceeding that requires an open exploration of the intimate aspects of family life and an ultimate judgment that one parent is preferable to the other'.[187] To the assertion that 'this is a "give-it-up" philosophy' there is the rejoinder that '[a] give-it-up attitude is constructive when it appears that the task is impossible of accomplishment with the resources that are available'.[188] There may be rationality, in other words, in resorting to sortition instead of producing finely calibrated distinctions in the endeavour to render indeterminacies determinate. We might invoke here the classic Hayekian argument that legal theorists and reformers are too often eager to render law complex in the belief that this is the way to achieve perfect justice in individual cases, when in fact both justice and rationality would be better served if regulators and decision-makers were encouraged to be wary of quests for complexity and perfection and to seek out instead the simple rule which offers the second-best solution.[189] 'Using simple, robust criteria for unfitness (physical

---

[185] Joseph Goldstein, Anna Freud, and Albert J. Solnit, *Beyond the Best Interests of the Child* (rev. edn., London: André Deutsch, 1980; orig. publ. 1973), 175. In a similar vein, see Joseph Goldstein, Anna Freud, Albert J. Solnit, and Sonja Goldstein, *In the Best Interests of the Child: Professional Boundaries* (New York: Free Press, 1986), 24.

[186] On consent, see further Goodwin (above, n. 3), 33–4.

[187] Mnookin (above, n. 33), 290.

[188] Brainerd Currie, *Selected Essays on the Conflict of Laws* (Durham, NC: Duke University Press, 1963), 121.

[189] The argument is developed in detail by Richard A. Epstein, *Simple Rules for a Complex World* (Cambridge, Mass.: Harvard University Press, 1995). See also F. A. Hayek, *The Road to Serfdom* (London: Routledge & Kegan Paul, 1944), 44, 54–65; and, for a comparable argument from the perspective of statistical theory, cf. Hillel J. Einhorn, 'Accepting Error to Make Less Error' (1986) 50 *Journal of Personality Assessment* 387–95 at 390–2.

neglect, physical abuse, sexual abuse, psychic disorders)', Elster argues, 'courts would be able to make swift rulings' in child custody cases.[190] If a court were to find neither parent to be unfit, a rule permitting resolution of the dispute by resort to lot would have 'the virtue of being simple and automatic'.[191] Complexity would, of course, be sacrificed—and the chances are that the parties themselves would prefer the court to take account of complexity (of every detail, that is, which might strengthen their own case). The point, however, is that the costs of engaging with complexities may be outweighed by the benefits of pushing those complexities to one side.

We might expect that temporal and monetary expenditure would be reduced if, in custody disputes where neither party appears to be unfit to take care of the children, courts were less inclined to seek out fine-tuned distinctions between the parties in terms of who might best advance the children's interests and more willing to make randomized determinations. There are also emotional costs which might be saved. It was noted earlier in this chapter that the endeavour to ascertain the best interests of children may sometimes be counter-productive in that it may lead to protracted litigation. Some children would be spared the pain of such litigation if courts were prepared to concede that, now and again, custody disputes are such close calls that a randomized decision would be no more, and possibly less, harmful than a quest for reasons to justify distinctions. It is not only the emotions of children which might be spared through resort to randomization. Where custody decisions are evidently close and courts struggle to produce reasons which tip the balance in favour of one party, the depression and loss of self-esteem suffered by the loser will, in many if not most instances, be immense. To be denied custody because one was unlucky in the draw would surely be a horrible and trivializing experience. I imagine, however, that it could be just as horrible and trivializing—and (this being the crucial point) would almost definitely be more protracted—an experience to be denied custody on the basis of reasons adduced to support some distinction, or distinctions, which more or less anyone would consider to be slight and which, to the losing party, are likely to be as unconvincing as they are devastating.

I have been trying to demonstrate that, in certain instances, it may be rational—even if it is not deemed acceptable—to resolve child custody disputes by resort to lot. Although my concern here is with rationality, it ought at least to be noted that other arguments may be advanced to support such a course of action. One such argument is that a non-weighted lottery will be impartial and so treat the disputing parties equally. This argument is developed by Elster, who claims that 'awarding custody by the flip of a coin would be fair to the parents, since the procedure would safeguard the important values of equal treatment and equal opportunity'.[192] In claiming as much, however, he appears to conflate equal treatment and

---

[190] Elster (above, n. 3), 170–1.   [191] Ibid. 170.
[192] Ibid. 171.

treatment as equals. 'Applicants who are rejected by the lottery', he observes, 'may well think that their right to a fair evaluation has been violated, but I do not believe they have any such right. They have a right to equal concern and respect, and that right is not violated by the lottery.'[193] It was noted in Chapter 3 that an allocative procedure will not accord equal concern and respect to candidates if it is insensitive to relevant differences between them. While a non-weighted lottery may ensure that parties contesting for child custody receive equal treatment *ex ante*, it will not guarantee what Dworkin would term their treatment as equals.[194]

Procedural Justice

The more that we emphasize the idea that it may be rational to resort to lotteries for legal decision-making purposes, the more that the disadvantages of randomness seem to demand our attention. The reason for this is that randomized legal decision-making, even where it appears to be a rational strategy, more often than not offends against conceptions of justice. Part of the problem, as was noted earlier, is that the idea of determining by lot issues of considerable social and legal significance is usually—though not always[195]—deemed to be objectionable on symbolic grounds.[196] There are at least three other problems.

First of all, to use a non-weighted lottery to resolve a legal dispute is to determine that the facts of the dispute should have no bearing on the outcome. Yet people invariably litigate because they believe the facts of their case to be significant. Few disputing parties will be happy to be told that the facts of the case are to count for nothing, even where there are good reasons for according the parties equal treatment.[197] As a variant on this point, consider the argument that, in the

---

[193] Ibid. 108. For an argument similar to Elster's, see James F. Childress, *Practical Reasoning in Bioethics* (Bloomington: Indiana University Press, 1997), 183–4.

[194] Though it will treat candidates as equals (and therefore Elster's claim would be valid) if there are no relevant differences between them. Consider also Federle (above, n. 29), 1549: 'Flipping a coin to resolve a conflict is possible only if there are two equally weighted interests; a coin toss neither acknowledges nor accommodates the possibility of a third set of interests that are held by the child.'

[195] A rather curious exception here is that of the draft lottery. Although many criticisms have been levelled at schemes designed randomly to select conscripts, rarely if ever is it argued that the draft lottery represents an inappropriate valuation of human life. Perhaps the reason for this is that the draft lottery is an illustration of resort to chance in a situation of crisis where, irrespective of the fact that lots are being drawn, it is generally recognized that human life is not being valued as it would be in more normal circumstances.

[196] It would not be quite accurate to characterize negative symbolic resonance purely as a problem of justice, for it could sometimes be the case—indeed, with regard to lottery decisions, it may quite often be the case—that an outcome is considered to be just and yet the method adopted to reach the outcome is considered humiliating: see Avishai Margalit, *The Decent Society* (Eng. trans. N. Goldblum, Cambridge, Mass.: Harvard University Press, 1996), 280–1; and cf. also Frank Henderson Stewart, *Honor* (Chicago: University of Chicago Press, 1994), 79–85.

[197] Cf. also Bix (above, n. 178), 106: '[W]e ask and expect judges to determine matters of blame and excuse, a delegation one would only make if one were confident that those judgments were based on decisions of what actually happened, as a matter of fact. The idea of the past being indeterminate sits very uncomfortably with us.'

United States, the Fourth Amendment exclusionary rule—which excludes the use of improperly obtained evidence at trial[198]—ought to be enforced randomly. 'For example, a judge could rule that a coin is to be flipped and if it comes up heads the relevant evidence is to be excluded and if it comes up tails the evidence will be allowed at trial.'[199] Although one might expect randomized application of the rule to lead to criminal defendants in similar circumstances being treated differently, it may in fact reduce the likelihood of differential treatment. In those cases where it is not clear what the exclusionary rule requires, we might broadly assume that, in the absence of a lottery decision, 'liberal judges would exclude the evidence and conservative judges would not. However, if lotteries were permitted, we would likely get a convergence between the decisions of the different judges.'[200] Whatever one makes of this line of argument, the strong likelihood remains that randomized application of the exclusionary rule would be considered objectionable, particularly by criminal defendants, because the decision as to whether evidence should be excluded or admitted would not be reached with reference to the manner in which it was obtained.

Secondly, a judge who resolves to decide by lot will probably be accused of acting irresponsibly. When, for example, a Manhattan criminal court judge tossed a coin to determine whether a pickpocket should receive twenty or thirty days imprisonment, the New York City Commission on Judicial Conduct removed him from office, holding that 'abdicati[on of] such solemn responsibilities, particularly in so whimsical a manner . . . is inexcusable and indefensible'.[201]

In relation to this second problem, it is worth noting Broome's argument that random selection is not really a refusal to judge.[202] Although a legal decision-maker who relies on a lottery does not offer a judgment concerning the relevant outcome, he or she does make the judgment that a randomized outcome is appropriate. Deciding by lot may, in fact, be a very honest, courageous, and resolute

---

[198] On the exclusionary rule, see generally Yale Kamisar, ' "Comparative Reprehensibility" and the Fourth Amendment Exclusionary Rule' (1987) 86 *Michigan L. Rev.* 1–50.

[199] Miller (above, n. 108), 92.   [200] Ibid. 93.

[201] Cited after David Wasserman, 'The Procedural Turn: Social Heuristics and Neutral Values', in Klaus F. Röhl and Stefan Machura (eds.), *Procedural Justice* (Aldershot: Dartmouth, 1997), 37–58 at 48. See also William G. Blair, 'Flip of Coin Decides Jail Term in Manhattan Criminal Case', *New York Times*, 2 Feb. 1982, § A, p. 1, col. 1. It was noted in Chapter 3 that judges have on various occasions been censured for resolving legal issues by lot. The fundamental problem with using lotteries to determine the length of sentences, as Wasserman notes ('Procedural Turn', 55 n. 8), is that the practice is likely to generate gratuitous inconsistency among similar cases. The Manhattan criminal court judge in question contended that resort to lot was justified because there was no principled basis for imposing a sentence of twenty in preference to thirty days, or vice versa. If, however, the judge was later faced with another pickpocket and the same dilemma as regards sentencing, and if he were to adopt the same solution but this time the coin toss produced the alternate sentence, an avoidable inconsistency would have been created. The inconsistency would have been avoidable because the judge could have adopted a consistent compromise solution: that is, he could have split the difference and resolved always to impose a twenty-five day sentence. The appeal of the lottery as a decision-making device tends to become particularly evident when indivisibility poses a problem and compromise solutions are either impossible or undesirable.

[202] See Broome (above, n. 4), 52.

thing to do. There is, however, rather more to the objection which Broome seeks to counter. Adherents to what was earlier termed the faith-in-reason perspective on American law have sometimes argued that a hallmark of sound adjudication, especially in the highest courts, is the maturing of collective judicial thought.[203] Delivering legal judgments—according to this perspective—requires not only that a decision be reached with regard to the problem at hand, but that analogous decisions arrived at by earlier courts be reconsidered with a view to improving upon the reasoning which was provided.[204] Where decisions are reached by lot, judicial wisdom is unlikely to mature, for randomization provides no feedback from which judges might learn. Where legal outcomes are procured in this way, indeed, precedent will serve little or no function.

The third, and perhaps the most significant, problem with the legal decision reached by lottery is that it will take no account of the requirements of procedural fairness. By providing reasons for our decisions, we render ourselves accountable to others.[205] Not only do 'reasons provide the basis for knowing how the decision was made and for judging whether it was properly made', but, 'if an error appears, the reasons help in seeking recourse to have the decision corrected'.[206] Reasons, in other words, provide disputing parties with something into which they can bite. Indeed, more basically, where reasons count there is a point to arguing one's case. Within legal contexts, lottery decisions are likely to be considered anathema precisely because they deny any such point. 'The opportunity to persuade a rational arbiter within the compass of permitted treatments could seem for the affected individual an elemental aspect of fairness. In our legal culture it is hard to think otherwise.'[207] If, for example, child custody decisions were made by the flip of a coin, disputing parties would be deprived 'of a process and a forum where their anger and aspirations might be expressed'.[208] In short, not only do randomized outcomes diminish the accountability of decision-makers, but they also remove the possibility of participation in the decision-making process by those for whom the outcome will matter most.

It might be argued that the inability to have any impact on a decision-making process will not cause too much alarm if one gets the outcome that one desires. So long as one wins, why be bothered that the decision-making method takes no account of facts and reasons? As for losers: '[t]hey lose a decision, but not the

---

[203] See Duxbury (above, n. 112), 240–1.

[204] For an exploration of this idea, see Ronald Dworkin, *Law's Empire* (London: Fontana, 1986), 228–32.

[205] See, generally, Robert Nozick, *The Nature of Rationality* (Princeton: Princeton University Press, 1993), 3–40.

[206] D. J. Galligan, *Due Process and Fair Procedures: A Study of Administrative Procedures* (Oxford: Clarendon Press, 1996), 432; and cf. also Genevra Richardson, 'The Duty to Give Reasons: Potential and Practice' [1986] *Public Law* 437–69 at 449.

[207] John E. Coons, 'Consistency' (1987) 75 *California L. Rev.* 59–113 at 110.

[208] Mnookin (above, n. 33), 290; and cf. also Elster (above, n. 3), 118–19, 158.

world. They may win on another occasion.'[209] One loses not because one is adjudged to have the worse or the weaker case but simply because one did not have the luck of the draw. This is precisely the sort of argument which theorists of procedural justice allege to be wrongheaded. At the heart of the procedural justice perspective rests the claim that disputing parties care as much, if not more, about the processes by which decisions are reached as they do about actual decisions. By and large, 'theories of procedural justice suggest that people focus on court procedures, not on the outcomes of their experiences. If the judge treats them fairly by listening to their arguments and considering them, by being neutral, and by stating good reasons for his or her decision, people will react positively to their experience, whether or not they receive a favorable outcome.'[210]

In advancing this general argument, procedural justice theorists point to a variety of characteristics or values which, if embodied within a legal process, should increase the likelihood of the process being considered procedurally fair. The capacity for parties to exert influence over the decision-making process is perhaps the most commonly emphasized of these characteristics.[211] Other important characteristics of procedural fairness include transparency of proceedings and impartiality of decision-makers.[212] Where a decision-making process disregards requirements of procedural fairness, theorists of procedural justice argue, it is unlikely that justice will generally be seen to be done or that citizens will readily accept the legitimacy of decisions reached.[213] Especially aggrieved will be those who receive unfavourable outcomes. Regard for fair procedures, on the other hand, 'can act as a cushion of support when authorities are delivering unfavorable outcomes. If unfavorable outcomes are delivered through procedures viewed as fair, the unfavorable outcomes do not harm the legitimacy of the legal authorities.'[214]

---

[209]   Sunstein (above, n. 142), 41.

[210]   Tom R. Tyler, *Why People Obey the Law* (New Haven: Yale University Press, 1990), 6.

[211]   On this particular characteristic see, e.g., John Thibaut and Laurens Walker, *Procedural Justice: A Psychological Analysis* (Hillsdale, NJ: Lawrence Erlbaum, 1975); Linda Musante, Marcia A. Gilbert, and John Thibaut, 'The Effects of Control on Perceived Fairness of Procedures and Outcomes' (1983) 19 *Journal of Experimental Social Psychology* 223–38; and P. Christopher Earley and E. Allan Lind, 'Procedural Justice and Participation in Task Selection: The Role of Control in Mediating Justice Judgments' (1987) 52 *Journal of Personality and Social Psychology* 1148–60.

[212]   On transparency, see e.g. John Thibaut and Laurens Walker, 'A Theory of Procedure' (1978) 66 *California L. Rev.* 541–66 (arguing, at p. 542, that 'the procedure most likely to produce justice is that procedure which facilitates the fullest possible report of inputs prior to determination'); and, on impartiality, see E. Allan Lind and Tom R. Tyler, *The Social Psychology of Procedural Justice* (New York: Plenum Press, 1988), 125–7. For other characteristics of procedural fairness, cf. Robert E. Lane, 'Procedural Goods in a Democracy: How One Is Treated Versus What One Gets' (1988) 2 *Social Justice Research* 177–92; and also Geoffrey M. Stephenson, *The Psychology of Criminal Justice* (Oxford: Blackwell, 1992), 237–9.

[213]   See Jonathan D. Casper, 'Having Their Day in Court: Defendant Evaluations of the Fairness of Their Treatment' (1978) 12 *Law and Society Review* 237–51 at 246–9; and Tyler (above, n. 210), 110–11.

[214]   Tyler (above, n. 210), 107. See also T. R. S. Allan, 'Procedural Fairness and the Duty of Respect' (1998) 18 *Oxford Journal of Legal Studies* 497–515.

Arguments for randomized legal decision-making are likely to look rather vulnerable when considered in the light of the procedural justice perspective. For although the lottery produces an outcome, it is inattentive to the main demands of procedural fairness. A randomized legal decision which is considered to be distributively just may still be unacceptable because it is not seen to be procedurally just. Greely probably has much the same point in mind when he states that:

Random selection . . . denies the citizen's demand for participation in and accountability of the method of allocation. In merit or need determinations, the potential recipient can argue with the allocating official about his satisfaction of the relevant criteria, and if the good is denied the citizen can blame the official. The lottery eliminates both options . . . The frustrations engendered by the unaccountable allocation of the lottery may be the greatest cost of random selection.[215]

The long and short of the matter is that arguments concerning the importance of procedural fairness tend to translate quite easily into criticisms, usually fairly robust criticisms, of proposals for legal decision-making by lot. Indeed, one might twist this observation around and state that aversion to the use of lotteries for legal decision-making purposes is indicative of commitment to standards of procedural fairness: that we generally do not want to resolve legal issues by lot is explicable by virtue of the fact that we generally do want legal processes which, among other things, ensure that outcomes are supported by reasons, are responsive to the arguments of claimants, provide decisions for which somebody can be held accountable and upon which future decision-makers might build, and offer answers that—irrespective of whether they might accurately be termed 'right'—are serious in the sense that the manner in which they are arrived at does not trivialize the subject-matter of the decision. One could highlight random selection as illustrative of the sort of legal process we do not want, in other words, so as to begin to develop our ideas about what sort of legal process we do want.

It would be easy and convenient to conclude this chapter, possibly even the book, on this last point. The moral of the story would be that random selection, although lacking prospects as a method of legal decision-making, is none the less an intriguing heuristic device for legal and political philosophers. Rather than rely on this conclusion, however, I intend to draw this chapter to a close by, first of all, raising some doubts about certain arguments related to procedural fairness and, secondly, arguing that we ought not to underestimate the resilience of the case for randomized legal decision-making. In Chapter 5, I shall endeavour to build upon this latter argument by considering how lotteries might profitably be put to greater use in certain legal decision-making contexts.

Procedural fairness is a rather ambiguous idea. Beliefs about what constitutes procedurally fair behaviour tend to be context-specific rather than general: not only will people have different expectations of decision-makers, but individual

---

[215] Greely (above, n. 3), 122–3.

conceptions of fairness tend to change as decision-making processes unfold.[216] Doubt can be cast, furthermore, on certain of the advantages of procedural fairness in official decision-making. Consider, for example, the so-called 'cushioning effects of fair procedure'.[217] That a fair procedure makes an unfavourable outcome tolerable is open to question. One might expect dissatisfaction with such a procedure to become evident if it persistently generates unfavourable outcomes.[218] Even in individual instances, fairness of procedure may fail to alleviate dissatisfaction with outcome. This tends to be the case, one psychological study has shown, where decision-makers have acted fairly in the sense that they have abided by relevant legal procedures but, in the eyes of the losing party, would have exhibited a greater sense of fairness had they moved beyond the legal rules and considered what, as a matter of equity, would have constituted procedurally just decision-making activity.[219] The very notion that there may be a distinction between what is procedurally just as a matter of law and what is procedurally just as a matter of equity rather reinforces the equivocality of procedural fairness. Should it be the case, it has been suggested, that decision-makers promote an equitable version of proceduralism by emphasizing the generation of fairness—in both procedure and outcome—through the exercise of discretion rather than through the following of rules, those who subscribe to a legalistic (or rule of law) conception of procedural justice might very well consider that conception to have been undermined.[220]

Also open to question is the idea, noted earlier, that fair procedures create the advantage of enabling—just as lottery decisions have the disadvantage of not enabling—disputing parties to express their anger and aspirations. The issue here is not whether a procedurally just legal process does provide parties with such an opportunity, but whether it is correct straightforwardly to assume that provision of this opportunity must be advantageous. The assumption appears to be that the advantage of a process which allows for presentation of one's case is that even those who lose will find the experience cathartic. But this is naive psychology. Aggression is not necessarily diluted by virtue of having been expressed. Indeed, in some circumstances aggressive behaviour tends to perpetuate itself. 'Aggressing the first time', Aronson contends, 'can reduce your inhibitions against committing other such actions; the aggression is legitimized, and it becomes easier to carry out such assaults. Furthermore . . . committing an overt

---

[216] For illustrations from different perspectives, see Daniel Kahneman, Jack L. Knetsch, and Richard Thaler, 'Fairness as a Constraint on Profit Seeking: Entitlements in the Market' (1986) 76 *American Economic Review* 728–41; and Kenneth A. Rasinski, 'What's Fair is Fair—Or is it? Value Differences Underlying Public Views About Social Justice' (1987) 53 *Journal of Personality and Social Psychology* 201–11.   [217] Tyler (above, n. 210), 107.

[218] A point which is acknowledged by Tyler, ibid.

[219] See Linda Musante, 'The Effects of Type of Evidence and Favorability of Verdict on Perceptions of Justice' (1984) 14 *Journal of Applied Social Psychology* 448–60.

[220] See Martin Loughlin, 'Procedural Fairness: A Study of the Crisis in Administrative Law Theory' (1978) 28 *Univ. Toronto LJ* 215–41 at 239–40.

act of aggression against a person changes one's feelings about that person, increasing one's negative feelings toward the target and therefore increasing the probability of future aggression against that person.'[221] Aggressive behaviour does not necessarily result in more of the same; whether or not it does will depend largely, I suspect, on the type of response that the behaviour provokes. For our purposes, the point which deserves emphasis is that it is simplistic to assume that recourse to a process which allows for expression of anger and aspirations will necessarily result in catharsis. Much will depend on how one considers the process to have reacted to one's plight. To walk away from the process having expressed one's anger and aspirations but having won nothing might do little, if anything, to quell inner turmoil.

One of the basic disadvantages of randomized decision-making, we have seen, is that it can sometimes generate what has been termed negative symbolic resonance. It appears that a basic argument in favour of procedural fairness is that it creates positive symbolic resonance. For example, it may be considered symbolically important that a legal process allows citizens to participate in, and endeavour to influence, decisions which affect them. The purpose of the process is then to try to ensure not only that justice is done, but that it is seen to be done. Claims concerning symbolic resonance are decidedly difficult to negotiate: it is no easier to refute the proposition that process values are symbolically important than it is to counter the argument that it is symbolically inappropriate to resolve legal disputes by lot—in short, it is difficult to know how to argue with the person who says that something is symbolically right or wrong. My own feeling is that, just as preoccupation with symbolism may cause us to underestimate the potential for the use of lotteries within legal decision-making contexts, so too it may lead us to overestimate the value of procedural fairness.[222] Consider, for instance, the emphasis that is placed upon participation as a procedural virtue. The fact of the matter is that '[p]articipatory governance ... is commonly overvalued. It is simply not possible in a society like ours for persons to participate in every significant stage of every significant decisional process that might significantly affect them. And even where possible, it would not necessarily be appropriate, given such other desiderata as expertise and confidentiality.'[223] More generally, it seems questionable whether people, certainly *qua* litigants, commonly do value procedure as much as or more than outcome, or even whether procedure and outcome are genuinely separable from each other.[224]

[221] Elliot Aronson, *The Social Animal* (7th edn., New York: W. H. Freeman & Co., 1995), 261.

[222] Others have claimed that it is fundamentally irrational to emphasize the symbolic importance of procedural fairness: see Elster (above, n. 34), 10; and Brian Barry, *Democracy, Power and Justice: Essays in Political Theory* (Oxford: Clarendon Press, 1989), 396–8.

[223] Summers (above, n. 135), 43.

[224] See Elster (above, n. 3), 120–1; and cf. also Thomas C. Grey, 'Procedural Fairness and Substantive Rights', in J. Roland Pennock and John W. Chapman (eds.), *Nomos XVIII: Due Process* (New York: New York University Press, 1977), 182–205; and Larry Alexander, 'Are Procedural Rights Derivative Substantive Rights?' (1998) 17 *Law and Philosophy* 19–42.

The discussion here has proceeded on the assumptions that legal decision-making by lot could never be presented in a symbolically positive light or be considered procedurally fair. Yet neither assumption ought to be left entirely unquestioned. In relation to child custody adjudication, one can at least 'imagine a coin-tossing procedure coming to symbolize the equal worth of the parents, as well as the child's right to a speedy decision'.[225] As regards procedural justice, there is certainly some evidence that disputing parties will be more likely to regard as procedurally fair an adjudicative process over which the decision-maker has no control—such as a lottery—as compared with a process which the decision-maker is able to administer in an entirely arbitrary fashion.[226] It is, of course, highly unlikely that parties to a legal dispute will ever be faced with a choice between a decision-making procedure over which nobody has control and one over which the decision-maker has unfettered control. Anyone who has regularly to resolve between children the type of squabble that does not allow for compromise, however, will know that this sort of choice can realistically (and very effectively) be posed to resolve some non-legal disputes.

These claims concerning the possible symbolic virtue and procedural fairness of legal decision-making by lot are very obviously tentative. The case for such decision-making would look decidedly far-fetched were they to be cited as primary supporting evidence. But then, how might one make a case for resort to lotteries in legal decision-making contexts? What other supporting evidence do we have? The case for more extensive use of lotteries within legal decision-making contexts will most likely look bizarre no matter how we try to advance it. The argument, however, that resort to lot will sometimes be the proper course of action for the honest rationalist deserves, I think, more than cursory consideration. As decision-makers, we quite often fall prey to myopia, inconsistency, emotivism, and other cognitive quirks; sometimes, we cannot see the difference between sufficient and excessive information—indeed, it is often the case that the more information we have, the better we believe our position to be. Rarely, when making decisions of considerable social significance, are we quick to come to the conclusion that to acquire more information will in all probability prove costly and distortive.[227] Rather than give up, or cut our losses, we more often than not persist in our efforts to approximate what we believe to be the behaviour of a rational decision-maker. Yet such a decision-maker would recognize something that often escapes us: that our capacity to assimilate information, and to develop reasons on the basis of that information, is limited. Reason and

---

[225] Elster (above, n. 3), 171.

[226] See Blair H. Sheppard, David M. Saunders, and John W. Minton, 'Procedural Justice From the Third-Party Perspective' (1988) 54 *Journal of Personality and Social Psychology* 629–37 at 634–6.

[227] See, generally, Daniel Kahneman, Paul Slovic, and Amos Tversky, *Judgment Under Uncertainty: Heuristics and Biases* (Cambridge: Cambridge University Press, 1982).

ethics, like rationality itself, are bounded entities.[228] That we may recognize the bounded nature of our decision-making faculties and yet, when confronted by indeterminacy, keep faith with those faculties—in spite of the fact that there is available, in the form of the lottery, a more rational method by which to produce an outcome—can largely be explained, I believe, by reference to notions of symbolism and justice. That symbolism and justice may explain our behaviour, however, does not necessarily make that behaviour honest. It may be good political strategy—a useful lie[229]—to prefer the rituals, rather than to accept the limits, of legal decision-making. '[F]rom the point of view of quest for truth,' however, 'such a method is worthless.'[230] In studying legal decision-making it is possible, Tribe has argued, to pursue rationalism to excess.[231] Although I shall defer from assessing that argument, my own distinctly speculative claim here has been that when we engage in legal decision-making, we will sometimes pursue pseudo-rationalism to excess.

CONCLUSION

We saw in Chapter 3 that the primary advantages of social decision-making by lot are subject to qualification. In this chapter, I have outlined the primary disadvantages of randomized decision-making. Out of the discussion of these disadvantages, however, there has emerged a fairly positive case for lottery use. Just as I found it impossible to advance arguments in favour of randomization without acknowledging their shortcomings, I have likewise not been able to explore arguments concerning the disadvantages of randomness without considering how they might be countered. No doubt I risk being accused of adversariality by concluding this chapter with a fairly elaborate argument in favour of lottery use—as if according the last word, as it were, to the case for random decision-making. But there is a straightforward reason for doing this: the arguments in favour of using lotteries for legal decision-making purposes are generally weaker than the counter-arguments. It would be as simple as it would be pointless to write in denunciation of resort to sortition in order to resolve legal disputes. With whom, after all, would I be in disagreement? The primary objective of this book is to encourage serious reflection on a counter-intuitive idea. Arguments concerning the appropriateness of random selection as a method of dispute resolution will, in

---

[228] On bounded rationality as a determinant of social choice, see Herbert A. Simon, 'A Behavioral Model of Rational Choice' (1954) 69 *Quarterly Journal of Economics* 99–118; and on the notion of bounded ethics, cf. Daniel C. Dennett, *Darwin's Dangerous Idea: Evolution and the Meanings of Life* (Harmondsworth: Penguin, 1995), 494–510.

[229] See Plato, *Laws* 2. 663.

[230] Hans Kelsen, *What is Justice? Justice, Law, and Politics in the Mirror of Science* (Berkeley, Calif.: University of California Press, 1957), 173.

[231] Laurence H. Tribe, 'Trial by Mathematics: Precision and Ritual in the Legal Process' (1971) 84 *Harvard L. Rev.* 1329–93.

most instances, cause us to react uneasily. I hope to have demonstrated that it is at least intellectually worthwhile to consider why we should generally react in this way and whether such a reaction is always justifiable. In the next chapter, I shall endeavour to go one step further and suggest that it may make practical as well as intellectual sense to accord serious attention to the idea of randomized legal decision-making.

Before proceeding to that chapter, we might briefly consider one more conjecture. Sometimes, when one swims, one finds that the coolness of the water on initial entry takes one's breath away. The experience is an uncomfortable one, and seasoned outdoor swimmers—certainly if one lives in a place more akin to Manchester than Malibu—will know that, when faced with cool water, most people either try to enter it in stages so as gradually to get used to the temperature or just defiantly take the plunge. The point is that, however one enters the water, once one is in—and so long as one swims—the discomfort will certainly diminish, and most probably vanish. When negotiating cold water, we tend to be thankful for our ability to acclimatize. In other contexts, however, our capacity for acclimatization can trouble us. This much is evident from the fact that, in considering whether or not to accept arguments and proposals, we occasionally express concern that acceptance may represent the thin end of the wedge, or place us on a slippery slope.[232] Sometimes we worry that acceptance of some state of affairs will have a morally impoverishing effect. Such anxiety is most commonly expressed in relation to proposals for the commodification of 'non-market' goods: should we ever reach a point where we consider commercial adoption or the sale of human organs to be legally acceptable, it is sometimes asked, what sort of species will we have become?[233] On occasions we do, however, enter markets— just as we enter the cold-water pool—with a sense of unease and yet fairly quickly (and without coming to any harm) find ourselves acclimatized. The history of life insurance reveals as much.[234]

Perhaps resistance to proposals for randomized legal decision-making is partially explicable in terms of acclimatization. Possibly part of the worry is that were we—on an experimental basis, say—to decide to resolve certain types of legal issue by resort to lot, to dip our toes in the water, we would soon find ourselves swimming in the pool, comfortable with what once filled us with dread. I find this conjecture difficult to evaluate. However, what I would argue—indeed, what I hope the next chapter demonstrates—is that the analogy on which I have

---

[232] On the notion of the slippery slope in argumentation, see Bernard Williams, *Making Sense of Humanity and Other Philosophical Papers, 1982–1993* (Cambridge: Cambridge University Press, 1995), 213–23.

[233] See, e.g., Margaret Jane Radin, *Contested Commodities* (Cambridge, Mass.: Harvard University Press, 1996), 79–101.

[234] See Viviana A. Zelizer, 'Human Values and the Market: The Case of Life Insurance and Death in 19th-Century America' (1978) 84 *American Journal of Sociology* 591–610; and cf. also Duxbury (above, n. 21), 336.

relied to articulate the conjecture falls apart on close inspection. In contemplating whether to enter or stay out of the water, we have an all-or-nothing choice; in considering whether or not to use lotteries for legal decision-making purposes, the choice appears to be more complex—that is, it is not, or rather does not have to be, simply a matter of either resolving to decide by lot or refraining from deciding by lot. Instead, with lotteries, there can be degrees of commitment.

5

Lotteries within Legal Frameworks

It was stated earlier that this book would drift from historical study to analytical inquiry and, ultimately, to normative proposals. No attempt has been made rigidly to demarcate these three objectives, so although this chapter is concerned with the last objective the normative thrust of this project has been adverted to on various occasions already. In this chapter, I shall outline a fairly modest and distinctly provisional case for greater reliance on lotteries within specific (primarily legal) contexts. It seems reasonable, from the outset, to question why anybody should wish to do such a thing.

1. WHY NORMATIVITY?

This question might be prompted by two reservations, one general and one quite specific. The general reservation concerns the very point of normative legal theory. Why do it? In Chapter 4, we considered Schlag's argument that American academic lawyers deify the role of reason in law to the extent that they seem generally to be unwilling to contemplate the possibility that, within the legal decision-making process, the role of reason may become exhausted. Schlag develops this argument further, claiming that American law professors, being so enamoured of reason, conceive their purpose to be that of suggesting how the legal system might be reformed so as to meet the demands of reason with ever greater precision. The law reviews of the American law schools contain article upon article, he insists, offering the same normative message: that legal actors (judges, legislators, or whoever) ought to endeavour to become something other than what they currently are—more principled, more prudent, more candid, more tolerant, more race-conscious, more open to theories of interpretation, more economically minded, or whatever—so that the legal process might function better. The great tragedy for the American law professor is that the message goes unheeded. 'By and large, neither judges nor any other bureaucratic decision makers are listening to academic advice that they are not already prepared to believe.'[1]

American legal scholarship is beset, in other words, by normative redundancy. Legal academics are prone to 'wishful thinking'—to persisting with their recommendations as if the legal profession really were paying attention—but the truth is

---

[1] Pierre Schlag, *Laying Down the Law: Mysticism, Fetishism, and the American Legal Mind* (New York: New York University Press, 1996), 70.

that judges and other legal officials 'simply do not have the time, the inclination, or the patience to read' the law reviews.[2] On realizing that their exhortations have failed to influence legal practice, academic lawyers tend to seek solace in one another, boosting their collective sense of self-importance by taking one another's ideas seriously. In truth, however, the game is up: recognition 'that normative legal thought is an economy of self-referential instrumentalist rhetorical structures ... is likely to lead [legal academics] to a certain degree of disenchantment ... [T]his disenchantment is already well on its way'[3]—to the extent, indeed, that 'the participants can no longer sustain the beliefs, or suspensions of disbelief, necessary to make the practice [of legal scholarship] meaningful to them or to others'.[4] Normativism in legal scholarship is reaching, if it has not already reached, a dead end.

If Schlag's diagnosis is correct, then the normative dimension to this project is—as it would be to any jurisprudential project—ill-judged. For at least three reasons, however, the diagnosis might be doubted.[5] Schlag makes an unconvincing case, first of all, because he seems unable to disentangle himself from normative legal scholarship. 'Until normative legal thought begins to deal with its own paradoxical postmodern rhetorical situation,' he states, 'it will remain something of an irresponsible enterprise.'[6] He further asserts that the value of normative legal thought 'is now very much in need of some serious intellectual demonstration'[7] and that '[t]o understand law, one must appreciate and understand the identity of the subjects who invoke its name'.[8] These assertions are, if nothing else, normative. Secondly, if normative legal scholarship in the United States really is moribund, one would expect that in the United Kingdom—where, as compared with their American counterparts, academic lawyers have been able to exert considerably less influence upon the legal system—such scholarship would have withered away long ago. Yet this is not the case.[9] In short, the proposition that normative legal scholarship in America has run, or even that it is running, out of steam is not substantiated and—in light of experience on this side of the Atlantic—lacks credibility. Indeed, thirdly, normative scholarship, for all that it may often prove to be otiose, appeals to academic lawyers because non-normative scholarship, by comparison, delivers very little indeed. When addressing the question of what it is that legal academics ought to do instead of engaging in normative legal scholarship, Schlag provides answers which are vague and

---

[2] Pierre Schlag, 'Normativity and the Politics of Form' (1991), in Paul F. Campos, Pierre Schlag, and Stephen D. Smith, *Against the Law* (Durham, NC: Duke University Press, 1996), 29–99 at 59. On the impotence of academic moralism in relation to law, see also Richard A. Posner, *The Problematics of Moral and Legal Theory* (Cambridge, Mass.: Belknap Press, 1999), 38–44, 68–90.
[3] Schlag (above, n. 1), 35–6.   [4] Ibid. 70.
[5] The criticisms which follow are developed in two book reviews which I have produced dealing with Schlag's work: see (1997) 60 *Modern L. Rev.* 874–7; and 'Legal Dons in the Dock', *Times Higher Education Supplement*, 27 Mar. 1998, p. 25.
[6] Schlag (above, n. 1), 37–8.   [7] Ibid. 76.   [8] Ibid. 163.
[9] See P. S. Atiyah, *Pragmatism and Theory in English Law* (London: Stevens & Sons, 1987), 165–83.

unconvincing. Such academics, he states, ought to 'attempt to help destabilize normative legal thought'.[10] 'For those with the inclination and the capacity' to engage in such attempts, 'there are a tremendous number of questions to answer, questions that . . . no one has yet *dared* to ask'.[11] To what end, however, ought we to destabilize normative legal scholarship? And what questions should we be asking? Schlag responds with bewilderment to the suggestion that there must be some purpose to the debunking of normativism: the notion 'that one should not merely criticize or destroy, but try to be constructive as well' is, he believes, 'perplexing'.[12] Asked, in the course of an interview, with what he would replace normative legal scholarship, Schlag replies: 'I just cut down some parasites on my ponderosa pines. And if somebody were to ask me, "What are you going to put in its [*sic*] place?" I'd say, "Nothing. Haven't I done enough?" '[13] Elsewhere, he responds to the question with a more elaborate analogy:

If you take someone's neurosis away, are you being *destructive* (of that person's way of doing things) or are you being *constructive* (of a new organically healthy person)? If you were being destructive when you took away the person's neurosis, are you then obliged to do something more afterwards—something constructive? What would this additional constructive moment look like, and how would it help? Indeed, how often does an analysand terminate successful therapy with the statement, 'Yes, I understand I'm fine now. There's just one more question, doctor: What should I do?'[14]

Neither of these analogies is convincing. Citizens depend upon legal systems and want to be happy with the ways in which those systems operate; academic lawyers generally appreciate this and so engage in normative legal scholarship because they recognize that if law is to serve people better there is often a need not simply for the removal of defects but also for the replacement of those defects with something else. The comparison of legal scholarship with the treatment of an infested garden tree or a course of therapy fails to accommodate this insight. That legal academics should make it their business to highlight shortcomings within legal systems and suggest how those systems might be changed for the better is perfectly understandable. No doubt there will often be a good deal of naivety to such suggestions, and no doubt they will often fall on stony ground. It seems highly unlikely, however, that the impulse to be normative should dissipate.

It is, of course, one thing to defend normative legal scholarship in general, but something else entirely to make a specific case for greater use of lotteries within legal decision-making contexts. How might such a case be made? The most obvious answer to this question is to be derived from the argument which has just been offered in favour of normative legal scholarship: there will be

---

[10] Schlag (above, n. 2), 99.
[11] Pierre Schlag, 'Clerks in the Maze', in Campos *et al.* (above, n. 2), 218–36 at 236.
[12] Schlag (above, n. 1), 169 n. 7.
[13] Comment attributed to Pierre Schlag in 'Waiting for Langdell, I' (interview with the authors), in Campos *et al.* (above, n. 2), 15–28 at 28.   [14] Schlag (above, n. 1), 169–70 n. 7.

good reason to make a case for more extensive use of lotteries within legal decision-making contexts if it should appear that such use is likely to change the legal system for the better. The problem which arises here is that arguments concerning how novel uses of lotteries for decision-making purposes might improve legal processes will be speculative and contestable. Indeed, all of the arguments to be encountered in this chapter concerning how lotteries might be incorporated into decision-making processes are questionable at one level or another. This, however, hardly constitutes a reason for not considering such arguments. If nothing else, these arguments are deserving of theoretical scrutiny because we ought to be sure that we do not dismiss them too casually. That they can be dismissed too casually is surely not in doubt. Arguments for taking seriously the idea that lotteries might be used within legal decision-making contexts have already emerged at various points throughout this study. In Chapter 4, for example, it was argued that merely to contemplate the randomized resolution of important legal disputes is likely to prove instructive if only because our aversion to this procedure will be generated to a certain degree by our sense of what legal decision-making ought to entail. The spectre of the lottery as a legal device, in other words, may turn out to be heuristically significant. It was also suggested in that chapter that it may sometimes be rational, even if it is considered unrealistic, to make greater use of randomized legal decision-making. In this chapter, I shift from an abstract consideration of the benefits which may be associated with this mode of decision-making and argue more concretely that, in certain contexts, the introduction of lottery elements into legal processes might be practically advantageous. The primary difficulty with this thesis is that it cannot seriously be advanced without frank acknowledgement of the fact that resort to lotteries for legal decision-making purposes will quite frequently offend against commonplace conceptions of justice. It is important also to recognize that the incorporation of lotteries into broader decision-frameworks will often be considered impracticable. The purpose of this chapter is to try to ascertain that, in limited circumstances, the use of randomizing techniques in legal contexts may have positive effects on people's incentives and might also, on occasions, turn out to be cost-efficient and (more controversially) just.

2. MODEST PROPOSALS

One of the reasons we tend to be resistant to recourse to sortition for the purpose of making decisions of social or legal significance is that we very often consider the lottery to be a device which is both pure and inflexible: we are prone to assuming, that is, that the lottery must only be capable of producing equiprobable outcomes and that, as a decision-making mechanism, it must operate in isolation. Neither assumption is warranted. Lotteries, it has been observed, do not have to generate equiprobable outcomes.[15] In searching for a middle ground between value-sensitivity and arbitrariness, decision-makers sometimes desire allocative devices or methods—the so-called 'quality adjusted life year' is illustrative of this point[16]— which can be applied in a mechanical or formulaic fashion but which can also accommodate distinctions between candidates. The weighted lottery is another such device, and social decision-makers—as was demonstrated in Chapter 3—may sometimes have good reasons for resorting to it. In this chapter, I am concerned not with the assumption of equiprobability but with the relationship between the lottery and other decision-making procedures. Central to my discussion is the idea that lotteries may be implemented so as to complement rather than to pose an alternative to other such procedures; indeed, my argument rests upon the assumption that resort to randomization within decision-making contexts is likely to be considered more acceptable where the lottery is used not in isolation but in combination with other devices for allocating goods and resolving disputes. That decision-making methods can be profitably combined is an idea which presents numerous avenues for study—indeed, all sorts of combinations might be envisaged. Here, however, I am concerned only with the combinative potential of lotteries.

Note that my suggestion is that lotteries may be usefully combined with other allocative and adjudicative methods.[17] Although I am concerned specifically with contrived combinations, it ought at least to be observed that such combinations often occur naturally. Chance, as was intimated in Chapter 1, might be expected to play a part at some level or another in all allocative procedures. In various ways, fate is likely to influence distributions of resources irrespective of what

---

[15] A point which is made implicitly in Chapter 4, section 2, but which we should perhaps spell out, is that even where the point of instituting a lottery is to generate equiprobabilistic outcomes, it is unlikely that all even-chance lotteries will be equally suited to the particular task in hand: see Henry E. Kyburg, Jr., 'Randomness and the Right Reference Class' (1977) 74 *Journal of Philosophy* 501–21 at 512–13; and, more generally, Peter C. Fishburn, 'Even-Chance Lotteries in Social Choice Theory' (1972) 3 *Theory and Decision* 18–40.

[16] The QALY approach to health care requires that decision-makers compare the cost of a treatment with the extent to which, and for how long, that treatment is expected to improve the quality of a patient's life. According to a sliding scale on which death counts as zero, each year of full health counts as one and each year of declining health as minus one. If, therefore, after treatment a patient enjoys a significant and long-lasting improvement in health, he or she accumulates units and scores high on the scale. The system obviously favours treatments which achieve the greatest increase in quality of life, over the longest period, for the least cost. For critical discussion of QALYs, cf. Lesley Fallowfield, *The Quality of Life: The Missing Measurement in Health Care* (London: Souvenir Press, 1990), 204–20; David J. Hunter, *Desperately Seeking Solutions: Rationing Health Care* (London: Longman, 1997), 70–3; John Harris, 'EQALYty', in Peter Byrne (ed.), *Health, Rights and Resources: King's College Studies, 1987–8* (London: King's Fund, 1988), 100–27; and R. A. Carr-Hill, 'Assumptions of the QALY Procedure' (1989) 29 *Social Science and Medicine* 469–77. For the argument that random allocation of health care resources is more just than allocation in accordance with the QALY system, see John Harris, 'Would Aristotle have Played Russian Roulette?' (1996) 22 *Journal of Medical Ethics* 209–15; and compare John McKie, Helga Kuhse, Jeff Richardson, and Peter Singer, 'Another Peep Behind the Veil' (1996) 22 *Journal of Medical Ethics* 216–21.

[17] Much the same suggestion is voiced, though not elaborated, by Guido Calabresi and Philip Bobbitt, *Tragic Choices* (New York: Norton & Co., 1978), 44 ('Pure lotteries . . . can frequently be appended *faute de mieux* to market and political decision procedures').

methods have been adopted to facilitate such distributions.[18] Although the 'lottery' element in many decision-making processes is nothing other than the ineradicable role played by chance, it will sometimes be the case that this element fulfils a specific purpose within such a process and may even be regarded as integral to the fairness of that process. One might expect, for example, that the rotation of tasks or entitlements is more likely to be considered fair if it appears that the person with whom the rota is to start has been selected randomly rather than strategically or on the basis of one or another criterion. Casual empiricism suggests, indeed, that when rotation is used as an allocative device, and particularly where it is used on an *ad hoc* basis, those in charge of the rota will often explicitly incorporate the lottery element into the procedure.

Consider also the phenomenon of queuing. Lotteries and queues are distinct allocative devices—allocation according to chance is something different from allocation according to temporal priority.[19] Nevertheless, it is quite often argued— especially, it appears, in literature dealing with health-care ethics—that the two devices couple naturally. The essence of this argument is that queuing entails 'a kind of "natural" random selection'[20] since ' "[f]irst come, first served" amounts to an on-going lottery'.[21] When, for example, hospital casualty departments dispense treatment on the basis of first come, first served, the order of the queue of patients will be attributable to the random sequence in which the various accidents and emergencies occur. As with random selection, queuing is sometimes seen to be an appropriate method by which to allocate resources where willingness to pay is considered to be an unsatisfactory criterion.[22] Indeed, economists observe

---

[18] Consider, for example, 'accidents of geography', as discussed by James F. Childress, 'Some Moral Connections Between Organ Procurement and Organ Distribution' (1987) 3 *Journal of Contemporary Health Law and Policy* 85–110 at 102–8.

[19] As with lotteries, queues can be weighted and so susceptible to manipulation. 'According to Polish regulations,' Czwartosz observed in the late 1980s, 'pregnant women and women with an infant in arms have a "right to buy without queueing up." Thus a woman with a baby in arms will do her shopping more quickly than when she leaves the baby at home. No wonder it is a normal thing in a shop to see many mothers with small babies.' Zbigniew Czwartosz, 'On Queueing' (1988) 29 *Archives Européenes de Sociologie* 3–11 at 6. According to Elster, queues tend to be susceptible to strategic manipulation where they do not evolve as a response to a natural occurrence (such as a short-age of, say, coronary care units) but rather are formed through voluntary decisions (e.g. to try to obtain scarce consumer goods or immigrant visas): see Jon Elster, *Solomonic Judgements: Studies in the Limitations of Rationality* (Cambridge: Cambridge University Press, 1989), 71. On queuing as a game of skill as opposed to a game of chance, see also the game-theoretic analysis of Leif Johansen, 'Queues (and "Rent-Seeking") as Non-Cooperative Games, Emphasizing Mixed Strategy Solutions', in *Collected Works of Leif Johansen*, ed. Finn R. Førsund (2 vols., Amsterdam: Elsevier, 1987), ii. 827–76.

[20] Gerald R. Winslow, *Triage and Justice* (Berkeley, Calif.: University of California Press, 1982), 146. While Winslow outlines this argument, he does not accept it (ibid. 192 n. 39). The argument does appear to be accepted, however, by John F. Kilner, 'A Moral Allocation of Scarce Lifesaving Medical Resources' (1981) 9 *Journal of Religious Ethics* 245–85 at 252.

[21] Paul Ramsey, *The Patient as Person: Explorations in Medical Ethics* (New Haven: Yale University Press, 1970), 252.

[22] See Brian Barry, *Democracy, Power and Justice: Essays in Political Theory* (Oxford: Clarendon Press, 1989), 402.

that a basic advantage of the queue is that it measures the amount of time that people are prepared to forfeit in order to obtain the resource in question.[23] Economists also observe, however, that a major problem with queuing is that the very process, by usually ensuring that time is spent unproductively, tends to impose a deadweight loss.[24]

The problem of deadweight loss is much less likely to occur where allocations are made randomly. In other respects, lotteries and queues are often considered to share certain advantages and drawbacks. Both systems, Winslow observes, are 'relatively simple to apply'.[25] He notes also, though expresses scepticism about, the argument that queuing tends to accord equality of opportunity owing to the fact that queues often naturally incorporate a lottery element.[26] It is understandable that the argument that queues will equalize opportunities because of their lottery-like quality should be treated with scepticism. For while queues may equalize opportunities, the opportunity costs borne by those queuing will often—depending upon the benefits which they might derive from not joining the relevant queue—differ from one person to the next. Besides imposing opportunity costs, queues may also discriminate against (among others) the aged, the infirm, and those with busy or inflexible schedules. Queuing, furthermore, can sometimes be manipulated, a consequence of which may be that the role of chance within the process is undercut. In his article, 'Who Shall Live When Not All Can Live?', first published in 1970,[27] Childress proposed 'that we use some form of randomness or chance (either natural, such as "first come, first served," or artificial, such as a lottery) to determine who shall be saved'.[28] Allocating scarce life-saving medical resources through the use of a lottery or by applying the principle of first come, first served—Childress saw little difference between the two procedures[29]—would be justifiable 'primarily because it preserves a significant degree of *personal dignity* by providing *equality* of opportunity'.[30] Reflecting on this

---

[23] See Yoram Barzel, 'A Theory of Rationing by Waiting' (1974) 17 *Journal of Law and Economics* 73–95; and Gary S. Becker, 'A Theory of the Allocation of Time' (1965) 75 *Economic Journal* 493–517 at 515–16.

[24] Which loss, furthermore, where people in the queue value their time unequally, will be felt in different ways: see D. Nichols, E. Smolensky, and T. N. Tideman, 'Discrimination by Waiting Time in Merit Goods' (1971) 61 *American Economic Review* 312–23.

[25] Winslow (above, n. 20), 103.

[26] '[Q]ueuing is often viewed as a way of according equal treatment in terms of equality of opportunity', Winslow observes (ibid. 101), since it is 'consider[ed] . . . to be roughly equivalent to random selection by use of a lottery'.

[27] James F. Childress, 'Who Shall Live When Not All Can Live?' (1970) 53 *Soundings* 339–55; repr. in Stanley Joel Reiser *et al.* (eds.), *Ethics in Medicine: Historical Perspectives and Contemporary Concerns* (Cambridge, Mass.: MIT Press, 1977), 620–6. The citations in the footnotes which follow are to the reprint.   [28] Ibid. 623.

[29] Though he did believe that there is some difference between the two procedures: ibid. 624–5 ('My proposal is that we extend this principle (first come, first served) to determine who among the medically acceptable patients shall live or that we utilize artificial chance such as a lottery or randomness. "First come, first served" would be more feasible than a lottery since the applicants make their claims over a period of time rather than as a group at one time.')   [30] Ibid. 623.

article and the many criticisms that it provoked, Childress conceded recently that he had 'oversimplified utilitarian selection'[31] and, in consequence, had failed to appreciate that allocation by randomization or through queuing might not always be fair. Childress states that not only would he now 'argue that medical utility should also be used to determine which candidate should receive the organ'[32] but that he would be less inclined to justify allocation through lots or queues by reference to equalization of opportunities. The problem is not simply that queuing systems can be manipulated—'for example, by putting patients on the [renal transplant] list before they become dialysis dependent'—but that 'the fairness of queuing (as well as of randomization) depends in part on background conditions. For example, some people . . . may receive inadequate medical advice about how early to seek transplantation.'[33]

That random selection may couple naturally with other allocative methods is, for the purposes of this study, less significant than the fact that this mode of selection may be deliberately combined with other such methods. In one way or another, such combinations might prove to be of value. At a very basic level, lotteries can be—and often are—combined with general decision-making criteria. We have observed in this study that non-weighted lotteries are inattentive to attributes such as need, merit, and productivity. Yet it is precisely because of this inattentiveness that these attributes are often deliberately incorporated into the lottery process. A random selection will usually be a selection from a pool of eligibles; determination of eligibility for entry into the pool will more often than not require that candidates satisfy some criterion of need, merit, productivity, or whatever.[34] The point is that, for the lottery to function effectively as a social decision-making device, it is often necessary that it be supplemented with criteria which make it possible to determine not who should be selected (which, of course, is the very purpose of the lottery) but who should be considered suitable for selection.

The proposition that lotteries may profitably be supplemented by decision-making criteria hardly seems controversial. Rather more difficult to support is the idea that it may sometimes be beneficial to incorporate lotteries into other decision-frameworks. We have encountered this idea already. Towards the end of Chapter 2, we considered the notion of a political system in which majoritarianism is qualified by randomization: under a scheme of lottery voting, political candidates do not win or lose elections on the basis of votes obtained, but are entered into a lottery whereby each candidate's chance of being selected is proportionate to the number of votes obtained. The candidate with the most votes

---

[31] James F. Childress, *Practical Reasoning in Bioethics* (Bloomington: Indiana University Press, 1997), 184.   [32] Ibid. 227.
[33] Ibid. 228; and cf. also Olga Jonasson, 'Waiting in Line: Should Selected Patients Ever Be Moved Up?' (1989) 21 *Transplantation Proceedings* 3390–4.
[34] See also Jon Elster, *Local Justice: How Institutions Allocate Scarce Goods and Necessary Burdens* (Cambridge: Cambridge University Press, 1992), 106–7.

will stand the greatest chance of winning but (ignoring the unlikely event that he or she has obtained all of the votes) will not necessarily win. Although, in Chapter 2, we considered what sorts of benefits might emerge out of a system of lottery voting, I did not elaborate on what is surely the fundamental drawback with such a system: that its implementation would very likely lead to a significant increase in the number of small political parties. 'With a combination of lottery voting and a large number of small parties, the laws of probability would ensure that even a large majority on a specific issue would often be reversed after the next election.'[35] The problem is probably more serious than this: were a system of lottery voting to lead to the emergence of numerous small parties, formation of government might prove difficult if not, on occasions, impossible to achieve.[36] This difficulty might arise in relation to local as it does with regard to national politics, since even regional assemblies usually have some sort of executive. (It is interesting, and perhaps not surprising, to discover that one proponent of lottery voting has fairly recently reiterated that the scheme was intended basically 'as a thought experiment to help us choose between . . . more familiar and time-tested models [of voting]' and conceded that the proposal was originally formulated in 'perhaps too exuberant' a fashion.)[37]

Lottery voting does not appear to constitute a particularly promising combination of decision-making devices. But then, what would be a promising combination? Possibly it will prove advantageous, on occasions, to combine lotteries with markets. Imposition of a price to be paid for entry into a lottery pool might sometimes be an effective method of dealing with scarcity. Szaniawski relates that '[i]n 1980 in Poland, because of the shortage of cars, their distribution between people who had paid in advance was decided upon by means of a lottery: a random device determined whether the car would be delivered to a given person in a year's time, or in two years' time, etc.'[38] No indication is given by Szaniawski as to whether or not this system of distribution was unpopular or why it was adopted in preference to the more obviously applicable principle of first come, first served. Szaniawski intimates that the point of introducing a lottery into the procedure was to reflect the fact that the preferences of those who had entered into the relevant market were indistinguishable: '[i]t was . . . assumed that all persons concerned had the same preferences, i.e. they wanted the cars delivered to them as early as possible'.[39] One might envisage, however, that those within the market for cars would consider the fairness of assuming equality of prefer-

---

[35] Elster (above, n. 19), 89–90.

[36] Although it ought to be noted that some European countries have maintained political stability notwithstanding the proliferation of small political parties.

[37] Akhil Reed Amar, 'Lottery Voting: A Thought Experiment' [1995] *Univ. Chicago Legal Forum* 193–204 at 194–5. That Amar has always conceived of lottery voting as a thought experiment is evident from his original study: see Akhil Reed Amar, 'Choosing Representatives by Lottery Voting' (1984) 93 *Yale LJ* 1283–1308 at 1308.

[38] Klemens Szaniawski, 'On Fair Distribution of Indivisible Goods', in Peter Geach (ed.), *Logic and Ethics* (Dordrecht: Kluwer, 1991), 275–88 at 288.   [39] Ibid.

ences to be outweighed by the unfairness of allocating in accordance with the luck of the draw instead of temporal priority.

Imposition of a price for entry into a lottery pool might sometimes make sense when a number of similarly situated commercial organizations are in competition for a scarce resource. Where, for example, there exists among economically powerful institutions competition for valuable commercial rights, it may in some instances be sensible from a revenue-raising standpoint to require that prospective competitors pay for entry into a lottery through which these rights will be allocated. I am not suggesting that a combined market-and-lottery procedure would necessarily be the best way to allocate such rights; I do not know, and lack the competence to determine, how this procedure might compare with currently favoured methods of allocation. My suggestion is simply that, in this type of allocative context, the market-and-lottery combination might prove now and again to be a feasible and economically sensible procedure. With certain scarce resources, such a procedure would in all likelihood be generally dismissed as unacceptable—given, for example, that proposals for either the random allocation or the sale of human tissue and organs are often considered objectionable,[40] an argument for the sale of rights to enter a lottery for the distribution of human tissues and organs might be considered in some quarters to be doubly objectionable.[41] Even when resources do appear to be suited to allocation through a combined market-and-lottery procedure, proposals for the use of that procedure will need to be framed carefully. It might, for example, be argued that the market-and-lottery method is well suited to the allocation of broadcasting licences. If, say, there exist concerns that allocation of licences on a purely commercial basis will have deleterious effects on broadcasting quality, the introduction of a randomizing element into the procedure will have the advantage of ensuring that licence-allocation is not wholly market-driven.[42] So long as a prospective broadcasting organization has paid the price for entry into the lottery, it will stand the same chance of being allocated a licence as any other organization within the pool.[43] The likelihood, however, is that organizations would be required to do

---

[40] For representative literature, see Marc D. Basson, 'Choosing Among Candidates for Scarce Medical Resources' (1979) 4 *Journal of Medicine and Philosophy* 313–33; George I. Mavrodes, 'Choice and Chance in the Allocation of Medical Resources: A Response to Kilner' (1984) 12 *Journal of Religious Ethics* 97–115; Ruth F. Chadwick, 'The Market for Bodily Parts: Kant and Duties to Oneself' (1989) 6 *Journal of Applied Philosophy* 129–39; and Leon R. Kass, 'Organs for Sale? Propriety, Property, and the Price of Progress' (1992) 107 *The Public Interest* 65–86.

[41] Though I would neither endorse the logic of this line of objection nor accept that arguments in favour of a market for entry into a lottery to allocate human tissue and organs are necessarily undeserving of serious scrutiny: see n. 42, below.

[42] Similarly, reason we should not dismiss outright the idea of allocating human tissue and organs through a combined market-and-lottery procedure is that the introduction of a randomizing element into the commercial allocation of human tissue and organs might have the effect of removing or reducing what are often perceived to be undesirable consequences of allocating such resources solely on the basis of ability and willingness to pay.

[43] I am, for the sake of simplicity, assuming that the lottery is not weighted. This, however, does not have to be the case.

more than simply pay to enter the lottery pool. It would probably be considered important to create regulatory safeguards to try to ensure, among other things, that all of the organizations within the pool would be able to provide, and would be committed to providing, broadcasting of a specified quality. Some years ago, a proposal for commercialized adoptions was denounced in an American newspaper for playing into the hands of child abusers;[44] yet, as one of the authors of the proposal responded, the creation of an adoptions market would not entail doing away with laws prohibiting child abuse.[45] By way of analogy, it might be observed that the introduction of a market-and-lottery procedure for allocating broadcasting licences would not entail the removal of regulations relating to the professional conduct of those entrusted with such licences. Were such a procedure to be implemented, it would no doubt be considered of vital importance that these regulations be kept in place—as would be the case with laws relating to child abuse were a market for adoptions to be established.

The basic problem with the use of a combined market-and-lottery procedure to distribute scarce resources is that it is likely to stymie competition. Should the resources in question be auctioned rather than distributed in accordance with this procedure, it might be expected that they will realize a price which is higher than that which the recipient pays for entry into the lottery[46] (although this price might not equal or exceed the total revenue raised by the market-and-lottery procedure). Not that a market-and-lottery system of allocation is necessarily anti-competitive. Resort to such a system might actually stimulate competition where demand for a resource is minimal owing to the fact that there is only a low probability that ownership of that resource will generate profit. The American experience of leasing federal land for oil and gas drilling appears to lend support to this observation. In the late 1950s, the Bureau of Land Management introduced a combined market-and-lottery scheme for the allocation of oil-drilling leases. To be entered into the lottery for leases, prospective lessees are required to pay a nominal application fee. Lessees must remain in possession of their leases for a minimum of one year and, during that time, pay a standard rent. After one year, they may assign their leases.[47] Parcels of leasehold land are not scarce: all entrants into the lottery can expect to be accorded one plot or another. But the available plots differ significantly in value. Furthermore, the value of any particular plot will not

---

[44] William L. Pierce, 'Baby Auction', *Wall Street Journal*, 22 Aug. 1986, p. 17. 'If I am a child pornographer,' Pierce asks, 'may I purchase a baby so that I will have a "model" or "rentable object" that can be reared to be compliant with my wishes?'

[45] Richard A. Posner, 'The Regulation of the Market in Adoptions' (1987) 67 *Boston Univ. L. Rev.* 59–72 at 66.

[46] See, more generally, Paul R. Milgrom and Robert J. Weber, 'A Theory of Auctions and Competitive Bidding' (1982) 50 *Econometrica* 1089–1122.

[47] Details of the scheme are taken from Abraham E. Haspel, 'Drilling for Dollars: The Federal Oil-Lease Lottery Program' (1985) 9 *Regulation: American Enterprise Institute Journal on Government and Society* 25–31. I assume that the duration of the oil-drilling leases is standard. Haspel's article provides no information on this point.

become apparent until an effort has been made to exploit it. Although entry into the lottery is cheap, tickets are restricted to one per United States citizen and 'the odds [of obtaining a valuable lease] are long. Even when the geologic data are promising, there is still a high risk that no deposits will be found.'[48] A competitive market for oil-drilling leases would probably exist were the most valuable plots of land identifiable prior to leasing and exploitation. The fact, however, that it is not possible to know in advance just which leases will generate profits rather than losses means that there is little incentive for potential lessees to engage in competitive bidding. Allocation of oil-drilling leases by lottery (the price of entry into which is low) is likely, by comparison, to be considered attractive. Not only does the scheme raise revenue for the government, but '[m]any seemingly unpromising tracts leased through the lottery have yielded significant amounts of oil and gas. Yet, because it was not possible to identify which tracts contained oil and gas prior to leasing, none of them would have attracted much bidding competition.'[49] The incentive to participate in the lottery derives from the fact that, although many oil-drilling leases have no resale value, a considerable number of these leases have 'later resold for hundreds of thousands of dollars'.[50] Whereas not many people will wish to bid competitively for leases the majority of which will generate loss, rather more might be willing to pay a small fee to be entered into a lottery for leases a few of which will prove highly profitable.

Thus far, we have been discussing markets combined with lotteries on the assumption that people will sometimes be prepared to pay to be considered for random selection. That market-and-lottery combinations might generate efficiency gains becomes more obvious, however, if we turn our attention to the fact that people may sometimes be prepared to pay for exemption from random selection. Payment for such exemption will often prove objectionable. If it were possible to pay to be excused from the process of random selection for jury service, for example, the criminal justice system would probably be susceptible to manipulation by those with the capacity to buy out jurors. Perhaps purchase of exemption will always be unacceptable where lotteries are used to assign essential communal duties. This supposition becomes somewhat questionable, however, if we consider the idea of a market in military service.

The idea is by no means novel. The practice of purchasing military commissions can be traced back to the fifteenth century.[51] Military offices were originally purchased as investments: according to Fortescue, speculators would invest money in mercenary bands, would then take office in those bands in accordance with the value of their investment, and would subsequently be indemnified from

---

[48] Ibid. 28.   [49] Ibid. 30.   [50] Ibid. 26.

[51] For an historical sketch, see A. E. Sullivan, 'The Rise and Fall of the Purchase System' (1949) 58 *Army Quarterly* 233–9; and, for a contemporary argument that certain public offices should— subject to careful regulatory supervision—be purchasable, cf. Gordon Tullock, 'Corruption Theory and Practice' (1996) 14 *Contemporary Economic Policy* 6–13.

the plunder raised by the mercenaries' activities.[52] In later centuries, the purchase system became a means by which to buy promotion.[53] The attractiveness of the system to the speculator remained, nevertheless, since '[i]f any man wished to realise his capital he could sell out, provided that he could find a buyer'.[54] That purchase entailed a right of resale ensured that governments would often be unable to exercise effective control over military staffing decisions.[55] Certainly in Britain, the inability of government effectively to regulate the purchase system contributed to the system's eventual abolition.[56] The practice of purchasing military commissions appears to have died out more generally because of developments in military strategy and technology. Such developments demanded, by the beginning of the nineteenth century, that the majority of military officers be subjected to formal training. 'The new training schools provided a substitute for the self-selection mechanism provided by purchase. The purchase system was replaced by a professionally trained and paid army to allow for more bureaucratic armies with direct monitoring.'[57]

The purchase system—buying one's way into office—is the primary example of a market in military service. A rather more interesting illustration of such a market for our purposes is the system which permits citizens who have been conscripted through random selection subsequently to purchase exemption. Rarely, if ever, has such a system proved popular. Although it appears that, during the nineteenth century, the citizens of Belgium accepted purchasable military commutation with moderate enthusiasm,[58] evidence from other countries suggests that support for the practice has been more or less wholly confined to the wealthy classes. In France, for example, where the right of all conscripts to purchase military exemption was introduced in the 1790s and abolished in the 1870s,[59] 'this bastard form of equality' came to represent the 'transition between Old Regime frank inequality and post-1870 personal, uncommutable [*sic*], untransferable obligation'.[60] Even in Belgium, certain politicians spoke out against a system which they considered to levy the money of the rich and the blood of the poor.[61]

The right to purchase exemption from military duty was perhaps most famously opposed in the United States during the Civil War. The first American

---

[52] See J. W. Fortescue, *A History of the British Army* (13 vols., London: Macmillan & Co., 1899–1930), i. 51.

[53] See, e.g., Anthony Bruce, *The Purchase System in the British Army, 1660–1871* (London: Royal Historical Society, 1980), 50–2.   [54] Fortescue (above, n. 52), i. 51.

[55] See Bruce (above, n. 53), 91–2.   [56] Ibid. 122–3.

[57] Douglas W. Allen, 'Compatible Incentives and the Purchase of Military Commissions' (1998) 27 *Journal of Legal Studies* 45–66 at 60.

[58] See Nuria Sales de Bohigas, 'Some Opinions on Exemption from Military Service in Nineteenth-Century Europe' (1968) 10 *Comparative Studies in Society and History* 261–89 at 268.

[59] See, generally, Francis Choisel, 'Du tirage au sort au service universel' (1981) 37 *Revue Historique des Armées* 43–60.   [60] Bohigas (above, n. 58), 261.

[61] Ibid. 266–7, also 261 (on commutation for money as 'l'impôt de sang pour le pauvre, impôt d'argent pour le riche').

draft lottery system was established with the enactment of the Enrollment and Conscription Act of 1863. The combination of anti-statist political sentiments and opposition to the war ensured that enforcement of this statute was bitterly, and often violently, resisted.[62] Resistance was intensified owing to the fact that the Act enabled any randomly selected conscript to avoid military duty by putting up $300 to pay a substitute. Banners held at the anti-draft riots which took place in Manhattan in July 1863, after the first lottery had taken place, proclaimed that the war was sustained by 'rich man's money and poor man's blood'.[63] The mood of discontent on the part of the rioters was captured by the New Yorker who asked why Abraham Lincoln should 'think that poor men are to give up their lives and let rich men pay three hundred dollars in order to stay home'.[64] Although the Enrollment and Conscription Act was enforced, the right to purchase release from service was widely resented; Americans have never since accepted such a statutory exemption.[65]

Why was this right considered to be so wrong? 'It's not that three hundred dollars was too cheap a price,' Walzer answers, 'or that dangerous jobs could not be sold for more or less than that amount on the labor market'; the answer, rather, is that the state ought not to 'impose a dangerous job on some of its citizens and then exempt others for a price'.[66] By doing just this, the state risked devaluing the very notion of civic duty, 'for it seemed to abolish the *public thing* and turn military service (even when the republic itself was at stake!) into a private transaction'.[67] More significant still, perhaps, was the fact that the system of payment for commutation generated the impression that the lives of the rich were more valuable than those of the poor. The idea that the purchase of exemption may devalue human life is explored more generally in Graham Greene's *The Tenth Man*. The basis of Greene's story is that prisoners subjected to a decimation order draw lots to determine which of their number will be executed. When the wealthy lawyer, Chavel, makes an unlucky draw, he offers everything he possesses to anyone who will take his place. Miraculously, one of the other prisoners, Janvier, accepts this offer and has Chavel bequeath his entire estate to Janvier's mother and sister in equal shares. By using his wealth in this way, Chavel incurs the resentment of other prisoners: '[w]e can't buy *our* lives ... Why should he?'[68] When, on

---

[62] See, generally, Jack Franklin Leach, *Conscription in the United States: Historical Background* (Rutland, Vt.: Tuttle, 1952), 278–352.

[63] Cited after Bohigas (above, n. 58), 261 n. 3.

[64] James McCague, *The Second Rebellion: The Story of the New York City Draft Riots of 1863* (New York: The Dial Press, 1968), 54. See also Ernest A. McKay, *The Civil War and New York City* (Syracuse, NY: Syracuse University Press, 1990), 213–14, 274.

[65] The US has since used other methods—most notably, during the Vietnam War, draft deferrals for college students—which have been widely regarded as class- or even race-discriminatory. If the right to purchase commutation is unjust, it might be argued, at least the injustice is transparent.

[66] Michael Walzer, *Spheres of Justice: A Defence of Pluralism and Equality* (Oxford: Blackwell, 1983), 99.   [67] Ibid.

[68] Graham Greene, *The Tenth Man* (London: The Bodley Head, 1985), 53.

release, he visits anonymously the women who now possess what was his fortune, he finds that the sister is consumed with hatred for the man who enabled Janvier to reveal his belief that wealth would matter more to his sister and mother than having a brother and son. Chavel's gesture serves to devalue not only the lives of Janvier and his other fellow prisoners but also the lives of Janvier's mother and sister.

History generally speaks against the market for exemption from conscription. But economics—more precisely, welfare economics—speaks very much in its favour. Imagine that there exists a draft lottery, along with a right for those conscripted—so long as there are available substitutes willing to be paid to take their place—to purchase exemption from service. For the purposes of raising an army, the advantage of voluntarism over conscription is that it 'more efficiently selects people for military service'.[69] A basic problem with selecting conscripts by way of a draft lottery is that some of the most able and willing soldiers will not be picked. But the draft lottery combined with a market for exemption might go some way to remedying this problem while also generating allocatively efficient exchanges. A significant number of those randomly selected for conscription may be eager and able to purchase exemption, while there will most likely be others who are eager, or at least willing, to be bought into military service. Pareto efficient transactions will occur where those seeking exemption pay those seeking inclusion to take their place in the military forces.[70] It is very likely, of course, that a draft lottery will have been initially instituted owing to the fact that there was a lack of volunteers for the military. Should this be the case, one might wonder from where it will be possible to find people willing to take the places of those seeking to purchase commutation. The answer is that we might expect some of those who would not volunteer to join the military to show more willingness were financial inducement to be offered.[71]

---

[69] Thomas W. Ross, 'Raising an Army: A Positive Theory of Military Recruitment' (1994) 37 *Journal of Law and Economics* 109–31 at 129.

[70] See Theodore Bergstrom, 'Soldiers of Fortune?', in Walter P. Heller, Ross M. Starr, and David A. Starrett (eds.), *Equilibrium Analysis: Essays in Honor of Kenneth J. Arrow*, ii (Cambridge: Cambridge University Press, 1986), 57–80. An allocation of resources is said to be Pareto optimal and therefore efficient if, and only if, any different allocation of those resources can make one person better off only to the cost of another. Although an allocation of resources may not be Pareto optimal, it may still promote efficiency if it is Pareto superior, i.e. if it makes at least one person better off and nobody worse off. Bergstrom demonstrates that transactions between those seeking exemption and those seeking inclusion will sometimes be Pareto optimal, at other times Pareto superior. See also John M. Marshall, 'Gambles and the Shadow Price of Death' (1984) 74 *American Economic Review* 73–86. On the problems with Pareto criteria, cf. Guido Calabresi, 'The Pointlessness of Pareto: Carrying Coase Further' (1991) 100 *Yale LJ* 1211–37 at 1215–17; and G. A. Cohen, 'The Pareto Argument for Inequality', in Ellen Frankel Paul, Fred D. Miller, Jr., and Jeffrey Paul (eds.), *Contemporary Political and Social Philosophy* (Cambridge: Cambridge University Press, 1995), 160–85.

[71] It ought to be noted that even if it is allocatively efficient to permit purchase of military exemption, such a practice might lead to a diminution in the quality of military recruits. One might anticipate such a diminution if it is the case that the best soldiers tend to be mature and intelligent, since a system which allows for the purchase of exemption is likely to ensure that a greater propor-

One might object that a scheme such as this would prove exploitative. Out of such an arrangement—to put the objection bluntly—there would emerge a military composed in the main of those too poor either to buy their way out or to resist being bought in.[72] I do not really know how to respond to this objection. Quite often it is voiced in relation to other resources the commodification of which is controversial. Were we to permit commercial adoptions and markets in human organs, it is sometimes asserted, the economically desperate would suffer physically and emotionally in providing these resources for the rich. I have argued elsewhere that exaggeration is often the primary ingredient of such assertions.[73] We ought to be hesitant, however, about arguing the same in relation to objections to a draft lottery which permits purchase of commutation. History shows, after all, that this type of arrangement has been considered to disadvantage the poor. Perhaps the sensible thing to do here is to conclude that this is where the matter ought to be left: for all that the military draft which combines the market and the lottery might be supported on the basis of allocative efficiency, it is obvious from past experience that any such proposal will meet with intense resistance.

Rather than conclude thus, however, I should prefer to offer the observation that it is quite frequently the case that the wealthy insure themselves somewhat to the cost of those who are less wealthy. To cite but two examples, the purchase of private health care and education may have a negative impact on the provision and quality of public health care and education. By no means is this to claim that such purchase will lower aggregate social welfare; the injection of additional resources into, for example, health care through private insurance is likely to have quite the opposite effect.[74] My point, however, is that such private purchase schemes may, as with the purchase of commutation, lead to specific (as opposed to aggregate) losses. It may not, of course, be possible to identify a specific person who loses as a consequence of one's buying private health care or education as one might identify one's replacement in, say, the army. This does not mean, however, that specific types of loss will not be borne. Among other things, private schemes may lure away some of the better personnel from the public systems. The private sector, furthermore, does not necessarily transfer wealth to the public sector in the same way as does the conscript to his substitute (although those who purchase private health care and education normally must continue, through taxation, to provide financial support for public services). None of this

tion of those soldiers are exempted (given that they will, more often than not, be economically capable of purchasing exemption) and replaced with younger and less intelligent recruits.

[72] There may also be a problem of quality: the exploitative nature of the scheme might ensure that many recruits turn out to be as pitiful and unsuitable as those which Justice Shallow provides for Falstaff. See *2 Henry IV*, III. ii.

[73] See Neil Duxbury, 'Do Markets Degrade?' (1996) 59 *Modern L. Rev.* 331–48 at 342–3; and Neil Duxbury, 'Trading in Controversy' (1997) 45 *Buffalo L. Rev.* 615–27 at 619–23.

[74] See, generally, Greg Clark, Tony Hockley, and Iain Smedley, 'The Insurance of Medical Risks', in *Risk, Insurance and Welfare: The Changing Balance Between Public and Private Protection* (London: Association of British Insurers, 1995), 8–25.

will be of relevance to the person who considers private health care and education to be just as objectionable as the draft lottery which allows for purchase of exemption. Yet when, in discussions, I have put forward the argument in favour of purchase of commutation, it has often been resisted by people who turn out not to object to private education and health insurance. That historical experience will most likely weigh decisively against any proposal for a draft lottery combined with a market for military exemption seems obvious. That this particular market-and-lottery combination is substantially different from various other forms of private insurance seems, to me at least, less obvious. In so far as a difference exists, it appears to be that to purchase commutation is to buy one's way out of a burden, whereas to purchase private health care or education is to buy one's way into a system which is likely to offer better quality of service than is made available by the government. Both purchasing exemption from military duty and purchasing the privilege of being able to bypass suboptimal public services can, however, be conceived as forms of private insurance.[75] The point which I wish to emphasize is that the operation of these private insurance systems may generate certain disadvantages (as well as possible advantages) for those who, for whatever reason, do not subscribe to them.

3. ADJUDICATING IN THE SHADOW OF A LOTTERY

Purchase of exemption from military service ought not to be allowed, Walzer suggests, for the same reasons that we do not permit purchase of exemption from jury duty.[76] Yet the principal argument against permitting trade in jury service—that such trade would very likely impede dispensation of justice—seems not to be relevant to the purchase of military commutation. Although a market in military exemption might not obstruct the pursuit of justice, however, it will—as ought to be clear from the foregoing discussion—most likely be considered intrinsically unjust. The only way in which I have been able to make a case for a market in military exemptions, indeed, is by playing down the notion of justice and emphasizing instead a particular conception of economic efficiency. Looking back over this study, it becomes apparent that arguments in favour of social decision-making by lot are quite often (though by no means always) supportable on what, broadly speaking, turn out to be efficiency grounds, whereas arguments against such decision-making are frequently premissed on appeals to some general idea of justice or fairness. We saw in Chapter 3, for example, that various arguments for resort to sortition emphasize how randomized processes can generate positive incentive effects, or save time and expense in decision-making. In Chapter 4, by

---

[75] See further Peter Diamond, 'Symposium on the Rationing of Health Care: 1. Rationing Medical Care—An Economist's Perspective' (1998) 14 *Economics and Philosophy* 1–26 at 23–5.
[76] See Walzer (above, n. 66), 101.

contrast, we observed that lotteries are often resisted in social decision-making contexts because they are considered to be inattentive to one or another dimension of justice. The belief that conceptions of efficiency and justice must exist in antagonism towards one another is fairly widespread.[77] Sometimes, however, justice may demand attentiveness to concerns about efficiency. This insight can, I believe, be deduced from section 4 of Chapter 4. I shall now try to develop this insight by arguing that a more efficient—that is, a less dilatory, protracted, and (in consequence) costly—legal process may also be more just (in the sense that it facilitates greater dispensation of justice), and that the introduction of a lottery element into an adjudicative process might, on occasions, reduce both inefficiency and injustice.

Perhaps the simplest way in which a lottery might assist adjudicators is as a heuristic device. Faced with a troubling decision between alternatives, I may toss a coin—not so as to let chance determine the matter, but to gauge my own reaction to the result of the toss. My reaction—whether I am pleased or disappointed with how the coin has landed—may give me an indication as to where my preferences actually lie.[78] Rather more ambitious is the proposal that a lottery may sometimes be introduced into a decision-making framework in order to improve adjudicative performance. One can envisage a situation in which adjudicators are accorded a specific amount of time within which to reach a decision. Imagine that there is introduced into this procedure a condition that, should a decision not have been reached once that time has passed, the matter in question will be settled by lot. Might the introduction of such a condition into a legal decision-making context be defensible?

The answer to this question is, I think, very rarely. Proposals to incorporate lotteries into adjudicative frameworks are likely to be beset by problems. While many of these problems are serious—while they may compel one to conclude, indeed, that such proposals must in all instances be unworkable—they can also, to some degree, be countered. The proposition being advanced here is by no means earth-shattering: it is merely that proposals for the more extensive use of lotteries within adjudicative frameworks might sometimes prove workable and beneficial. Yet even rendering this proposition plausible will prove difficult. In arguing that lotteries might profitably be incorporated into some legal decision-making frameworks, I shall outline the basic objections to such a proposal and also consider how these objections might be countered.

Before turning to these objections, let us consider the proposal in a little more detail. Decision-makers might sometimes settle a legal dispute more clearly and resolutely than they would otherwise do if recourse may be had to lot. Knowing

---

[77] See Neil Duxbury, *Patterns of American Jurisprudence* (Oxford: Clarendon Press, 1995), 402–5.

[78] See Edna Ullmann-Margalit and Sidney Morgenbesser, 'Picking and Choosing' (1977) 44 *Social Research* 757–85 at 776.

that the lottery decision would be beyond their influence, adjudicators might be more focused and cogent in resolving disputes than they would be were the option of resorting to lot unavailable. This argument may be elaborated by way of analogy. Game-theoretic jurisprudence teaches that the efficacy of legal rules is often attributable not to the fact that they are applied by courts, but to the fact that they constitute 'exit options' within bargaining processes.[79] Legal rules operate as exit options when they provide one party within a particular dispute or interaction with the power to bring negotiations to an end, and still receive something, by invoking a legal right. Where legal rules serve this purpose, they establish the contours of the negotiations that take place between the parties—for one party will always have the option to walk away from the bargaining process and yet receive a payoff. Contractual rules often work in this way. A buyer may, for example, have a right to perfect tender—a right, that is, to reject goods and force the seller to take them back where they do not conform to the contract. It may be the case that the goods in question are suited to the buyer's special needs, or that they can be returned only at considerable cost. In such an instance, the right to perfect tender is likely to set the initial conditions for bargaining between the parties: the buyer may well be prepared ultimately to keep the goods so long as the seller offers a sufficiently attractive discount; but if the seller does not offer such a discount, the buyer can exit the bargaining process and invoke the right to perfect tender. The power of the contractual rule here rests not, principally, in its actual application, but in the fact that it casts a shadow over the bargaining process. 'Pretrial bargaining', it has famously been observed, 'may be described as a game played in the shadow of the law. There are two possible outcomes: settlement out of court through bargaining, and trial, which represents a bargaining breakdown. The courts encourage private bargaining but stand ready to step from the shadows and resolve the dispute by coercion if the parties cannot agree.'[80] With regard to divorce settlements, Mnookin and Kornhauser observe thus:

---

[79] See generally Douglas G. Baird, Robert H. Gertner, and Randal C. Picker, *Game Theory and the Law* (Cambridge, Mass.: Harvard University Press, 1994), 221–43. The classic analysis of how the availability of exit options to economic actors may influence market activity is to be found in Albert O. Hirschman, *Exit, Voice, and Loyalty: Responses to Decline in Firms, Organizations, and States* (Cambridge, Mass.: Harvard University Press, 1970), 21–9.

[80] Robert Cooter and Stephen Marks with Robert Mnookin, 'Bargaining in the Shadow of the Law: A Testable Model of Strategic Behavior' (1982) 11 *Journal of Legal Studies* 225–51 at 225. Consider also Alexis de Tocqueville, *Democracy in America* (2 vols., New York: Vintage, 1990; vol. i orig. publ. 1835, vol. ii 1840), i. 140: 'The great end of justice is to substitute the notion of right for that of violence and to place a legal barrier between the government and the use of physical force. It is a strange thing, the authority that is accorded to the intervention of a court of justice by the general opinion of mankind! It clings even to the mere formalities of justice, and gives a bodily influence to the mere shadow of the law. The moral force which courts of justice possess renders the use of physical force very rare and is frequently substituted for it; but if force proves to be indispensable, its power is doubled by the association of the idea of law.'

Divorcing parents do not bargain over the division of family wealth and custodial prerogatives in a vacuum; they bargain in the shadow of the law. The legal rules governing alimony, child support, marital property, and custody give each parent certain claims based on what each would get if the case went to trial. In other words, the outcome that the law will impose if no agreement is reached gives each parent certain bargaining chips—an endowment of sorts.[81]

A somewhat imprecise analogy might be drawn between the phenomenon of bargaining in the shadow of the law and the idea of adjudicating in the shadow of a lottery.[82] Just as the option of resorting to the relevant legal rules may serve to engage the minds of disputing parties, so too the possibility of recourse to a lottery upon the expiry of a stipulated decision-making period may galvanize the minds of decision-makers. That the possibility of resort to a lottery might have this effect is attributable not only to the fact that adjudicators will be unable to influence the randomized outcome; there is also the matter of stigma. Were adjudicators to be faced with the prospect of either reaching a decision within a stipulated period or allowing that decision to be made randomly, they would—to adopt the terminology of modern behavioural legal analysis—be under pressure to comply with a social norm.[83] Although adjudicators will not (let us assume) be sanctioned should the decision-making period expire and the need arise for recourse to a lottery,[84] there will be a strong likelihood that they will generally be

---

[81] Robert H. Mnookin and Lewis Kornhauser, 'Bargaining in the Shadow of the Law: The Case of Divorce' (1979) 88 *Yale LJ* 950–97 at 968. It is not only rules, we might note, that possess the capacity to cast shadows over bargaining processes. For a discussion of other ways in which law casts shadows, see Marc Galanter, 'Justice in Many Rooms: Courts, Private Ordering, and Indigenous Law' (1981) 19 *Journal of Legal Pluralism* 1–47 at 7–10, 17–34.

[82] The imprecision of the analogy rests, first of all, in the fact that the outcome of an exit through a lottery will entail considerably more uncertainty than will exit through a clear-cut legal rule. The imprecision of the analogy rests also in the fact that whereas legal rules constitute exit options because they can normally be resorted to at any time throughout the bargaining process, exit to the lottery would only be available upon expiry of the stipulated period of adjudication.

[83] For illustrative jurisprudential literature on social norms, see the papers from the conference on 'Social Norms, Social Meaning, and the Economic Analysis of Law' (1998) 17 *Journal of Legal Studies* 537–823; 'Symposium: "Law, Economics, and Norms" ' (1996) 144 *Univ. Pennsylvania L. Rev.* 1643–2339; Eric A. Posner, 'The Regulation of Groups: The Influence of Legal and Nonlegal Sanctions on Collective Action' (1996) 63 *Univ. Chicago L. Rev.* 133–97; Lawrence Lessig, 'The Regulation of Social Meaning' (1995) 62 *Univ. Chicago L. Rev.* 943–1045; Robert C. Ellickson, *Order without Law: How Neighbors Settle Disputes* (Cambridge, Mass.: Harvard University Press, 1991); and, more generally, Jeffrey Rosen, 'The Social Police', *The New Yorker*, 20 and 27 Oct. 1997, pp. 170–81; and Jon Elster, *Alchemies of the Mind: Rationality and the Emotions* (Cambridge: Cambridge University Press, 1999), 145–64. Modern American behavioural legal theory is inspired, in the main, by recent developments in decision theory. A useful introduction to the theoretical literature which informs behavioural legal analysis is to be found in Linda D. Molm, *Coercive Power in Social Exchange* (Cambridge: Cambridge University Press, 1997), 160–5, 250–2. An earlier, and rather different version of American behaviouralist jurisprudence has its roots in legal realism. For discussion of this earlier incarnation, see Wilfred E. Rumble, Jr., *American Legal Realism: Skepticism, Reform, and the Judicial Process* (Ithaca, NY: Cornell University Press, 1968), 167–82.

[84] Of course, it could well be that legal provisions stipulate that adjudicators should, in this instance, be sanctioned. It is easier to outline the argument concerning stigmatization, however, if we leave aside this possibility.

considered to have failed to do what was required of them. In short, one might expect recourse to sortition to be commonly regarded as indicative of decision-making incompetence.

There are at least eight problems with the proposal for adjudication in the shadow of a lottery. The first of these problems, the problem of enforceability, appears to resist qualification or counter-argument. In the absence of a dictatorship, one might expect that such a system will only stand a chance of functioning effectively so long as the majority of citizens assent to it and adjudicators are, in the main, prepared to abide by it. Were adjudicators to agree to such a procedure, they would be adopting a strategy of precommitment: rather as Ulysses insists that he be bound to the mast of his ship so as not to succumb to the enchantment of the Sirens,[85] adjudicators would be relying on a strategy which combats the tendency, which some of them may exhibit, to veer off course when engaging in decision-making.[86] That an adjudicator might be willing to rely on such a strategy, however, would most likely require his or her recognition that a tendency to digress in the process of legal decision-making represents a problem. One can imagine many an adjudicator, particularly in the higher courts of common law jurisdictions, insisting not only that to digress is to be human, but that to deviate—in the pursuit, say, of questionable analogies or in the formulation of *obiter dicta*—is both an essential feature and virtue of the decision-maker's craft.

This last observation points us towards the second basic problem with the notion of introducing time limits and lotteries into legal decision-making procedures: such a strategy, assuming it were enforceable, might diminish the quality of adjudication. While such diminution may well occur in certain instances, it is possible on some occasions that adoption of the strategy will enhance the quality of decision-making. Decisions may be poorly conceived or reached in haste where they are made in awareness of a clock ticking away; but the presence of that clock might sometimes inspire adjudicators to focus more sharply on the problem at hand. Some years ago, the Faculty in which I work introduced a 'rule' that our board meetings should not last for longer than two hours. Prior to the introduction of this stipulation, board meetings had tended to meander: discussions more often than not strayed off point, many matters would remain unresolved, and items would frequently be shunted from one agenda to the next. That we were prepared to devote seemingly limitless time to the resolution of issues provided no guarantee that those issues would be considered thoroughly. While

---

[85] *Odyssey* 12. 40–128.

[86] See generally, on precommitment strategies, Jon Elster, *Ulysses and the Sirens: Studies in Rationality and Irrationality* (rev. edn., Cambridge: Cambridge University Press, 1984), 36–111; Stephen Holmes, *Passions and Constraint: On the Theory of Liberal Democracy* (Chicago: University of Chicago Press, 1995), 100–77, 202–35; and Jeremy Waldron, 'Precommitment and Disagreement', in Larry Alexander (ed.), *Constitutionalism: Philosophical Foundations* (Cambridge: Cambridge University Press, 1998), 271–99. I discuss precommitment further in Neil Duxbury, 'Liberalism, Self-Interest and Precommitment' (1996) 9 *Canadian Journal of Law and Jurisprudence* 383–95.

Faculty board meetings can still turn out to be ordeals, the general consensus among colleagues seems to be that we now constitute a more rigorous and focused decision-making body as compared with when we were not mindful of the possible imposition of a two-hour guillotine.

This example can be met with at least two lines of objection. It might be contended, first of all, that anecdotes concerning how the imposition of time constraints may improve the quality of debate among academics have no bearing on judicial decision-making. While it may make sense to impose, say, a two-hour guillotine on a body which has persistently taken too long to reach decisions which often turn out to be inconclusive or even incoherent, the imposition of a time limit on a decision-making body which does not generally function ineffi-ciently may lead to a deterioration in the quality of its decisions. It might also be argued that the imposition of time constraints on faculty boards—which, as compared with courts, will normally have more freedom to reopen previous debates—is likely to have less serious consequences. As compared with courts, faculty boards will probably have less cause to worry (though this is not to claim that they need not worry at all) about establishing unfortunate precedents.

Secondly, if the anecdote illustrates anything, it is only that the application of a time limit might have a beneficial effect on decision-making. The story reveals nothing about the use of a lottery. Where adjudicators decide within stipulated time constraints, however, the threatened imposition of a lottery might, on occa-sions, further strengthen their resolve to produce decisions which are clearly explained and to the point. The Manchester Law Faculty two-hour board 'rule' is not a real rule because meetings sometimes do extend beyond two hours and, when they do, no sanction is applied—indeed, there exists within the Faculty no sanction to be applied. Aware that an item of discussion is consuming an inordi-nate amount of time, nevertheless, the Dean may sometimes state that the issue will be discussed for only a few more minutes after which, should no decision have been reached, Faculty will move to a vote. Such a statement will, on occa-sions, have a focusing effect. One might anticipate that the proposal to move to a lottery rather than to a vote would have much the same effect: the resolve of deci-sion-makers to formulate a solution might be strengthened by virtue of the fact that they are uncertain of what the outcome will be if it is reached by a casting of lots.

It can be argued that the advantage of moving to a vote as compared with a lottery in such a situation is that it will usually ensure that the outcome reached most accurately reflects the aggregate preference of the particular decision-making body. In some decision-making contexts, however, the fact that voting is more responsive to preferences than is random selection may count against its adoption. Where, say, the members of a decision-making body split into a minor-ity and a majority group and decision-makers' voting preferences can be predicted with confidence, the imposition of a vote upon expiry of a stipulated period of discussion may very well cause members of the minority group to express dissatisfaction with the decision-making procedure. How, they might ask, can they be expected to deliberate effectively with members of the majority group, given that those within the majority hold the trump card of being able to win by voting? It is certainly not my argument that the lottery will always be preferable to the vote as a decision-making device of last resort. Voting, I suspect, will more often than not be preferable to random selection. But while the non-weighted lottery is by no means the only appropriate device of last resort in legal decision-making contexts, it may be that it is sometimes the best last resort because of the difficulty of predicting what the randomized outcome will be.

The third problem with adjudication in the shadow of a lottery is that the very possibility of resort to randomization may undermine respect for the legal process. A fundamental objection to the idea of legal decision-making by lot, we observed in Chapter 4, is that reasons will (assuming that the lottery is non-weighted) be irrelevant to outcomes. According to Fuller, 'the distinguishing characteristic of adjudication lies in the fact that it confers on the affected party a peculiar form of participation in the decision, that of presenting proofs and reasoned arguments for a decision in his favor . . . Whatever destroys the meaning of that participation destroys the integrity of adjudication itself.'[87] The introduction of a lottery into a legal decision-making framework might be regarded, however, as an example of a 'mixed or "impure" form of adjudication'[88]—about which Fuller was circumspect but not wholly negative.[89] That we ought, in principle, to be cautious about, but not thoroughly opposed to, the incorporation of lottery elements into legal decision-making procedures is explicable by virtue of the fact that such incorporation would not destroy what Fuller terms the integrity of adjudication: if adjudication were to take place in the shadow of a lottery, the procedure would still allow for the presentation and consideration of proofs and reasons.

There is, none the less, a risk that serious disputes will generally be considered to have been resolved inappropriately where decision-makers run out of time and a lottery is used. We might, however, expect such a risk to be minimal since, as already argued, the shadow cast by the lottery will make it most unlikely that adjudicators will fail to reach a decision within the time allotted to them. (It might fairly be remarked, indeed, that this study makes more of a case for the lottery's shadow than for the lottery itself.) I would argue, furthermore, that the creation of such a risk does not have to be cast in a negative light. Evidence of concern that an issue may ultimately be resolved by lot might be considered indicative of the importance attached to adjudication. A similar argument is sometimes advanced in relation to proposals for the use of lotteries as pure decision-making devices (as distinct from lotteries combined with other decision-frameworks). That a scarce resource is being allocated randomly may be sufficiently shocking

---

[87] Lon L. Fuller, 'The Forms and Limits of Adjudication' (1978) 92 *Harvard L. Rev.* 353–409 at 364.   [88] Ibid. 405.   [89] Ibid. 382, 405–6.

to prompt a concerted effort to ensure greater availability of the resource in question.[90] 'A lottery for the available artificial kidney machines', for example, 'brings into high relief the preliminary choice to provide an insufficient number of machines to serve everyone.'[91] To put the point very simply, certain of the consequences of using a lottery—or of creating the possibility of using a lottery—to resolve issues of social or legal significance may be salutary.

The fourth problem with the introduction of sortition into an adjudicative process was discussed in Chapter 3: the lottery may be a godsend to the lazy or the incompetent decision-maker. We need hardly dwell on this problem. Only a decision-maker who is content to be regarded as lazy or incompetent would make a habit of allowing the lottery to take effect. The likelihood of recourse to lot will be still more remote owing to the fact that the adjudicator who is minded persistently to rely on randomization will probably encounter discouragement and disapprobation from his or her peers. The fact, indeed, that legal decision-making is often the task of multi-member bodies makes such persistent reliance highly unlikely. Turning momentarily to a tangential matter, although we might confidently anticipate that decision-makers would, by and large, be unwilling to see lotteries employed to settle legal problems, it is difficult to know to what extent this reluctance would be shared by disputing parties. It might be expected that, on occasions, the possibility of decision by lot will discourage spurious litigation.[92] The fact, however, that a settlement might ultimately be determined by the luck of the draw could encourage some disputants with weak claims to litigate in the hope that proceedings may be prolonged to the point at which a non-weighted lottery is triggered: arrival at this point, after all, ensures them a 50 per cent chance of success. Conversely, while a disputant whose claim is unlikely to prevail on its merits may be attracted to the prospect of a lottery outcome, such a prospect may discourage some genuinely meritorious claimants from litigating because of the risk that justice will not be done.[93]

---

[90] See Willem K. B. Hofstee, 'Allocation by Lot: A Conceptual and Empirical Analysis' (1990) 29 *Social Science Information* 745–63 at 748.

[91] Calabresi and Bobbitt (above, n. 17), 42.

[92] 'It is amazing', one judge has recently observed, how the threat to distribute marital property between divorcing couples by the toss of a coin 'actually persuades the parties to be sensible and sort it out themselves'. Stephen Gerlis, 'Talking Shop: Divorce and the Counting of Spoons' (1998) 28 *Family Law* 47. See also Elster (above, n. 19), 170; and Barbara Goodwin, *Justice by Lottery* (Hemel Hempstead: Harvester Wheatsheaf, 1992), 166: 'If a lottery were instituted to decide "distributive" legal questions such as child custody, disputes over wills, boundary disputes, and so on, one can conjecture that litigation in these areas would diminish rapidly . . . Compromise distributions would be reached with less conflict because no one would wish to risk losing the whole of the disputed amount, or the desired object itself, by the throw of a dice.' More generally, on the idea that uncertainty encourages disputants to settle, cf. Hazel Genn, *Hard Bargaining: Out of Court Settlement in Personal Injury Actions* (Oxford: Clarendon Press, 1987), 97–123, 129–38.

[93] See further Timothy Swanson and Robin Mason, 'Nonbargaining in the Shadow of the Law' (1998) 18 *International Review of Law and Economics* 121–40.

The requirement that adjudication be conducted in the shadow of a lottery—we here encounter a fifth problem—may create an incentive to filibuster. Where a decision-maker is in total and passionate disagreement with all of his colleagues, the lottery may represent the only chance of an outcome being reached with which he would find himself in agreement. That decision-maker might therefore obstruct constructive dialogue so as to run down the clock and ensure that the lottery is initiated. One might try to discourage such a strategy by providing that the lottery must be weighted in accordance with the preferences of the various adjudicators. Thus weighted, the lowest probability of desired outcome will be accorded to the decision-maker who is out on a limb. That decision-maker, however, is still likely to consider filibustering to be his best option. One can only speculate as to how frequently such a scenario might arise in legal decision-making contexts. It will probably very rarely be the case that a legal decision-maker disagrees with his colleagues so intensely that he can see no point in persisting with deliberation; it might be expected, indeed, that where a decision-maker believes that a compromise, or that some other form of progress, can be made through dialogue, he is unlikely to be determined to ensure that a lottery outcome is reached.

The sixth problem concerns practicalities. What sort of lottery should we have? How much time should legal decision-makers be given before the lottery is instituted? And precisely which decision-making bodies ought to adjudicate in the shadow of a lottery? I do not believe that any of these questions can be answered satisfactorily in the abstract. The questions of whether or not a lottery ought to be weighted, and what sort of randomizing device should be used, seem to require answers relative to context. Perhaps all that we might assert confidently is that, whatever lottery were used, transparency in application would be a desideratum. Those awaiting legal decisions might be expected from the very outset to be uneasy with the prospect of outcomes being settled randomly; one would expect such unease to be compounded were the relevant lotteries not conducted openly and their outcomes simply announced. To offer some general pronouncement, furthermore, on how long legal decision-makers should be given before the lottery takes effect would be unwise. Assuming—and we have observed already that this assumption cannot be made lightly—that the use of randomization as a last resort has been assented to, disagreement would very likely emerge with regard to just how much time should pass before responsibility for determining an outcome is removed from decision-makers and entrusted to a lottery. The fact that opinions will probably differ on the matter of how much time decision-makers should be given, however, does not mean that a period of time cannot be agreed upon and stipulated; it would, in short, be silly to assume that the likelihood of disagreement poses an insurmountable problem.

Rather more difficult to tackle is the question of where decision-makers might be expected to adjudicate in the shadow of a lottery. The discussion which has unfolded here, it will have been noted, has focused on civil claims rather than on criminal proceedings. No doubt many criminal trials could, in theory, be settled by lot—indeed, in the past, such has been the practice. Wedberg, for example, shows that the resolution of military trials by lot can be traced back to Roman law and, in Nordic countries, remained an accepted (if rarely used) procedure up until the eighteenth century.[94] It is unlikely, however, that such a procedure would be considered acceptable for the purpose of deciding criminal cases today, even if recourse to a lottery was envisaged only as a last resort. There are numerous reasons for suspecting as much. One reason is that the element of censure which comes with a criminal conviction tends to be rather more significant, for want of a better word, than that which attaches to a finding of civil liability.[95] The stigmatizing effects of a criminal conviction, for example, often last well beyond the point at which punishment is imposed, whereas this is less frequently the case where civil liability has been established.[96] The idea that lotteries might be introduced into criminal law frameworks is likely to meet with considerable resistance, accordingly, because of what is at stake: if, on the expiry of a time limit, questions of guilt can be determined by lot, defendants in particular stand to lose a great deal; if, on the expiry of such a limit, issues of civil liability can be decided by lot, litigants also may stand to lose a great deal—but not, in most instances, as much as do criminal defendants.[97]

Another reason to suspect that proposals for the possibility of resort to lot in criminal proceedings will meet with even greater resistance than will such proposals in civil cases is that it would be difficult, indeed probably impossible, to weight a lottery so that it reflects the criminal burden of proof. With regard to the civil standard of proof—proof on the balance of probabilities—an equiprobable lottery might, in the event that decision-makers fail to produce an outcome in the time available to them, be considered to accord each party an appropriate

---

[94] Birger Wedberg, *Tärningkast om liv och död: Rättshistoriska skisser* (Stockholm: Norstedt & Söners, 1935), 10–13. 'Only after the enactment of the [Swedish] war laws of 1868', Wedberg notes, 'did decimation disappear from our military penal law. Over the past 250 years, however, during which this manner of punishment has been validated by written law, I cannot present any case where it has been used—unless one concedes that the punishment of the soldiers who were involved in the Dalklarnes rebellion [of 1742] counts as such: [according to Malmström], "those who had been found guilty of participating in the recruitment riots of 1742 were punished by the whip, of the other recruits every thirteenth [was whipped] according to the lottery" ' (ibid. 12–13). Cf. also ibid. 23–7 (on the random imposition of the death penalty in 18th- and early 19th-cent. Swedish criminal law).

[95] See, e.g., Andrew von Hirsch, *Censure and Sanctions* (Oxford: Clarendon Press, 1993), 6–19, 24–7; and also S. E. Marshall and R. A. Duff, 'Criminalization and Sharing Wrongs' (1998) 11 *Canadian Journal of Law and Jurisprudence* 7–22 at 12–17. In civil litigation, an element of censure comparable with that which accompanies many criminal convictions may attach to some punitive damage awards: cf. Peter Jaffey, 'Restitutionary Damages and Disgorgement' (1995) 3 *Restitution L. Rev.* 30–48 at 40.

[96] On the long-term effects of criminal conviction, see Nigel Walker, *Punishment, Danger and Stigma: The Morality of Criminal Justice* (Oxford: Blackwell, 1980), 142–63; and also Andrew von Hirsch and Martin Wasik, 'Civil Disqualifications Attending Conviction: A Suggested Conceptual Framework' (1997) 56 *Cambridge LJ* 599–626.

[97] See further Mike Redmayne, 'Standards of Proof in Civil Litigation' (1999) 62 *Modern L. Rev.* 167–95.

chance of success.[98] When, however, the relevant standard is proof beyond reasonable doubt, questions arise concerning whether the lottery should be weighted to reflect this standard and, if it ought to be so weighted, how this might be done. The basic difficulty with weighting a lottery in this context is that answers to the question of just how large a doubt there should be before the doubt compels an acquittal will vary from one case—often, indeed, from one juror or magistrate—to another. The indeterminacy of 'beyond reasonable doubt' may therefore militate against adjudication in the shadow of a lottery in criminal cases.

Adjudication in the shadow of a lottery is perhaps most appropriate in instances where decision-makers are entrusted not with the determination of matters of guilt or even of liability, but with the allocation of scarce resources among candidates who all appear to be equally qualified for those resources and who are likely to benefit from receiving them sooner rather than later. This form of decision-making might prove especially welcome, in other words, where dilatoriness on the part of decision-makers may cause those awaiting their decisions to suffer unduly. We observed in Chapter 3 that delay in the allocation of medical resources can reduce the quality, or even result in the loss, of some of the lives of candidates for those resources. If such resources were to be allocated in the shadow of a lottery, decision-makers would have an incentive to think clearly and quickly about distributive criteria and differences among candidates, while the presence of the lottery would prevent inordinate delay. It should be clear from section 4 of Chapter 4 that a similar argument might be advanced in relation to child custody adjudication.

An obvious objection to this line of reasoning is that it encourages haste on the part of adjudicators. The objection illustrates a point which has been adverted to at various junctures throughout this study: we often seem to be more ready to condemn the ill consequences of haste on the part of decision-makers than we are to lament the similarly unfortunate consequences of leisureliness. Leaving this observation aside, I would in any event emphasize that my concern here is with the encouragement not of haste but of more expeditious decision-making where procrastination is proving to be a problem. Such encouragement would probably require that lotteries be imposed not upon specific decision-making bodies, but in particular types of case. Justifying the incorporation of lotteries into certain decision-frameworks and not into others would no doubt be difficult (though, again, not necessarily impossible).

The seventh problem with the proposal for adjudication in the shadow of a lottery is that, in real terms, such a system might not save time. Although the system might ensure that courts generally dispense with cases more quickly than

---

[98] Acceptance of this argument depends upon the belief that, in civil litigation, there is no need to apply a standard of proof substantially greater than 0.5. For doubt concerning this belief see, e.g., David T. Wasserman, 'The Morality of Statistical Proof and the Risk of Mistaken Liability' (1991) 13 *Cardozo L. Rev.* 935–76 at 937.

they would otherwise do, those courts may find themselves deciding more cases if the presence of the lottery provides a spur to litigation. Even if such a system really did save time, furthermore, it may be questioned whether it would save very much time, given that the lottery would only cast a shadow over the adjudicative proceedings. Many delays in legal proceedings have nothing to do with dilatoriness on the part of decision-makers but are, rather, attributable to events and problems which occur outside the courtroom.[99]

The eighth and final problem is that it is possible to construct a fairly convincing argument to the effect that certain courts should never—no matter what type of legal issue they are addressing—be required to adjudicate in the shadow of a lottery. We noted in the previous chapter that appeal courts in particular are very often expected to produce decisions which do not simply settle the matter in hand but which also build or improve upon the efforts of earlier courts in deciding analogous cases. One might speculate that if appeal courts laboured in the shadows of lotteries, opportunities for the maturing of legal principle, and collective judicial thought, would diminish. Where judges are burdened by the lottery, to steal a classic image from Lord Mansfield, the law is less likely to work itself pure.[100]

It may also be the case that higher courts will rarely, if ever, be able to determine outcomes by lot owing to the fact that they typically concern themselves with hard cases. The fact of the matter is that many hard cases centre upon disputes and issues that cannot satisfactorily be formulated as problems suitable for resolution through random selection. Consider, for example, the case of *The Regents of the University of California* v. *Allan Bakke*.[101] If a lottery had been used in this case, precisely what would it have decided? Whether or not Bakke should have been admitted to the University of California at Davis medical

---

[99] See further Daniel Kessler, 'Institutional Causes of Delay in the Settlement of Legal Disputes' (1996) 12 *Journal of Law, Economics and Organization* 432–60.

[100] See *Omychund* v. *Barker* (1744) 1 Atk. 21, 23; and cf. also Ronald Dworkin, *Law's Empire* (London: Fontana, 1986), 400–13.

[101] (1978) 443 US 265. The facts of the case are thus: the medical school of the University of California at Davis, a state university, set aside sixteen of the 100 places in the entering class for educationally and economically disadvantaged individuals from four racial-ethnic groups (African-American, Asian, American-Indian, and Mexican-American). Bakke, a white candidate, applied for one of the remaining eighty-four places and was rejected. Since his test scores were relatively high, the medical school conceded that it could not prove that he would have been rejected if the sixteen places reserved for the minority groups had been open to him. Bakke sued the university, alleging that his exclusion from the entering class resulted from racial discrimination in violation of the equal protection clause of the Fourteenth Amendment of the United States Constitution, Title VI of the Civil Rights Act of 1964 (which forbids racial discrimination by recipients of federal financial assistance), and the California Constitution. The California Supreme Court upheld Bakke's equal protection claim, holding that racial criteria could not be used to determine admission to a state educational institution, but declined to consider his other grounds. The US Supreme Court affirmed the judgment of the California Supreme Court in so far as it ordered that Bakke be admitted to the Davis medical school, but reversed the judgment in so far as it enjoined the University from taking any account of race in its admissions decisions. Commentary on the case is voluminous: for but two examples, see Ronald Dworkin, *A Matter of Principle* (Oxford: Clarendon Press, 1986), 293–315; and Richard A. Posner, *The Economics of Justice* (Cambridge, Mass.: Harvard University Press, 1981), 387–407.

school? Whether or not the University's race-discrimination policy was constitutional? Whether or not the policy contravened Title VI of the Civil Rights Act? Whether or not race is a factor which can be taken into account in admissions decisions? If a lottery had been used simply to determine whether or not Bakke should have been admitted to the medical school, most of the key issues raised by the case would have remained unanswered. Yet if lotteries had been used to tackle all of the key questions highlighted by the case, an incoherent decision might have been produced.

Leaving aside hard cases, resolution of legal issues by lot may sometimes be inappropriate owing to the fact that a court might be expected not merely to produce an outcome but also to operate in a supervisory capacity. Rather than being a passive arbiter over social affairs, that is, a court will sometimes establish what Chayes terms 'an ongoing remedial regime',[102] producing decisions which are intended to influence the future behaviour of the disputants and also the conduct of parties other than the disputants. '[T]he trial judge', according to Chayes, 'has increasingly become the creator and manager of complex forms of ongoing relief, which have widespread effects on persons not before the court and require the judge's continuing involvement in administration and implementation.'[103] Randomized outcomes do not necessarily preclude courts from operating in a supervisory role: a judge could decide by the toss of a coin, say, and then establish an ongoing remedial regime on the basis of that decision. An outcome determined by lot, however, might not support the particular remedial regime that a court wishes to impose. A court which functions in a supervisory capacity, furthermore, in effect takes on an extra layer of responsibility; a decision-making body which runs out of time, thereby leaving the outcome to chance, might not be considered sufficiently responsible to impose and maintain an ongoing remedial regime once that outcome has been determined.

It has been noted that the introduction of lotteries into legal processes might actually delay decision-making. But even if the possibility of resort to a lottery were to speed up legal decision-making, the desirability of such a strategy might be questioned. Although the costs of legal decision-makers dragging their feet may often be substantial, dilatoriness will usually, as I have already intimated, be regarded as a lesser evil than is haste. '[L]et it be again remembered,' Blackstone remarked, 'that delays, and little inconveniences in the forms of justice, are the price that all free nations must pay for their liberty in more substantial matters.'[104] Those who concur with Blackstone will no doubt consider bizarre the idea that adjudication in the shadow of a lottery deserves to be defended because such a

---

[102]   Abram Chayes, 'The Role of the Judge in Public Law Litigation' (1976) 89 *Harvard L. Rev.* 1281–1316 at 1301.

[103]   Ibid. 1284. For an application of this insight to British public law adjudication, see Martin Loughlin, *Legality and Locality: The Role of Law in Central–Local Government Relations* (Oxford: Clarendon Press, 1996), 400–10.

[104]   *Commentaries on the Laws of England*, IV. xxvii. 350.

scheme might encourage expeditious decision-making. Even if the scheme were to operate thus, they might ask, why should it ever be considered a good thing?

To this question I have two answers. The requirement that adjudication takes place in the shadow of a lottery might make good sense, first of all, where stakes are low. The proposition that decision-making bodies which deal solely with small claims disputes ought to abide by a procedure which discourages or even precludes protracted deliberation strikes me as fairly uncontroversial. Those entrusted to make difficult decisions of social importance are likely to be able to fulfil this duty competently only so long as responsibility for making relatively simple and unimportant decisions is delegated to others.[105] Even those who make the delegated decisions, however, may become overburdened; the imposition of a time limit, upon expiry of which a lottery takes effect, may generally prevent them from dwelling on particular disputes for too long. We noted earlier Fuller's view that the distinguishing characteristic of adjudication rests in the fact that it confers on affected parties the right to present proofs and reasoned arguments to support their cases. Yet Fuller did not insist that, for there to be integrity in adjudication, reasons for decisions must always be given: 'Does the integrity of adjudication require that reasons be given for the decision rendered? I think the answer is, not necessarily. In some fields of labor arbitration . . . it is the practice to render "blind" awards. The reasons for this practice probably include a belief that reasoned awards are often misinterpreted and "stir up trouble," as well as the circumstance that the arbitrator is so busy he has no time to write opinions.'[106] Blind awards can, of course, be rendered by resorting immediately to lot. Where, however, decision-makers wish to engage in a degree of reasoning, but are too busy to undertake lengthy reasoning or to write opinions, adjudication in the shadow of a lottery might be an appropriate adjudicative strategy.

There is also, I think, a tentative case for adjudication in the shadow of a lottery where stakes are high. It was suggested earlier that we might conceive of this form of adjudication as a strategy of precommitment. Just as individuals may act on their environments or call upon others in such a way as to avoid succumbing to various weaknesses of will, so too institutions may commit themselves to procedures or mechanisms which ought to prevent them from lapsing into bad habits. Where courts are in the business not merely of settling disputes but of articulating and developing legal doctrines and principles, however, do there exist any bad habits which might be remedied by resort to time limits and lotteries? Will not resort to such devices do more harm than good? The answers to these questions may well be, respectively, no and yes. Let us, however, consider the opposing answers.

In section 4 of Chapter 4, it was argued that it may sometimes be rational to resolve legal issues by lot. In developing this argument, I emphasized the deleterious effects that protracted litigation and adjudication can have on those who await legal

---

[105] See, e.g., Exodus 18: 13–27; and also Bernard S. Jackson, 'Modelling Biblical Law: The Covenant Code' (1995) 70 *Chicago-Kent L. Rev.* 1745–1827 at 1806–26.
[106] Fuller (above, n. 87), 387.

decisions. What I did not emphasize is the fact that such litigation and adjudication may have adverse effects on the legal system itself. A dominant theme within modern jurisprudential thought is the idea that judicial ambition ought generally to be applauded. 'Law as integrity', according to Dworkin,

> requires a judge to test his interpretation of any part of the great network of political struc-
> tures and decisions of his community by asking whether it could form part of a coherent
> theory justifying the network as a whole. No actual judge could compose anything
> approaching a full interpretation of all of his community's law at once. That is why we are
> imagining a Herculean judge of superhuman talents and endless time. But an actual judge
> can imitate Hercules in a limited way. He can allow the scope of his interpretation to fan
> out from the cases immediately in point to cases in the same general area or department of
> law, and then still farther, so far as this seems promising.[107]

Judges do well, then, to aspire to Herculean ideals. Were judges generally to be so aspirational, however, they would risk increasing their workload while deciding fewer cases. It is sometimes argued that the primary purpose of a particular court—the United States Supreme Court, say, or the House of Lords—is to formulate and develop principles, and that the court in question will probably perform poorly if it decides too many cases. In the United States during the 1950s, this criticism was levelled at the Warren Court by proponents of the legal process perspective.[108] '[T]oo many of the Court's opinions', Henry Hart wrote in 1959, 'are about what one would expect could be written in twenty-four hours ... [F]ew of the Court's opinions, far too few, genuinely illumine the area of law with which they deal.'[109] No doubt expediency in judicial decision-making can be a problem. At the other extreme, however, appeal courts which seek in every instance to elaborate principle might be expected to grant certiorari even more infrequently than such courts currently do. The court which is dedicated to the elaboration of reasons, to put the point crudely, is likely to dispense less justice than is the court which is more willing to leave issues unexplored.

This insight informs Sunstein's argument in favour of judicial resort to what he terms incompletely theorized agreements. Rather than aspiring to Herculean ideals, Sunstein contends, judges will often be economical in the exposition of principle owing to the fact that this tends to be the best way to avoid provoking unnecessary debate and disagreement. '[W]hen people diverge on some (relatively) high level proposition, they might be able to agree when they lower the level of abstraction.'[110] By eschewing deliberative ambition—by refusing to develop dialogue any further than is necessary for the purpose of resolving the problem at hand—people 'can help minimize conflict . . . and save a great deal of

---

[107] Dworkin (above, n. 100), 245.

[108] See generally Duxbury (above, n. 77), 237–41.

[109] Henry M. Hart, Jr., 'The Supreme Court, 1958 Term—Foreword: The Time Chart of the Justices' (1959) 73 *Harvard L. Rev.* 84–125 at 100.

[110] Cass R. Sunstein, *Legal Reasoning and Political Conflict* (New York: Oxford University Press, 1996), 37.

time and expense'.[111] This observation holds in legal decision-making contexts, Sunstein believes, much as it does elsewhere.

The main strand of Sunstein's argument—that judicial reliance on incompletely theorized agreements may facilitate social stability and mutual respect among citizens—strikes me as contentious.[112] Such reliance might, for example, generate dissatisfaction among citizens if it leads to the perception (whether warranted or not) that judges are failing properly to discharge their duties when tackling controversial issues of considerable social importance.[113] I am not here concerned, however, with this strand of his argument; I am concerned, rather, with his claim that '[i]ncompletely theorized agreements may be the best approach [to decision-making] that is available to people of limited time and capacities'.[114] As compared with dedication to reasoned elaboration, judicial resort to incompletely theorized agreements might reduce the costs of adjudication and litigation and lead to a (quantitatively) greater dispensation of justice. Should it be considered desirable to encourage incomplete theorization in legal decision-making—and it is crucial to emphasize that it is by no means obvious that such encouragement is desirable—the requirement that adjudication be subject to a time limit and the possible imposition of a lottery might be one way of creating an appropriate incentive for decision-makers. There may be a case for adjudication in the shadow of a lottery, in short, where there exists considerable support for the argument that a decision-making body ought generally to be providing not more but fewer reasons in an effort to deal with a greater number of cases (albeit in less detail).[115]

[111] Ibid. 39.
[112] See Neil Duxbury, 'Ambition and Adjudication' (1997) 47 *Univ. Toronto LJ* 161–74 at 165–70.
[113] The argument concerning incompletely theorized agreements bears a fairly close resemblance to Rawls's idea of an overlapping consensus: see John Rawls, *Political Liberalism* (New York: Columbia University Press, 1993), 133–72. Sunstein contends that the resemblance is superficial, not least because '[t]he overlapping consensus is itself highly theorized and a matter of abstractions'. Cass R. Sunstein, 'From Theory to Practice' (1997) 29 *Arizona State LJ* 389–404 at 392. For criticism of Sunstein's contention, see Duxbury (above, n. 112), 166–7. I also suggest (ibid. 163 n. 6) that Sunstein rather caricatures Dworkin as a proponent of high-level theorization in judicial decision-making. The argument is developed much more forcefully and convincingly by Alexander Kaufman, 'Incompletely Theorized Agreement: A Plausible Ideal for Legal Reasoning?' (1996) 85 *Georgetown LJ* 395–415 at 406–15. See also Ronald Dworkin, 'In Praise of Theory' (1997) 29 *Arizona State LJ* 353–76 at 368–74.   [114] Sunstein (above, n. 110), 42.
[115] It is worth noting that, as compared with appellate courts in common law jurisdictions, the French Cour de Cassation decides a significantly greater volume of cases while demonstrating far less concern with the elaboration of reasons for decisions. See generally Adolphe Touffait and André Tunc, 'Pour une motivation plus explicite des décisions de justice notamment de celles de la Cour de Cassation' (1974) 72 *Revue Trimestrielle du Droit Civil* 487–508. More often than not, the Cour de Cassation has been criticized for deciding too many cases with excessive brevity. '[W]hen the Cour de Cassation makes a new point, changes the law,' it has been observed, 'it does not take one more word than for a routine decision. Whereas the English court will dig for plausible precedents, look around for a new rule, test it against reason—whereas the American court will do about the same and add considerations of social justice—the French will authoritatively assert the new rule as if it had been common knowledge for years.' Jean-Louis Goutal, 'Characteristics of Judicial Style in France, Britain and the USA' (1976) 24 *American Journal of Comparative Law* 43–72 at 59.

CONCLUSION

I tried to show in Chapter 4 that it may be intellectually beneficial to consider seriously arguments for legal decision-making by lot. The basic contention advanced in this chapter is that such arguments may even have some practical significance. Proceeding from the assumption that randomization is more likely to be considered acceptable within decision-making contexts where sortition is used not in isolation but in combination with other devices for allocating goods and resolving disputes, I have developed two basic claims: first, that rights to buy into or out of lotteries may sometimes be justifiable on allocative grounds; and, secondly, that it might on occasions be appropriate to stipulate that adjudication should take place in the shadow of a lottery. To both of these arguments there attaches a considerable number of qualifications. I hope not to have underestimated the degree to which these arguments might be considered objectionable. But I hope also to have shown that the combination of lotteries with other decision-making devices and procedures might sometimes generate significant efficiency gains or have positive effects on incentives.

The exoticism of another system of thought, Foucault wrote in a very different context, tends to demonstrate the limitations of one's own.[116] We ought to take seriously the notion of introducing lotteries into legal frameworks not merely because there may be contexts in which the idea could be pursued to practical advantage, but also because it is an idea which demands that we be imaginative when thinking about law. No doubt it is possible to develop a jurisprudence of randomized decision-making which exhibits vision, ambition, subtlety, and skill far superior to anything achieved here. Should this book serve to encourage any such development, it will have achieved enough.[117]

---

[116] Michel Foucault, *The Order of Things: An Archaeology of the Human Sciences* (Eng. trans. A. M. Sheridan, London: Tavistock, 1970 (1966)), p. xv.

[117] For a considerably more piquant expression of much the same sentiment in relation to an infinitely more enlightening work, see Ludwig Wittgenstein, *Philosophical Investigations* (Eng. trans. G. E. M. Anscombe, Oxford: Blackwell, 1978 (1953)), p. viii.

Conclusion

It might be considered that the basic point of this project has been to turn a ludicrous idea into a dubious one. Certainly this estimation makes sense if one takes the primary objective of the book to be normative. Possibly I have courted such an estimation: the organization of this study perhaps invites readers to focus most carefully on its normative dimension. Normativity, however, is not the driving force of the book. The point of the project is, basically, to encourage reflection on a theme. All the better, of course, if the normative arguments which have been advanced render this theme more engaging; but it would be a pity if these arguments were to eclipse the historical and analytical inquiries which take up the bulk of the study.

I have tried to illustrate the advantages and drawbacks of randomized social decision-making, and to demonstrate that arguments concerning such decision-making more often than not require qualification. I hope to have shown that this form of decision-making is both historically significant and analytically complex. Detailed scrutiny of, in particular, randomized legal decision-making compels us to confront difficult, sometimes uncomfortable, questions concerning the role of reason in law and how we conceptualize justice. Although we are often understandably wary of resorting to lotteries to determine outcomes of legal significance, furthermore, the idea that randomization might be employed more extensively within legal decision-making contexts ought not to be dismissed cursorily.

Given that the substance of this book was summarized in the Introduction, it seems almost pointless to conclude by doing the same again. Instead, by way of conclusion, I offer but one straightforward observation. Rigid application of some particular decision-making criterion to settle disputes might render adjudication less fraught with complexity and ambiguity. Depending on the criterion used, such application might even make the process of adjudication less partial. If the criterion is easy to apply, moreover, the costs of decision-making are likely to be reduced. One criterion which offers all of these qualities is random selection. Decision-making by lot is likely to be simple, objective, and cheap. 'Cast lots, and settle a quarrel, and so keep litigants apart.'[1] Randomized decision-making will, however, be unreasoned. If a single argument rests at the heart of this book it is that, in law, faith in reason is sometimes maintained at too high a cost. The lottery, possibly more than any other decision-making device, demands that this argument be accorded serious consideration.

[1] Proverbs 18: 18.

Index